Journal of Prisoners
on Prisons

I0027729

... allowing our experiences and analysis to be added to the forum that will constitute public opinion could help halt the disastrous trend toward building more fortresses of fear which will become in the 21st century this generation's monuments to failure.

Jo-Ann Mayhew (1988)

Volume 21
Number 1 & 2
2012

JOURNAL OF PRISONERS ON PRISONS

EDITORIAL STAFF:

Editor-in-Chief:	Bob Gaucher	Issue Editors:	Stephen C. Richards
Associate Editors:	Susan Nagelsen		Michael Lenza
	Charles Huckelbury	Prisoners' Struggles Editor:	Kevin Walby
Managing Editors:	Justin Piché	Book Review Editor:	Pat Derby
	Mike Larsen		

EDITORIAL BOARD:

Ramona Brockett	Sara Falconer	Michael Lenza	Stephen C. Richards
Panagiota Chrisovergis	Sylvie Frigon	Tara Lyons	Viviane Saleh-Hanna
Elizabeth Comack	Bob Gaucher	MaDonna Maidment	Judah Schept
Howard Davidson	Kristen Gilchrist	Joane Martel	Renita Seabrook
Claire Delisle	Anne-Marie Grondin	Erin McCuaig	Rashad Shabazz
Patrick Derby	Kelly Hannah-Moffatt	Dawn Moore	Lisa Smith
Leah DeVellis	Stacey Hannem	Melissa Munn	Dale Spencer
Giselle Dias	Charles Hucklebury	Peter Murphy	Brian Chad Starks
Danial Dos Santos	Jennifer Kilty	Susan Nagelsen	Karen Emily Suurtamm
Aaron Doyle	Mike Larsen	Justin Piché	Kevin Walby
		Stephen Reid	Matt Yeager

The *Journal of Prisoners on Prisons* is published twice a year. Its purpose is to encourage research on a wide range of issues related to crime, justice, and punishment by prisoners and former prisoners. Donations to the *JPP* are gratefully received.

SUBMISSIONS:

Prisoners and former prisoners are encouraged to submit original papers, collaborative essays, discussions transcribed from tape, book reviews, and photo or graphic essays that have not been published elsewhere. The *Journal* does not usually publish fiction or poetry. The *Journal* will publish articles in either French or English. Articles should be no longer than 20 pages typed and double-spaced or legibly handwritten. Electronic submissions are gratefully received. Writers may elect to write anonymously or under a pseudonym. For references cited in an article, the writer should attempt to provide the necessary bibliographic information. Refer to the references cited in this issue for examples. Submissions are reviewed by members of the Editorial Board. Selected articles are corrected for composition and returned to the authors for their approval before publication. Papers not selected are returned with editor's comments. Revised papers may be resubmitted. Please submit bibliographical and contact information, to be published alongside articles unless otherwise indicated.

SUBCRIPTIONS, SUBMISSIONS AND ALL OTHER CORRESPONDENCE:

Journal of Prisoners on Prisons
c/o Justin Piché, Assistant Professor
Department of Criminology, University of Ottawa
Ottawa, Ontario, Canada K1N 6N5

e-mail: jpp@uottawa.ca
website: www.jpp.org

SUBCRIPTION RATES FOR 2013:	One Year	Two Years	Three Years
Prisoners	$15.00	$28.00	$40.00
Individuals	$30.00	$56.00	$80.00
Prison Libraries & Schools, Libraries & Institutions	$60.00	$110.00	$150.00

Canadian subscriptions payable in Canadian dollars. Canadian orders include 5 percent HST. Subscriptions outside Canada payable in U.S. or Canadian dollars. Add four dollars for postage.

INDIVIDUAL COPIES AND BACK ISSUES:

$15 each for single issues / $25 each for double issues (Canadian $ in Canada – U.S. $ outside of Canada) available from University of Toronto Press Distribution.

University of Toronto Press Inc.
5201 Dufferin Street
Toronto, Ontario, Canada M3H 5T8

phone: 1-800-565-9523
fax: 1-800-221-9985
e-mail: utpbooks@utpress.utoronto.ca
website: www.utpress.utoronto.ca/utp_D1/home.htm

Co-published by the University of Ottawa Press and the *Journal of Prisoners on Prisons*.

© **Journal of Prisoners on Prisons, 2012**
All rights reserved. This includes the right to reproduce this journal or portions thereof in any form. Opinions expressed herein are not necessarily those of the publishers, editors, or sponsors.

ISSN 0838-164X
ISBN 978-0-7766-0940-9

In This Issue

PREFACE FROM THE MANAGING EDITORS

Convict Criminology
and the Journal of Prisoners on Prisons
Mike Larsen and Justin Piché

The *Journal of Prisoners on Prisons* (JPP) emerged in response to the underrepresentation of the voices of the criminalized in criminological and public discourse on punishment more broadly, and their marginalization within the International Conference on Penal Abolition specifically (Gaucher, 2002). Nearly a quarter century since the publication of the journal's first issue in 1988, it remains the case that the voices of those most affected by criminalized conflicts and harms – including those incarcerated in the community and inside prisons walls, as well as those they have harmed – are often silenced in academia, advocacy, public debate and the penal process itself. This being the case, it is vital that the work of the *JPP* and similar efforts continue to expand their reach to challenge common assumptions about, and dominant responses to, criminalized activities and statuses.

For fifteen years, Convict Criminology (CC) has shared many of the same commitments as the *JPP*, most notably privileging the voices of current and former prisoners in debates concerning penality (Ross and Richards, 2003). Convict Criminologists have also made numerous other contributions, including mentoring countless numbers of criminalized individuals as they have made the transition from prisons to their communities, as well working towards the development of reform-oriented penal policies and practices.

Recognizing the importance of privileging the accounts of the criminalized and acknowledging the many challenges they face in attempting to disseminate their firsthand knowledge (see Piché, 2008), many from the CC Group have made sustained contributions to the *JPP* by reviewing submissions as members of the Editorial Board, and introducing inside and outside students to prison writing by using journal issues as part of their university courses. Convict Criminologists have also submitted and published articles in the *JPP*.

For us, this special double issue celebrating "The First Dime and Nickel of Convict Criminology" edited by Stephen C. Richards and Michael Lenza represents a continuation of the shared commitment by, and work of, the *JPP* and the CC Group that aims to merge the experiences of the criminalized with criminological literature to shed light on contemporary penal policies and practices. We are particularly excited about this collection as a number of the articles introduce readers to some of the emerging voices within CC who illuminate important issues pertaining to punishment and reentry through ethnographic contributions that will challenge even the most critical of thinkers to reflect upon their pre-conceived notions concerning those who are excluded from society. Moving forward, the contributions of current and former prisoners to the discussion on punishment remain vital if we are to, in the words of *JPP* contributor Jo-Ann Mayhew, "help halt the disastrous tend toward building more fortresses of fear which will become in the 21st century this generation's monuments to failure".

REFERENCES

Gaucher, B. (ed.) (2002) *Writing as Resistance: The Journal of Prisoners on Prisons Anthology 1988-2002*, Toronto: Canadian Scholars' Press.

Piché, J. (2008) "Barriers to Knowing Inside: Education in Prisons and Education on Prisons", *Journal of Prisoners on Prisons*, 17(1): 4-17.

Ross, J. I. and S. C. Richards (eds.) (2003) *Convict Criminology*, Belmont (CA): Wadsworth.

EDITORS' INTRODUCTION

The First Dime and Nickel of Convict Criminology
Stephen C. Richards and Michael Lenza

In prison convicts learn a lot of lingo. They have their own language to discuss how sentences add up. A person is lucky to have sentences run concurrent, compared to consecutive, which is "running wild". Years ago old-time convicts, when asked about how much time they had to serve in prison, would talk of doing nickels, dimes and quarters. They might say they have three convictions, for example five years for burglary, ten years for a felony with a firearm and twenty-five years for murder. This meant they were pulling a train, with two boxcars and a caboose. They would go to the parole board first for the nickel, then the dime, then the quarter. Each sentence served independently was a pocket full of change if they were still alive to tell the tale.

DEDICATION OF THIS ISSUE

We decided to dedicate this issue to two Convict Criminologists that devoted their professional careers to helping convicts, some of whom have served the kinds of sentences noted above, each in their own way. John Irwin and Thomas Bernard were professors that encouraged the publication of convicts and ex-convicts, while contributing to the Convict Criminology (CC) Perspective themselves.

John Irwin
John Irwin, Professor of Sociology and Criminology at San Francisco State University, passed away in 2010. John was an ex-convict who served time in California. In 1957, he got out of prison and attended San Francisco State University, graduating from UCLA in 1961. He then completed his Ph.D. in Sociology at UC Berkeley in 1968. He was a professor for twenty-seven years.

For forty years he wrote about prisons. The main themes he explored included convict culture, prisoner typologies, conditions of confinement, political manipulation of the public's fear of crime and the creation of a felony underclass in the United States. He is best known for his ethnographies of prison life and innovative typologies of convict roles and identities. Richards (2009a, p. 176) notes:

3

> In all of Irwin's books he writes about people, the folks you meet in prison.
> In The Rogue (unfinished memoir) he wrote about his own experience in
> prison as a convict in the 1950's [...] His analytical invention of prisoner
> typologies began with his own incarceration and became more refined in
> each book.

His typologies included thieves, hustlers, dope fiends, heads, disorganized
criminals, state-raised youth, man in the lower class, square johns, petty
hustlers, derelicts, junkies, crazies, cornerboys, lowriders, aliens, gays, thugs,
gangbangers, outlaws, state-raised prisoners, crazies and sex offenders.
John's books include *The Felon* (1970), *Prisons In Turmoil* (1980), *The Jail*
(1985), *It's About Time* (1994, with James Austin), *The Warehouse Prison*
(2005), Lifers (2009) and *The Rogue* (unfinished memoir). He was also a
major contributor in *Struggle for Justice* (1971) and *Scenes* (1977).

John Irwin was one of the founders of CC. For many of us in the
CC Group, John served as a mentor, confidant and friend. At the annual
meetings of the American Society of Criminology (ASC) John Irwin had the
academic reputation and connections to join in discussions with any group
he choose to, yet one could almost always find him sitting at a table with
one or two ex-convict graduate students or professors. Richards (2009a, pp.
173-174) observes:

> Every year, at conferences and events, before or after Convict Criminology
> sessions, I introduce John to new felons, most of them graduate students
> struggling to complete their degrees, and wondering when they might exit
> the closet and publicly announce their personal truth. John helps them to
> prepare for their "coming out", where they introduce themselves to the
> audience by relating their criminal activity, convictions, and prison time,
> to their research. Once they step out of the closet they are members of the
> Convict Criminology Group.

> John takes them aside, engages them in conversation, and gives each
> one personal attention. He is very straight forward, as he tests their
> transparency, their courage to retain their own identity, despite the stigma
> they suffer, and the temptation to conceal their past. Irwin understands that
> most felons prefer not to talk about their crimes, convictions, and time in
> prison, especially in public. The problem is the charade may become an

elaborate subterfuge; the ex-convict slides into respectability, and then becomes a prisoner again of the secrets they keep. Their professional lie becomes a performance that inhibits their work and limits their ability to write about the subject they are determined to bury.

John had little patience for pretence. He would ask very direct questions: What was your crime? Where did you do time? What do you miss about prison?

Thomas Bernard

Thomas Bernard, a Professor of Criminal Justice and Sociology at the Pennsylvania State University, died in 2009. He received his B.A. in Mathematics at the University of Notre Dame in 1968, M.S. in Administration of Justice at Southern Illinois University in 1975 and Ph.D. in Criminal Justice at the State University of New York at Albany in 1981. Tom was a non-con member of the CC Group. Over the years he attended and participated in many of our sessions at conferences. He is best known for his books *Vold's Theoretical Criminology* (2002), *Consensus-Conflict Debate* (1983) and *The Cycle of Juvenile Justice* (2010).

We especially remember Tom for the many books he edited or co-authored with convict authors. He is responsible for developing the talents of many and helping to get their writing published including K. C. Carceral's *Behind a Convict's Eyes* (2003) and *Prison, Inc.* (2005), James Paluch's *Life for a Life* (2003), Victor Hassine's *Life Without Parole: Living and Dying in Prison* (2011), as well as others. Tom was especially interested in publishing the work of convicts doing long or life sentences. He recruited a crew of academic colleagues, including Robert Johnson, Leanne Fiftal Alarid, Bruce Bikle, Alene Bikle, John Irwin, and Stephen Richards to help with the editing, revising and publications of numerous convict authors.

THE BIRTH OF CONVICT CRIMINOLOGY

CC was born of the frustration ex-convict professors and graduate students felt when reading the academic literature on prisons. In our view, most academic textbooks and journal articles reflected the ideas of prison administrators, while largely ignoring what convicts knew about the day-to-day realities of imprisonment. Instead, these works tended to gloss over the horrors of prison, inventing a sanitized presentation, without the smell of fear and noise of desperation known so well by the men and women that live in cages. Ross *et al.* (2012, p. 160) elaborate on this critique noting:

> Many prison studies tended to approach the subject abstractly, or from secondary data sources, with little detail or differentiation among security levels, state or federal systems, or regional jurisdictions. When details were provided, for example on prison conditions or subculture within a prison, the data and sources were often outdated. Most studies were conducted without even entering the prison concerned or interviewing the prisoners.

In reply, these former prisoners now academics working at universities teaching sociology, criminology, criminal justice, social work and related disciplines developed a new criminological perspective to better represent the reality they knew in prison before they entered university.

We have related the long story of how CC began in previous publications (see Richards and Ross, 2001; Ross and Richards, 2003; Jones *et al.*, 2009; Ross *et al.*, 2012). The short story is that in 1997 a small group of ex-convict professors gave papers on a panel at the ASC conference. This session was entitled "Convicts Critique Criminology: The Last Seminar". Ross *et al.* (2012, p. 162) note:

> This was the first time a collection of ex-convict academics had appeared openly on the same panel at a national conference. The session drew a large audience including national media. That evening, over dinner, James Austin, John Irwin, Stephen Richards, and Chuck Terry discussed the importance and possibilities of ex-con professors working together to conduct "inside studies" of prisons and other criminological matters. This group and the scholarly work they produced eventually became known as "convict criminology".

The papers presented at this first conference and those thereafter led to the book *Convict Criminology* (2003). Ross *et al.* (2012, pp. 162-163) note:

> In the spring of 1998, Richards spoke with Jeffrey Ian Ross, a former prison worker currently with the University of Baltimore, about the possibility of editing a book using manuscripts produced by ex-con academics. Almost

immediately, Ross and Richards sent out formal invitations to ex-convict professors and graduate students, and well-known critical authors of work on corrections. In short order, a proposal was written that would eventually result in the book, *Convict Criminology* (Ross & Richards, 2003). This was the first time ex-convict academics had appeared in a book together that included discussion of the authors' own criminal convictions, their time in prison, and their experiences in graduate school and as university professors.

Since 1997, the CC Group has organized nearly fifty sessions, panels, roundtables and workshops at numerous academic events in the United States and abroad. These appearances have included plenary sessions at the meetings of the American Society of Criminology, the Academy of Criminal Justice Sciences and the American Correctional Association. For example, in 2008, an ASC Presidential Plenary Session on Convict Criminology was held, featuring Dave Curry, John Irwin, Stephen Richards and Jeffrey Ian Ross.

THE FIRST DIME AND NICKEL

The first fifteen years of CC was very productive based on the number of research studies conducted and published. These include books, journal articles, and chapters in edited books. In general the work has been critical of the criminal justice system, especially the treatment of prisoners and parolees. Writing as a collective, with different combinations of co-authors, the Convict Criminologists have critiqued and challenged existing policies and practices, as they built their own "New School of Convict Criminology" (Richards and Ross, 2001, 2004; Ross and Richards, 2003; Richards *et al.*, 2008, 2009, 2010, 2011; Jones *et al.*, 2009; Ross *et al.*, 2010, 2012).

The CC Group has also been very active examining and analyzing existing public policy concerning a wide array of criminal justice issues concerning felons, convicts and ex-convicts. Numerous CC essays have been published with policy recommendations, including this issue (see Richards *et al.*; Grigsby; Murphy *et al.*; Oliver; Ekunwe and Jones). Authors have discussed prison conditions (Irwin, 1970, 1980, 2005, 2009; Richards, 1995; Jones and Schmid, 2000; Austin *et al.*, 2001; Ross and Richards, 2003, 2004; Terry, 2003; Tregea and Larmour, 2009; Richards *et al.*, 2010; Austin and Irwin, 2012), jails (Irwin, 1985), private prisons (Hogan and Richards, 2006), the classification of prisoners (Richards and Ross, 2003), violence in prison (Austin *et al.*, 2001; Carceral, 2003, 2005: Carceral *et al.*, 2008; Hassine, 2011), medical care in prisons (Murphy 2003, 2005), and super max prisons (Richards, 2008). We have also published pieces on the death penalty (Lenza, 2005), prisoner reentry to the community (Richards, 1995; Richards and Jones, 1997, 2004; Ross and Richards, 2009; Leyva and Bickel, 2010; Richards *et al.*, 2011, 2012), the mass incarceration movement in the United States (Rose *et al.*, 2010), ethnography and autoethnographic research (Irwin, 1987; Lenza, 2011), money, policies and crime (Lenza and Jones, 2010), women guarding men (Richards *et al.*, 2002; Murphy *et al.*, 2008), folk knowledge of medical marijuana use for alcoholism (Lenza, 2007), medical marijuana (Lenza, 2012), community punishments (Richards, 1998, 2009), as well as ex-cons applying for university faculty positions (Ross *et al.*, 2010). Additional essays and research have included employment barriers for felons (Murphy *et al.*, 2011, 2012), felon disenfranchisement in America (Murphy *et al.*, 2006), prisons (Newbold 1982, 1989, 2007) and crime (Newbold, 1992, 2000) in New Zealand, controlling state crime in the United States (Richards and Avery, 2000), and many related topics (see the CC website at http://www. convictcriminology.org).

THIS ISSUE

Building on the contributions noted above and introducing new voices emerging within the CC Group, this issue is divided into three parts. *Part I: Defining Convict Criminology* leads with a group statement by Stephen C. Richards, Jeffrey Ian Ross, Greg Newbold, Michael Lenza, Richard S. Jones, Daniel S. Murphy, and Robert S. Grigsby entitled "Convict Criminology, Prisoner Reentry and Public Policy Recommendations". The second article by John F. Frana, Michael Lenza and Ryan D. Schroeder, "Convict Criminologists in the Classroom", is a survey of student views regarding the prospects of having an ex-convict teaching their criminal justice courses. James Burnett and D J Williams report how they used CC to develop a rehabilitative initiative in "Convict Criminology and Community Collaboration: Developing a Unique Program to Empower Vulnerable Youth in Idaho". In "Fundamental Problems in Criminal Justice Knowledge Production" Michael Lenza challenges the way research is constructed and conducted in mainstream criminology and criminal justice. The section concludes with a piece by Robert S. Grigsby exploring how CC might chart a path forward in "Convict Criminology and Social Justice Advocacy: Toward Radical Change".

Part II: Prisoners in the Community begins with an essay by Daniel S. Murphy, Stephen C. Richards and Brian Fuleihan entitled "Policy Options to Mitigate the Criminal Record Barrier to Employment". It is followed by Richard Hendricksen and Alan Mobley's "A Tale of Two Convicts: A Reentry Story About the Impacts of Ethnicity and Social Class". This autoethnographic piece brings to life how structural inequality and the destructive systematic indifference of how our criminal justice system affects the ability of individuals to reintegrate into society. In "A Convict Criminology Perspective on Sex Offender Laws: America's "War against Sex Offenders"" by Brian Oliver and "Interrelated Problems of Silencing Voices and Sexual Crime: Convict Criminology Insights for Reducing Victimization" by D J Williams and James Burnett some of the unique challenges faced by those convicted of sexual offences are discussed. The last piece is an autobiographical account by Jesse De La Cruz entitled "Detoured: My Journey from Darkness to Light" that reflects upon his personal journey from being a convict in San Quentin to becoming an ex-convict graduate student in California.

Part III: Convict Criminology Beyond Borders reports our recent efforts to educate ourselves about prison conditions in other countries, and establish collaborations with ex-convicts in Great Britain and Finland. Andreas Aresti reports on "Developing a Convict Criminology Group in the UK". Matti "Kid" Hytönen recounts how ex-convicts established a group in Finland to help prisoners and former prisoners reenter society in partnership with government in "An Ugly Fairy Tale with an Ending of Hope: The Founding of KRIS in Finland". Its continued success is in part due to their recognition of the promise of prisoners returning to society to use their knowledge and experiences to help others and their communities. The last article, "Finnish Criminal Policy: From Hard Time to Gentle Justice", by Ikponwosa O. Ekunwe and Richard S. Jones provides the historical background for one of the most progressive criminal justice systems in the Western world. The issue concludes with three short *Response* pieces by Katherine Irwin, Robert Johnson, and Mike Larsen and Justin Piché that reflect on the past and future of CC.

THINKING ABOUT THE FUTURE
OF CONVICT CRIMINOLOGY

The CC Group continues to grow. Every year we add ex-con and non-con academics to our ranks. We know that we depend on the support of hundreds of non-con professors and administrators working at universities in the United States and many other countries that help ex-convict students and faculty, sometimes at the risk of their own careers. Despite our success, we know of ex-convicts being denied admission to undergraduate programs or admitted and denied dormitory rooms. We know of college graduates denied admission to graduate programs or having their graduate student stipends suspended after the states passed new laws (e.g. Missouri and Kentucky). We also know Ph.D. students who have been denied an opportunity to defend their dissertations (e.g. Texas) and ex-convict professors denied tenure or promotion in numerous states. Unfortunately, some private and public universities are uncomfortable with both ex-convict students and faculty.

The fact is that ex-convict professors are still just a few dozen, including those in the United States, United Kingdom, New Zealand, Canada, France and Finland. Regardless of the state or the country for that matter, we have learned over the past fifteen years that, while it may be safer to play it low profile, it compromises our ability to support all the prisoners coming out of prison that manage to gain admittance to a university. At many universities the ex-con professors work to advise and mentor the many ex-con students that ask for help. Most of us spend a lot of time attending to the academic dreams of felons and ex-convicts that find us because our work is public. Our hope is that every large university in the country comes to realize that they need to hire ex-con professors or at the very least academic advisers to serve felons, as much as they hire people to advise women, minorities and non-traditional students.

Nevertheless, while we celebrate the fifteenth anniversary of CC with this issue, the future of our movement is not assured. While our contributions to the critical literature on criminology and prisons continue, and we have a few more ex-convict tenured professors, we still have no academic home. Ideally, we need at least one Endowed Chair in Convict Criminology to guarantee the future of our group, along with the over seven million men and women presently under correctional supervision who need to know their voices and experiences matter.

REFERENCES

Austin, J., M. A. Bruce, L. Carroll, P. L. McCall and S. C. Richards (2001) "The Use of Incarceration in the United States: American Society of Criminology National Policy Committee White Paper", *Critical Criminology*, 10(1): 17-41.

Austin, J. and J. Irwin (2012) *It's About Time: America's Imprisonment Binge* (fourth edition), Belmont (CA): Wadsworth.

Bernard, T. J. (1983) *The Consensus-Conflict Debate*, New York: Columbia University Press.

Bernard, T. J. and M. C. Kurlychek (2010) *The Cycle of Juvenile Justice*, New York: Oxford University Press.

Bernard, T. J., G. B. Vold and J. B. Snipes (2002) *Vold's Theoretical Criminology*, London: Oxford University Press.

Carceral K. C. (2005) *Prison, Inc.: A Convict Exposes Life Inside a Private Prison*, New York: New York University Press.

Carceral K. C. (2003) *Behind a Convict's Eyes: Doing Time in a Modern Prison*, Belmont (CA): Wadsworth.

Carceral, K.C., C. D. Rose, S. C. Richards and T. J. Bernard (2008) Moving Beyond the Officer-prisoner Model of Control", in R. K. Ruddell and N. E. Fearn (eds.), *Correctional Violence*, Richmond (KY): Newgate Press, pp. 231-248.

Hassine, V. (2011) *Life Without Parole: Living and Dying in Prison Today*, London: Oxford University Press.

Hogan, R. G. and S. C. Richards (2006) "Private Prison Problems", *Journal of Prisoners on Prisons*, 15(1): 53-64.

Irwin, J. (2009) *Lifers: Seeking Redemption in Prison*, London: Routledge.

Irwin, J. (2005) *The Warehouse Prison: Disposal of the New Dangerous Class*, Los Angeles: Roxbury.

Irwin, J. (1987) "Reflections on Ethnography", *Journal of Contemporary Ethnography*, 16: 41-48.

Irwin, J. (1985) *The Jail*, Berkeley: University of California Press.

Irwin, J. (1980) *Prisons in Turmoil*, Boston: Little Brown.

Irwin, J. (1970) *The Felon*, Englewood Cliffs (NJ): Prentice-Hall.

Jones, R. S., J. I. Ross, S. C. Richards and D. S. Murphy (2009) "The First Dime: A Decade of Convict Criminology", *Prison Journal*, 89(2): 151-171.

Lenza, M. (2012) "Medical Marijuana", in D. Schultz (ed.), *Encyclopedia of American Law and Criminal Justice*, New York: Facts On File.

Lenza, M. (2011) "The Critical Role of Ethnography and Autoethnographic Research: Validating Voices of Prisoners and Former Prisoners within Postmodern Theories and Methods", in O. E. Ikponwosa and R. S. Jones (eds.), *Global Perspectives on Reentry*, Tampere (FI): Tampere University Press, pp. 146-172.

Lenza, M. (2007) "Toking Their Way Sober: Alcoholics and Marihuana as Folk Medicine", *Contemporary Justice Review*, 10(3): 307-322.

Lenza, M. and R. S. Jones (2010) "Money, Criminology and Criminal Justice Policies: The Impacts of Political Policies, Criminality, and Money on the Criminal Justice in the United States", in Martine Herzog-Evans (ed.), *Transnational Criminology Manual* (volume 1), Netherlands: Wolf Legal Publishers, pp. 313-332.

Lenza, M., D. Keys and T. Guess (2005) "The Prevailing Injustices in the Application of the Missouri Death Penalty (1978-1996)", *Social Justice*, 32(2): 151-166.

Leyva, M. and C. Bickel (2010) "From Corrections to College: The Value of a Convict's Voice", *Western Criminology Review*, 11(1): 50-60.

Murphy, D. S. (2005). "Medical Care in the Federal Bureau of Prisons: Fact or Fiction", *California Journal of Health Promotion*, 3(2): 3-37.

Murphy, D. S. (2003) "Aspirin Ain't Gonna Help the Kind of Pain I'm In: Health Care in the Federal Bureau of Prisons, in J. I. Ross and S. C. Richards (eds.), *Convict Criminology*, Belmont (CA): Wadsworth, pp. 246-266.

Murphy, D. S., B. Fuleihan, S. C. Richards and R. S. Jones (2011) "The Electronic "Scarlet Letter": Criminal Backgrounding and a Perpetual Spoiled Identity", *Journal of Offender Rehabilitation*, 50(3): 101-118.

Murphy, D. S., A. Newmark and A. Philip (2006) "Felon Disenfranchisement in the United States", *Juvenile Justice and Criminal Justice Policy*, 3: 1-24.

Murphy, D. S., C. M. Terry, G. Newbold and S. C. Richards (2008) "A Convict Criminology Perspective on Women Guarding Men", *Justice Policy Journal*, 4(2): 1-36.

Newbold, G. (2007) *The Problem of Prisons: Corrections Reform in New Zealand*, Wellington (NZ): Dunmore.

Newbold, G. (2000) *Crime in New Zealand*, Palmerston North (NZ): Dunmore.

Newbold, G. (1992) *Crime and Deviance*, Auckland (NZ): Oxford University Press.

Newbold, G. (1989) *Punishment and Politics: The Maximum-security Prison in New Zealand*, Auckland (NZ): Oxford University Press.

Newbold, G. (1982) *The Big Huey*, Auckland (NZ): Collins.

Paluch, J. (2003) *Life for a Life: Life Imprisonment*, London: Oxford University Press.

Richards, S. C. (2009a) "John Irwin", in K. Hayward, S. Maruna and J. Mooney (eds.), *Fifty Key Thinkers in Criminology*, London: Routledge, pp. 173-178.

Richards, S. C. (2009b) "A Convict Perspective on Community Punishment: Further Lessons from the Darkness of Prison", in J. I. Ross (ed.), *Cutting the Edge: Current Perspectives in Radical/Critical Criminology and Criminal Justice* (second edition), Edison (NJ): Transaction, pp. 122-144.

Richards, S. C. (2008) "USP Marion: The First Federal Super-max", *Prison Journal*, 88(1): 6-22.

Richards, S. C. (1998) "Critical and Radical Perspectives on Community Punishment: Lessons from the Darkness", in J. I. Ross (ed.), *Cutting the Edge: Current Perspectives in Radical/Critical Criminology and Criminal Justice* (first edition), New York: Praeger, pp. 122-144.

Richards, S. C. (1995) *The Structure of Prison Release: An Extended Case Study of Prison Release, Work Release, and Parole*, New York: McGraw-Hill.

Richards, S. C., J. Austin and R. S. Jones (2004a) "Thinking About Prison Release and Budget Crisis in the Blue Grass State", *Critical Criminology*, 12(3): 243-263.

Richards, S, C., J. Austin and R. S. Jones (2004b) "Kentucky's Perpetual Prisoner Machine: It's About Money", *Review of Policy Research*, 21(1): 93-106.

Richards, S. C. and M. J. Avey (2000) "Controlling State Crime in the United States of America: What Can We Do About the Thug State?", in J. I. Ross (ed.), *Varieties of State Crime and Its Control*, Monsey (NY): Criminal Justice Press, pp. 31-58.

Richards, S. C. and R. S. Jones (2004) "Beating the Perpetual Incarceration Machine", in S. Maruna and R. Immarigeon (eds.), *After Crime and Punishment: Pathways to Offender Reintegration*, London: Willan Publishers, pp. 201-232.

Richards, S. C. and R. S. Jones (1997) "Perpetual Incarceration Machine: Structural Impediments to Post-prison Success", *Journal of Contemporary Criminal Justice*, 13(1): 4-22.

Richards, S. C. and M. Lenza (2012) "Day Reporting Centers", in Jeffrey Ian Ross (ed.) *Encyclopedia of Street Crime in America*, Thousand Oaks (CA): Sage.

Richards, S. C., M. Lenza, G. Newbold, R. S. Jones, D. Murphy and R. Grigsby (2010) "Prison as Seen by Convict Criminologists", in M. Herzog-Evans (ed.), *Transnational Criminology Manual* (volume 3), Nijmegen (Netherlands): Wolf Legal Publishers, pp. 343-360.

Richards, S. C., G. Newbold and J. I. Ross (2009) "Convict Criminology", in M. J. Miller (ed.), *21st Century Criminology: A Reference Handbook* (volume 1), Thousand Oaks (CA): Sage, pp. 356-363.

Richards, S. C. and J. I. Ross (2004) "The New School of Convict Criminology", *Journal of Prisoners on Prisons*, 13: 11-26.

Richards, S. C. and J. I. Ross (2003) "Convict Perspective on the Classification of Prisoners", *Criminology & Public Policy*, 2(2): 243-252.

Richards, S. C. and J. I. Ross (2001) "The New School of Convict Criminology", *Social Justice*, 28(1): 177-190.

Richards, S, C., J. I. Ross and R. S. Jones (2008) "Convict Criminology", in G. Barak (ed.), *Battleground: Criminal Justice*, Westport (CN): Greenwood, pp. 106-115.

Richards, S. C., J. I. Ross, G. Newbold, M. Lenza, R. S. Jones, D. S. Murphy and R. S. Grigsby (2012) "The Challenge of Pragmatic Solutions: Convict Criminology, Prisoner Reentry, and Public Policy", in R. Immarigeon and L. Fehr (eds.), *Pathways for Prisoner Reentry: An ACA Reader*, Alexandria (VA): American Correctional Association.

Richards, S. C., J. I. Ross, G. Newbold, M. Lenza, R. S. Jones, D. S. Murphy and R. S. Grigsby (2011) "Convict Criminology: Prisoner Re-entry Policy Recommendations", in I. O. Ekunwe and R. S. Jones (eds.), *Global Perspectives on Re-entry*, Tampere (FI): University of Tampere Press, pp. 198-222.

Richards, S. C., C. M. Terry and D. S. Murphy (2002) "Lady Hacks and Gentlemen Convicts", in L. F. Alarid and P. Cromwell (eds.), *Contemporary Correctional Perspectives: Academic, Practitioner, and Prisoner*, Los Angeles: Roxbury, pp. 207-216.

Rose, C. D., V. Beck and S. C. Richards (2010) "The Mass Incarceration Movement in the USA", in M. Herzog-Evans (ed.), *Transnational Criminology Manual* (volume 2), Nijmegen (Netherlands): Wolf Legal Publishers, pp. 533-551.

Ross, J. I. and S. C. Richards (2009) *Beyond Bars: Rejoining Society After Prison*, New York: Alpha/Penguin Group.

Ross, J. I. and S. C. Richards (2003) *Convict Criminology*, Belmont (CA): Wadsworth.

Ross, J. I. and S. C. Richards (2002) *Behind Bars: Surviving Prison*, New York: Alpha/Penguin Group.

Ross, J. I., S. C. Richards, G. Newbold, R. S. Jones, M. Lenza, D. S. Murphy, R. G. Hogan and G. D. Curry (2010) "Knocking on the Ivory Towers' Door: The Experience of

Ex-convicts Applying for Tenure-track University Positions", *Journal of Criminal Justice Education,* 21(3): 1-19.

Ross, J. I., S. C. Richards, G. Newbold, M. Lenza, R. S. Grigsby (2012) "Convict Criminology", in W. DeKeseredy and M. Dragiewicz (eds.), *The Routledge Handbook of Critical Criminology*, London: Routledge, pp. 160-171.

Terry, C. M. (2003) The Fellas: Overcoming Prison and Addiction, Belmont (CA): Wadsworth.

Tregea, W. and M. S. Larmour (2009) *The Prisoners' World: Portraits of Convicts Caught in the Incarceration Binge*, New York: Lexington Books.

ABOUT THE SPECIAL ISSUE EDITORS

Stephen C. Richards, PhD, is an ex-convict now Professor of Criminal Justice at the University of Wisconsin-Oshkosh. His work has appeared in numerous academic journals. The author of five books, his most recent books include *Behind Bars: Surviving Prison* (2002), *Convict Criminology* (2003) and Beyond Bars (with Jeffrey Ian Ross) (2009). Richards is a Soros Senior Justice Fellow and member of the American Society of Criminology National Policy Committee. He is lead organizer of the Convict Criminology Group.

Michael Lenza, PhD, is an ex-convict who is now an Associate Professor of Criminal Justice at the University of Wisconsin-Oshkosh. He has published on the death penalty, research ethics, medical marijuana, a historical political view of the development of mass incarceration in the USA, as well as theory and research methods. He is currently working on the institutional foundations of violence in the American context, and utilizing postmodern autoethnograpic theory and methods to provide voice to prisoners.

PART I

DEFINING CONVICT CRIMINOLOGY

Convict Criminology, Prisoner Reentry and Public Policy Recommendations *

Stephen C. Richards, Jeffrey Ian Ross,
Greg Newbold, Michael Lenza, Richard S. Jones,
Daniel S. Murphy and Robert S. Grigsby

INTRODUCTION

"Convict Criminology" (CC) began in the United States in the mid-1990s and has grown over the years (Richards and Ross, 2001, 2003a, 2003b, 2004, 2005, 2007; Ross and Richards, 2002, 2003, 2009; Murphy *et al.*, 2008; Richards *et al.*, 2008, 2010, 2011a, 2011b; Jones *et al.*, 2009; Ross *et al.*, 2010). CC started out of the frustrations many of us felt when reading the academic literature on prison and prisoner reentry. In our view, much of the published work on correctional facilities reflected the ideas of prison administrators and largely ignored what convicts knew about the day-to-day realities of confinement. Many prison studies tended to approach the subject abstractly, or from secondary and often outdated sources, with little detail or differentiation among security levels, state or federal systems, or regional jurisdictions. Some studies were conducted without even entering a prison or interviewing prisoners. In response, former prisoners with PhDs, along with some allied critical criminologists, began conducting ethnographic and autoethnographic research (Lenza, 2011) that reflected a more hands-on approach to the analysis of prison life and its aftermath.

Convict criminologists, working at universities across the United States and in other countries, are informed by personal experiences as former prisoners and/or correctional workers, along with traditional training as academics in sociology, political science, criminology and related disciplines. The object of CC is to educate the public, academics and policy makers about the realities of confinement, as well as the social and psychological impediments to community reentry. Additionally, we serve as role models, mentors, and advisors for prisoners and formerly incarcerated persons who are completing college degrees in the social sciences.

PRISON REENTRY POLICY RECOMMENDATIONS

Convict criminologists do not claim to have a monopoly on knowledge about jails and correctional institutions, but we generally make policy recommendations. Indeed, we borrow selectively from conservative, liberal, critical and radical criminological/criminal justice approaches alike. With this in mind, the following sections briefly outline our prisoner reentry policy recommendations. Many of these suggestions, based on years of formal and observational research, were originally introduced in previous publications (Richards, 1995, 1998, 2008; Richards and Jones, 1997, 2004; Jones and Schmid, 2000; Richards and Ross, 2001; Austin and Irwin, 2001; Austin *et al.*, 2001, 2003a, 2003b; Ross and Richards, 2003; Richards *et al.*, 2004a, 2004b, 2010, 2011a, 2011b; Irwin, 2005, 2009; Jones *et al.*, 2009; Ross, 2008; Ross *et al.*, 2010). These policy recommendations are offered as a blueprint for rethinking the way prisoner release to the community is organized in the United States.

Our policy recommendations for reentry start before the individual is convicted and sentenced. The reason is that it is difficult separating out pre-custody, custody and post-release in the real world. We know that current reentry programs are largely a failure. Repeatedly, prisoners are granted parole only to be violated soon thereafter and returned to prison often for minor technical infractions. In order to break this cycle we need to rethink the entire incarceration process, as well as procedure for release and recall. We need to make serious and pragmatic recommendations about the changes to be implemented. The following proposals are based on what we have learned from our own personal experiences and from the many interviews we have conducted with prisoners and parolees over the past 15 years. In this article, we propose twelve steps towards a new direction in corrections in the United States:

1. Reduce the U.S. prison population;
2. Increase the scope and range of restorative justice programs;
3. End the 'war on drugs';
4. Demilitarize the criminal justice system;
5. End punishment packages;
6. Restore voting rights to felons and prisoners;
7. Close old and functionally obsolete prisons;
8. Restore federally funded higher education to all prisons;
9. Properly prepare prisoners for release;
10. Improve medical services;
11. Provide community resource centers; and
12. Provide residential treatment centers.

1. REDUCE THE U.S. PRISON POPULATION

Approximately one in 31 American adults is under criminal justice control. Such figures disproportionately impact minority populations resulting in one in 27 Hispanics, and one in 11 Blacks under the supervision of the state. If current trends continue, one in three Black males can expect to be imprisoned in their lifetime (Pew Center, 2009). Every year over 600,000 American men and women leave prison to re-enter society.

Where imprisonment is concerned, the United States incarcerates four to five times as many citizens per head of population as other modern democracies such as Canada, England, Australia and New Zealand (Department of Corrections, 2001; Newbold and Eskridge, 2005). In large part, the American prison population has grown dramatically because prisoners receive long sentences for minor crimes, including simple possession of drugs or common assault (Miller, 1996, pp. 10-47), followed by long periods of community supervision after release with strict conditions, rigorous monitoring and hair-trigger violation components. Parolees may be summarily returned to prison for breaking technical rules of supervision.

We advocate dramatic reductions in the national prison population. We argue for imprisonment only as a last resort for serious crimes, where the convicted person cannot be safely supervised in the community. This can be done by recognizing that imprisonment should be reserved for only the most dangerous criminals. For example, many drug addicts could be offered community-based residential drug treatment, instead of imprisonment. Violent offenders could receive shorter sentences, followed by longer terms on parole, depending upon their disposition for future violence (see Irwin, 2009, pp. 6-15). Perhaps some of the longest sentences should be served by persons guilty of serious corporate and white-collar crimes that have resulted in serious injury or economic loss for many people. Most prisoners, regardless of their crimes, could become eligible for parole review after three years in prison. Recall to prison should only occur after serious or repeated breaches of parole conditions. A reduction in the national prison population could be accomplished by restructuring sentence administration and substituting many prison sentences with probation, fines, and community service.

2. INCREASE THE SCOPE AND RANGE OF RESTORATIVE JUSTICE PROGRAMS

We recommend extending and rethinking the many ways community restorative justice services can be successfully employed (Richards, 1998, 2009; Richards and Jones, 1997, 2004; Ross and Richards, 2009), particularly for young and Aboriginal offenders. Restorative justice (Daly, 2006; Strang *et al.*, 2006) is a process that recognizes and builds upon traditions of solving conflicts through communal communicative processes – common within indigenous populations such as those in North America, New Zealand, Australia and Israel (Zehr, 2002, 2004). Unlike modern state-oriented criminal justice processes, restorative justice focuses on the harm to individuals and the offenders' obligation to repair the damage done. Ideally, restorative justice creates a voluntary, safe, and respectful environment for the victim, the offender, and community representatives to meet, discuss issues surrounding the offending, and reach a mutually acceptable solution (Zehr, 2002).

Because restorative justice requires the willing participation of both the offender and the victim, and meetings can be difficult and expensive to organize, their practical utility is limited. Moreover, restorative justice is less suited to hardened, serious recidivists, to offenders with multiple victims, or to those convicted of 'victimless' crimes. Restorative justice methods are, however, ideally suited for young first-time offenders who may not fully appreciate the personal pain that their actions have caused. Participation in restorative justice may mitigate, but should not be used to completely void, the punitive consequences of criminal actions (Daly, 2006, 2008; Maxwell *et al.*, 2006; Ministry of Justice, 1995).

3. END THE 'WAR ON DRUGS'

The United States has lost its much-vaunted 'war on drugs' (Chambliss, 1995; Miller, 1996; Austin and Irwin, 2001). Rather than ending America's drug problem, the 'war on drugs', which began in 1970, has led to an "imprisonment binge" (Austin and Irwin, 2001; Austin *et al.*, 2001) with millions of men and women incarcerated, and an immense burden to taxpayers in the form of police, courts, jails, prisons, and welfare payments to the dependant families of prisoners. In 1980, there were 40,000 Americans in prison or jails on drug charges. With the ongoing intensification of the 'war on drugs' since 1980, by 2009 the number had grown to 500,000 Americans in prison or jail on drug charges alone. In 2005, African Americans represented about 14 percent of unlawful drug users, yet they represent 34 percent of those arrested for drug offenses and 53 percent of those sentenced to prison for drug offenses (Mauer, 2009; Sheldon, 2001). We are long overdue in recognizing that the 'war on drugs' is a flawed policy, causing more social harm through its implementation than the actual harm from the drugs themselves (Miron and Zwiebel, 1995).

Today, there is a growing recognition that a return to medical solutions such as opiate maintenance is a viable and promising alternative to prohibitionist policies. Opiate maintenance programs in Canada and Europe have been shown to reduce crime, improve the health of addicts and greatly reduce involvement with black markets for opiates (Blanken *et al.*, 2010; Lindesmith, 1947; Oviedo-Joekes *et al.*, 2009; Uchtenhagen, 2010; Van den Brink, 2009). The Swiss program, allowing doctors to prescribe heroin, morphine or methadone to addicts resulted in a 60 percent reduction in the number of criminal offenders, while income from illegal activities of addicts fell from 69 percent to 10 percent. At $30 per patient per day, the net economic benefit to society was established through a cost-benefit analysis because of reduced criminal justice and health care costs (Nadelmann, 1998, p. 120). The American 'war on drugs' needs to end and be completely replaced by harm reduction and/or medical model of treatment. By decriminalizing personal drug possession and usage, and returning the treatment of drug addiction to our health care system instead of our criminal justice system, we can reduce the harm associated with drug usage and its associated costs (see Drucker, 1995; De Jarlais, 1995; Nadelmann, 1998).

4. DEMILITARIZE THE CRIMINAL JUSTICE SYSTEM

Since the invention of the penitentiary in the 18th Century, prison systems in the United States and elsewhere in the world have become authoritarian regimes roughly organized on the police or military model. This model has been reflected in the uniforms and ranking of staff, and use of nomenclature such as "superintendent", "officer", and "warden". Even parole officers, although dressed in civilian clothing in many states, carry badges and firearms like police detectives. The military-type imagery of law enforcement is enhanced by the use of terms such as "war on crime" and "war on drugs", with the perpetrators thus depicted as the "enemy". The result is an occupational mindset based on fighting wars and vanquishing enemies. In such an atmosphere, containment and control easily take precedence over correction and rehabilitation.

We suggest that a new direction in American corrections might begin with changing the job titles of correctional "officer" to correctional "worker" and parole "officer" to parole "worker". These professional titles (like that of social "worker") would ideally be accompanied by a college degree and a license. We see the upgrading of the professional status and competency of staff, together with a shedding of the authoritarian model, as an important first step in effective prison reform.

5. END PUNISHMENT PACKAGES

Many courts are now handing out multiple sentences in what Morris and Tonry (1990) have called "punishment packages", that include both prison time and so-called "alternative" sentences. Initially, probation, restitution, fining and community service were intended as alternatives to incarceration. Community supervision (e.g. probation or court-ordered treatment for substance abuse) was developed as a means to divert minor or first-time offenders from prison. With the exception of fining and restitution, combining prison sentences with non-custodial sanctions defeats the meaning and purpose of the alternative remedy.

We recommend that apart from financial penalties, imprisonment and community-based alternatives should be mutually exclusive sentencing options, meaning they should not be imposed at the same time. There should be an end to the stacking or piling-on of sanctions. Moreover, we suggest that restitution, fines and court costs should only be imposed upon those with reasonable means of repayment. For those who cannot pay, community service may be an option. Further, we suggest that court-ordered child support payments be suspended while a person is in jail or prison, unless the court can demonstrate that the prisoner has assets or income to pay the bills.

6. RESTORE VOTING RIGHTS TO
ALL FELONS AND PRISONERS

Another matter that concerns us is voting rights. The United States is one of the few advanced industrial countries that deny most prisoners in jail (even before they are convicted of felonies) and convicted felons in prison, on parole, or in some states for the rest of their life, the right and opportunity to vote in elections. If the government wishes prisoners to become responsible and contributing members of society, it should endow prisoners with the same democratic rights as other citizens.

People do not lose their sense of fairness and justice just because they go to prison. Their life experiences are often unique and varied, and their opinions and values are no less valid than those of any other person. Moreover, because law and order is often such a key component of election campaigns, the voice of the criminal is of critical significance. Criminals, generally, have a practical and realistic view of criminal justice issues, nurtured by years of personal experience. The enfranchisement of prisoners is thus a fundamental component of any society, which calls itself "democratic".

7. CLOSE OLD AND FUNCTIONALLY OBSOLETE PRISONS

Prison conditions have steadily deteriorated over the past thirty years, largely because of growing correctional populations, rising incarceration costs, ageing institutions and a thinning of resources. Many American jurisdictions, struggling under the weight of heavy correctional population increases, have been forced to keep archaic institutions open in order to contain the burgeoning numbers. Prisoners in old penitentiaries may be forced to sleep two or even three to a cell, or on the floor along a tier. In most medium- and minimum-security facilities prisoners sleep in dormitories. Such conditions create huge management problems, with the result that up to 20 percent of the population of some institutions has to be kept in solitary confinement under administrative or punitive segregation. Here, with almost nothing in the way of vocational or educational resources, they languish until their sentences expire (Austin and Irwin, 2001; Austin *et al.*, 2001; Irwin, 2005, 2009; Richards, 2008; Ross, 2008).

We oppose the warehousing of prisoners in old penitentiaries and reformatories. Over many decades, the design and operation of these archaic "big house" prisons has dehumanized prisoners, contributing to higher levels of intimidation, serious assault, and sexual predation than in newly constructed facilities. As is the case in many other advanced industrialized countries, a reduced prison population detained in smaller institutions could be accomplished by constructing or redesigning prison units. In small correctional facilities where prisoners are held in single-celled units of no more than 60 people, maintaining control and security is easier and the incidents of sexual predation is close to zero. New Zealand, along with a number of European countries, follows this model (see Newbold, 2007).

Accordingly, we recommend that American correctional authorities work towards the replacement of "big house" prisons with smaller, more management-friendly facilities. Modern prisons should be divided into small, discrete, administrative units of about 60. Small-unit management provides staff with an opportunity to get to know the prisoners, their names, their needs and their ability for self-improvement. Having a collection of such units upon a single site allows for the development of a variety of larger industries and work programs for the development of the prisoners' employment skills.

8. RESTORE FEDERALLY FUNDED
HIGHER EDUCATION TO ALL PRISONS

All prisons should offer prisoners serving sentences over one year the opportunity of accessing education programs appropriate to their competence and aptitude. These might involve courses taught inside the prison or at nearby colleges. The federal government should help underwrite tuition costs. Alternatively, states might consider a program that waives the first year of tuition, or room and board, at state-supported schools and universities, for men and women just released from custody.

The state would save money by assisting former prisoners to attend college, rather than having them living on welfare and returning to prison. It now costs, depending on the state and level of security, from $15,000 to $100,000 to keep one adult in a correctional facility for a year. For example, it might cost $15,000 a year to keep a person in a minimum-security camp, while the expense for high-security or super-max solitary confinement might approach $100,000 per year. If assisting prisoners with the cost of higher education helps them to get jobs, pay taxes, support their families and avoid further imprisonment, the potential savings can be significant (Richards and Ross, 2007).

Federal funding might also be used to begin innovative college programs inside prisons. The important idea is that the federal government has a responsibility to help return college programming to prisons. In Wisconsin, for example, a program called "Inviting Convicts to College" has been in place since 2004, training pairs of undergraduate student intern instructors to go inside prisons to teach a free college course entitled "Convict Criminology" (Richards *et al.*, 2006, 2008a, 2008b; Rose *et al.*, 2005, 2010a, 2010b). The courses use the books *Convict Criminology* (Ross and Richards, 2003) and *Beyond Bars* (Ross and Richards, 2009) to educate and inspire the prisoners. Classes are taught two hours a week, for 14 weeks, and are supervised by ex-convict professors.

Prisoners exiting prison use the course as a bridge to entering college, with the final weeks including instruction on completing university admission and financial aid forms. The prisoners learn that admission to college, as well as financial aid grants and loans, can be a viable parole plan. The program has already helped a number of prisoners to enter universities where they receive ongoing advice and mentoring from members of the Convict Criminology Group.

9. PROPERLY PREPARE PRISONERS FOR RELEASE

Preparation for release should begin the day a person enters prison and should intensify as his or her discharge date approaches. Prisoners should be processed from high to low-security levels as part of a carefully planned "staged release program". This means a prisoner who enters a maximum-security prison (penitentiary) is provided an opportunity to earn his or her way down the ladder to medium-security (correctional institution), then minimum-security "in custody" (prison camp), and finally minimum-security "out custody" where he or she qualifies for home furloughs and release to work a job or attend college in the community during the day and return to prison camp at night.

In order to assist prisoner development, institutions need to invest in libraries, vocational and educational programs, social work services, and medical care. This requires increased funding, a commitment to helping prisoners, community co-operation, and a steady flow of information and feedback between the prisons and community corrections concerning conditions on the street. These programs should include liberal visitation privileges, home furloughs for well-behaved prisoners, and family and employment counseling.

All prisoners should have a detailed plan prepared by a dedicated release planner, before discharge. This may be a work-release or parole plan. The release planner should arrange for persons nearing release to obtain drivers' licenses and social security cards. Prisoners with outstanding consumer or tax debt could receive legal counseling on filing for bankruptcy. The plan should include specific reference to family, place of residence and employment or school. Also, pre-release preparation may include escorted home visits for men to see their children and spouses or ex-spouses, if deemed safe and appropriate.

Another recommendation concerns the need for work-release facilities within or near prisons, operating with low supervision. Few work-release clients require the intensive supervision used in controlled movement facilities. We suggest that work-release centers currently operated by the federal government and non-profit agencies may provide a model for the guidance of state correctional administrators contemplating such a move.

Irrespective of work-release, however, we urge that individuals getting out of prison should have enough "gate money" to provide for up to three months' living expenses as a guard against financial desperation and relapse. All persons exiting correctional institutions should have clothing suitable for the climate and environment into which they are entering, and access to subsidies for work-related clothing and equipment expenses. Some of the costs involved could be recouped from prison wages, with the balance provided by the state.

Finally, all states should consider funding prison, residential, and counseling services administered, operated, and staffed by ex-convicts who hold college degrees in social work, social science, or related subjects. Former prisoners know and understand the difficulties of leaving prison and re-entering the community. Their expertise is an available resource rarely utilized and desperately needed if we are ever to make a dent in the rate of recidivism.

10. IMPROVE MEDICAL SERVICES

We believe that providing proper medical care for persons in custody is a fundamental duty of the state. As things stand, one of the most terrifying scenarios is to be a prisoner in the United States with a serious illness. The standard of treatment for sickness and pain is generally poor, and there is much unwarranted suffering, sometimes leading to untimely death, within our penal institutions. We recommend that independent qualified hospital staff, outside the command structure of corrections departments, regulate all prison medical care. We also recommend that prisoners with serious or terminal medical conditions be transferred to community hospitals, where they can receive better medical treatment, at a reduced cost.

However, recognizing that prevention is better than cure, and that many entering prisons come from backgrounds of poverty with limited access to medical services, we also recommend that all prisoners be provided with education in health and nutrition. By giving prisoners proper training in health, prison-related health care expenses could be reduced and the health status of the prisoner would improve over the course of incarceration. Thus, it would be more likely to be maintained after release. Additionally, the adoption of a healthy lifestyle may lead to a reduction in criminal or drug-related activity, and reducing recidivism (see Murphy, 2003, 2005).

11. PROVIDE COMMUNITY RESOURCES CENTERS

If we really want to help people coming out of prison, we need to provide for the likelihood of their success. When they are released, they should thus be free of petty or punitive parole supervision. This means not only a relief from intrusive scrutiny, but also provision of appropriate professional services. Through a process of assisted decision-making, prisoners should be enabled to make responsible choices about the kinds of help – vocational, domestic, medical, drug and alcohol treatment – that they may need.

Accordingly, we suggest that probation and parole workers be assigned office space at well-equipped Community Resource Centers, which would provide services to help people find jobs, get training, go to school, secure affordable housing, and readjust to family life. This deployment would serve the needs of both ex-convicts and the local community. These centers could serve a broad spectrum of people with fewer state or federal employees. Some resource workers might specialize in people coming out of jails or prisons, while others would focus on the disabled, homeless or unemployed. These services would help offenders adjust to the "free world", thus reducing their chances of returning to a life of crime.

12. PROVIDE RESIDENTIAL TREATMENT CENTERS

The current punitive system of justice incarcerates people without addressing seriously the factors that led to the offending in the first place. The public demands that criminals be punished for their crimes, but for a correctional system to be effective, it must also alter criminal behavior patterns and mindsets. Drug related crime presents a special challenge, because in this case, addictive precursors to criminal activity also have to be neutralized.

We encourage authorities to consider thinking about the prevention of criminal and addictive activity in a new way: through state-run Residential Treatment Centers (RTCs). RTCs may operate as a substitute for imprisonment or as a means of assisting prisoners at the very end of their time in prison, or when they return to the community. There are a number of ways of running RTCs, but the Delancey Street Foundation in San Francisco and its sister organization, the Salisbury Street Foundation in New Zealand, are possible models (see Hough, 2003; Newbold, 2007; Newbold and Hough, 2009).

RTCs generally offer residential treatment of twelve months or more for selected offenders, within a system of graduating privilege and freedom. Residents are assisted into jobs and accommodation upon release, and receive ongoing support on an ad hoc basis once they are discharged. Organizations of this type are no 'magic bullet' for the problem of recidivism, but when properly operated and resourced they can have a significant impact on the post-prison lives of some offenders. Because RTCs are less expensive to run than prison they are a worthwhile investment for any jurisdiction serious about reducing reoffending.

We suggest different states might begin pilot programs where they convert one or more prisons into an RTC. The RTC would be staffed by more social workers, teachers and health care workers, and fewer correctional officers. This would give the states large facilities where they could treat thousands of persons at one time.

They might also explore allowing free citizens to voluntarily request commitment as a means to receive treatment for alcoholism, drug addiction or other behavioral problems that may be associated with criminal offenses. People might ask for help because they know their problems will eventually lead to arrest. For example, people that drink and drive, or have become addicted to street drugs or doctor prescribed medications, or have developed a pattern of losing their temper, would ask for treatment. The RTC would be operated to serve a diverse population of people, including those assigned by court, jail or prison, as well as those that know they have a problem and request admission, without any arrest or conviction.

CONCLUSION

In this article, we have proposed policy recommendations for rethinking incarceration and the reentry process in the United States. Our proposals have ranged from suggestions relating to sentencing, prison alternatives, changing the job orientations of correctional employees, improvements in the physical conditions of prisons, preparation of prisoners for release, and finally the availability of integrative programs and services for prisoners after readmission to the free world.

Nevertheless, we have left a number of topics unaddressed. We have not discussed the experience of arrest, pre-trial lockup and court processing (see Ross and Richards, 2002, pp. 1-46). We have not touched on the spoiled identity of felons resulting from online public access to criminal records in the United States (Murphy *et al.*, 2010), the plight of 'lifers' in the prisons (Irwin, 2009) and many other topics.

As Convict Criminologists, we contend that state agencies routinely fail to address simple problems that contribute to high incarceration, re-offending and reincarceration rates in the United States. In effect, state agencies have created a "perpetual incarceration machine" (Richards and Jones, 1997, 2004) that recycles the same people repeatedly through the same processes without improving their life-chances. In failing to adequately prepare prisoners for life after incarceration, prisons set in motion a self-motivating cycle. Unless the traditional and popular notions about crime and punishment, which form the basis of the existing system, are questioned, meaningful change will not be possible. In our view, if the taken-for-granted is not contested to the point where state agencies become ready to rise to the challenge of finding pragmatic solutions, recidivism will remain at its currently high levels, while the prison system will continue to replicate its record of dismal underachievement and failure.

ENDNOTE

*Earlier versions of this paper were published in Ikponwose O. Ekunwe and Richard S. Jones (eds.) (2011) *Global Perspectives on Re-entry*, Tampere (FI): University of Tampere Press, and Russ Immarigeon and Larry Fehr (eds.) (2011) *Pathways for Prisoner Reentry: An ACA Reader*, Alexandria (VI): American Correctional Association.

REFERENCES

Austin, J., M. A. Bruce, L. Carroll, P. L. McCall and S. C. Richards (2001) "The Use of Incarceration in the United States: ASC National Policy Committee White Paper", *Critical Criminology*, 10(1): 17-41.

Austin, J. and J. Irwin (2001) *It's About Time: America's Imprisonment Binge*, Belmont (CA): Thomson Learning.

Austin, J., S. C. Richards and R. S. Jones (2003a) "New Ideas for Reforming Parole in Kentucky", *Offender Programs Report*, 7(2): 19-20, 22, 24.

Austin, J., S. C. Richards and R. S. Jones (2003b) "Prison Release in Kentucky: Convict Perspective on Policy Recommendations", *Offender Programs Report*, 7(1): 1, 13-16.

Blanken, P., W. van den Brink, V. M. Hendriks, I. A. Huijsman, M. G. Klous, and E. J. Rook (2010) "Heroin-assisted Treatment in the Netherlands: History, Findings, and International Context", *European Neuropsychopharmacology*, 20: S105-S158.

Chambliss, W. J. (1995) "Another Lost War: The Costs and Consequences of Drug Prohibition", *Social Justice*, 22: 101-124.

Daly, K. (2006) "The Limits of Restorative Justice", in D. Sullivan and L. Tifft (eds.), *Handbook of Restorative Justice: A Global Perspective*, Abington (UK): Routledge.

Daly, K. (2008) "Girls, Peer Violence, and Restorative Justice", *Australian and New Zealand Journal of Criminology*, 41(1): 109-137.

Department of Corrections (2001) *About Time: Turning People Away From a Life of Crime and Reducing Re-offending*, Wellington (NZ).

Des Jarlais, D. C. (1995) "Harm Reduction: A Framework For Incorporating Science Into Drug Policy", *American Journal of Public Health*, 85: 10-12

Drucker, E. (1995) "Harm Reduction: A Public Health Strategy", *Current Issues in Public Health*, 1: 64-70.

Hough, D. (2003) *A History and Analysis of the Salisbury Street Foundation in Christchurch*, Unpublished Master of Arts Thesis, Christchurch: University of Canterbury – New Zealand.

Irwin, J. (2009) *Lifers: Seeking Redemption in Prison*, London: Routledge.

Irwin, J. (2005) *The Warehouse Prison: Disposal of the New Dangerous Class*, Los Angeles: Roxbury.

Jones, R. S. and T. Schmid (2000) *Doing Time: Prison Experience and Identity Among First Time Inmates*, Stamford (CT): JAI Press.

Jones, R. S., J. I. Ross, S. C. Richards and D. S. Murphy (2009) "The First Dime: A Decade of Convict Criminology", *Prison Journal*, 89: 151-171.

Lenza, M. (2011) "The Critical Role of Ethnography and Autoethnographic Research: Validating Voices of Prisoners and Former Prisoners Within Postmodern Theories and Methods", in I. O. Ekunwe and R. S. Jones (eds.), *Global Perspectives on Reentry*, Tampere (FI): Tampere University Press, pp. 146-172.

Lenza, M. and R. S. Jones (2010) "Money, Criminology and Criminal Justice Policies: The Impacts of Political Policies, Criminality, and Money on the Criminal Justice in the United States", in Martine Herzog-Evans (ed.), *Transnational Criminology Manual* (volume 1), Netherlands: Wolf Legal Publishers, pp. 313-332.

Lindesmith, A. R. (1947) *Opiate Addiction*, Bloomington (IN): Principia Press.

Maxwell, G., A. Morris and H. Hayes (2006) "Conferencing and Restorative Justice", in *Handbook of Restorative Justice: A Global Perspective*, Abington (UK): Routledge.

Mauer, M. (2009) *Racial Disparities in the Criminal Justice System*, Washington (DC): The Sentencing Project.

Ministry of Justice (1995) *Restorative Justice: A Discussion Paper*, Wellington (NZ).

Miller, J. (1996) *Search and Destroy: African-American Males in the Criminal Justice System*, Cambridge (UK): Cambridge University Press.

Miron, J. A. and J. Zwiebel (1995) "The Economic Case Against Drug Prohibition", *Journal of Economic Perspective*, 9(4): 175-192.

Morris, N. and M. Tonry (1990) *Between Prison and Probation*, New York: Oxford University Press.

Murphy, D. S. (2005) "Health Care in the Federal Bureau of Prisons: Fact or Fiction", *California Journal of Health Promotion*, (3)2: 23-37.

Murphy, D. S. (2003) "Aspirin Ain't Gonna Help The Kind of Pain I'm In: Health Care in the Federal Bureau of Prisons", in J. I. Ross and S.C. Richards (eds.), *Convict Criminology*, Belmont (CA): Wadsworth, pp. 247-265.

Murphy, D. S., B. Fuleihan, S. C. Richards and R. S. Jones (2010) "The Electronic "Scarlet Letter": Criminal Backgrounding and a Perpetual Spoiled Identity", *Journal of Offender Rehabilitation*, 50(3): 101-118.

Murphy, D. S., C. M. Terry, G. Newbold and S. C. Richards (2008) "A Convict Criminology Perspective on Women Guarding Men", *Justice Policy Journal*, 4(2): 1-36.

Nadelmann, E. A. (1998) "Commonsense Drug Policy", *Foreign Affairs*, 77(1): 111- 126.

Newbold, G. (2007) *The Problem of Prisons*, Wellington (NZ): Dunmore.

Newbold, G. and C. Eskridge (2005) "History and Development of Modern Correctional Practices in New Zealand", in C. B. Fields and R. H. Moore, Jr. (eds.), *Comparative and International Criminal Justice: Traditional and Nontraditional Systems of Law and Control*, Long Grove (IL): Waveland.

Newbold, G. and D. Hough (2009) *Salisbury St Foundation, 1979-2009*, Christchurch (NZ): Salisbury St Foundation.

Oviedo-Joekes, E., S. Brissette, D. C. Marsh, P. Lauzon, D. Guh and A. Anis (2009) "Diacetylmorphine versus Methadone for the Treatment of Opioid Addiction", *New England Journal of Medicine*, 361(8): 777-786.

Pew Center on the States (2009) *One in 31: The Long Reach of American Corrections*, Washington (D.C.): The Pew Charitable Trusts – March.

Richards, S. C. (2009) "A Convict Perspective on Community Punishment: Further Lessons from the Darkness of Prison", in J. I. Ross (ed.), *Cutting the Edge: Current Perspectives in Radical/Critical Criminology and Criminal Justice* (second edition), Edison (NJ): Transaction, pp. 122-144.

Richards, S. C. (2008) "USP Marion: The First Federal Super-max", *Prison Journal*, 88(1): 6-22.

Richards, S. C. (1998) "Critical and Radical Perspectives on Community Punishment: Lessons from the Darkness", in J. I. Ross (ed.), *Cutting the Edge: Current Perspectives in Radical/Critical Criminology and Criminal Justice* (first edition), New York: Praeger, pp. 122-144.

Richards, S. C. (1995) *The Structure of Prison Release: An Extended Case Study of Prison Release, Work Release, and Parole*, New York: McGraw-Hill.

Richards, S. C., J. Austin and R. S. Jones (2004a) "Thinking About Prison Release and Budget Crisis in the Blue Grass State", *Critical Criminology,* 12(3): 243-263.

Richards, S, C., J. Austin and R. S. Jones (2004b) "Kentucky's Perpetual Prisoner Machine: It's About Money", *Review of Policy Research*, 21(1): 93-106.

Richards, S. C., D. Faggiani, J. Roffers, R. Hendricksen and A. J. Krueger (2008a) "Convict Criminology Courses at the University and in Prison", *Journal of Prisoners on Prisons*, 17(1): 43-60.

Richards, S. C., D. Faggiani, J. Roffers, R. Hendricksen and A. J. Krueger (2008b) "Convict Criminology: Voices from Prison", *Race/Ethnicity: Multidisciplinary Global Context*, 2(1): 121-136.

Richards, S. C. and R. S. Jones (2004) "Beating the Perpetual Incarceration Machine", in S. Maruna and R. Immarigeon (eds.), *After Crime and Punishment: Pathways to Offender Reintegration*, London: Willan Publishers, pp. 201-232.

Richards, S. C. and R. S. Jones (1997) "Perpetual Incarceration Machine: Structural Impediments to Post-prison Success", *Journal of Contemporary Criminal Justice*, 13(1): 4-22.

Richards, S. C., M. Lenza, G. Newbold, R. S. Jones, D. S. Murphy and R. S. Grigsby (2010) "Prison as Seen by Convict Criminologists", in M. Herzog-Evans (ed.), *Transnational Criminology Manual* (volume 3), Nijmegen (Netherlands): Wolf Legal Publishers, pp. 343-360.

Richards, S. C., C. D. Rose and S. O. Reed (2006) "Inviting Convicts to College: Prison and University Partnerships", in *The State of Corrections: 2005 Proceedings ACA Annual Conferences*, Lanham (MD): American Correctional Association, pp. 171-180.

Richards, S. C. and J. I. Ross (2007) "The New School of Convict Criminology: How Might Prison College Programs Rehabilitate Prisoners?", in L. F. Alarid and P. Reichel, *Corrections: A Contemporary Introduction*, Boston (MA): Allyn and Bacon.

Richards, S. C. and J. I. Ross (2005) "Convict Criminology", in M. Bosworth (ed.), *Encyclopedia of Prisons and Correctional Facilities*, Thousand Oaks (CA): Sage, pp. 169-175.

Richards, S. C. and J. I. Ross (2004) "The New School of Convict Criminology", *Journal of Prisoners on Prisons*, 13: 11-26.

Richards, S. C. and J. I. Ross (2003a) "Ex-convict Professors Doing Prison Research", in *The State of Corrections: 2002 Proceedings ACA Annual Conferences*, Lanham (MD): American Correctional Association, pp. 163-168.

Richards, S. C. and J. I. Ross (2003b) "Convict Perspective on the Classification of Prisoners", *Criminology & Public Policy*, 2(2): 243-252.

Richards, S. C. and J. I. Ross (2001) "The New School of Convict Criminology", *Social Justice*, 28(1): 177-190.

Richards, S. C., J. I. Ross, G. Newbold, M. Lenza, R. S. Jones, D. S. Murphy and R. S. Grigsby (2011a) "Convict Criminology: Prisoner Re-entry Policy Recommendations",

in I. O. Ekunwe and R. S. Jones (eds.), *Global Perspectives on Re-entry*, Tampere (FI): University of Tampere Press, pp. 198-222.

Richards, S. C., J. I. Ross, G. Newbold, M. Lenza, R. S. Jones, D. S. Murphy and R. S. Grigsby (2011b) "The Challenge of Pragmatic Solutions: Convict Criminology, Prisoner Reentry, and Public Policy", in R. Immarigeon and L. Fehr (eds.), *Pathways for Prisoner Reentry: An ACA Reader*, Alexandria (VA): American Correctional Association.

Richards, S, C., J. I. Ross and R. S. Jones (2008) "Convict Criminology", in G. Barak (ed.), *Battleground: Criminal Justice*, Westport (CN): Greenwood, pp. 106-115.

Rose, C. D., S. O. Reed and S. C. Richards (2005) "Inviting Convicts to College: A Free College Preparatory Program for Prisoners", *Offender Programs Report*, 8(6): 81, 91-93.

Rose, C. D., K. Reschenberg and S. C. Richards (2010a) "Inviting Convicts to College", *Journal of Offender Rehabilitation*, 49(4): 293-308.

Rose, C. D., K. Reschenberg and S. C. Richards (2010b) "Where Are We Now? An Update on the Evolution of the Inviting Convicts to College Program", *Offender Programs Report*, 14(3): 33-34, 43-45, 47.

Ross, J. I. (2008) *Special Problems in Corrections*, Upper Saddle River (NJ): Pearson/Prentice-Hall, pp. xi-xiv.

Ross, J. I. and S. C. Richards (2009) *Beyond Bars: Rejoining Society After Prison*, New York: Alpha/Penguin Group.

Ross, J. I. and S. C. Richards (2003) *Convict Criminology*, Belmont (CA): Wadsworth.

Ross, J. I. and S. C. Richards (2002) *Behind Bars: Surviving Prison*, New York: Alpha/Penguin Group.

Ross, J. I., S. C. Richards, G. Newbold, R. S. Jones, M. Lenza, D. S. Murphy, R. G. Hogan and G. D. Curry (2010) "Knocking on the Ivory Towers' Door: The Experience of Ex-convicts Applying for Tenure-track University Positions", *Journal of Criminal Justice Education*, 21(3): 1-19.

Sheldon, R. (2001) *Controlling the Dangerous Classes*, Boston: Allyn and Bacon.

Strang, H., L. Sherman, C. M. Angel, D. J. Woods, S. Bennett, D. Newbury-Birch and N. Inkpen (2006) "Victim Evaluations of Face-to-Face Restorative Justice Conferences: A Quasi-experimental Analysis", *Journal of Social Issues*, 62(2): 281-306

Uchtenhagen, A. (2010) "Heroin-assisted Treatment in Switzerland: A Case Study in Policy Change", *Addiction*, 105(1): 29-37.

Van den Brink, W. (2009) "Heroin Assisted Treatment", *British Medical Journal*, 1326-1326.

Zehr, H. (2004) *Critical Issues in Restorative Justice*, Monsey (NY): Criminal Justice Press.

Zehr, H. (2002) *The Little Book of Restorative Justice*, Intercourse (PA): Good Books.

ABOUT THE AUTHORS

Stephen C. Richards, PhD, is an ex-convict now Professor of Criminal Justice at the University of Wisconsin-Oshkosh. His work has appeared in numerous academic journals. The author of five books, his most recent books include *Behind Bars: Surviving Prison* (2002), *Convict Criminology* (2003) and *Beyond Bars* (with Jeffrey Ian Ross) (2009). Richards is a Soros Senior Justice Fellow and member of the American Society of Criminology National Policy Committee. He is lead organizer of the Convict Criminology Group.

Jeffrey Ian Ross, PhD, is an Associate Professor in the Division of Criminology, Criminal Justice and Forensic Studies, and a Fellow of the Center for International and Comparative Law at the University of Baltimore. He has researched, written, and lectured on national security, political violence, political crime, violent crime, corrections and policing for over two decades. Ross' work has appeared in many academic journals and books, as well as popular outlets. He is the author, co-author, editor or co-editor of thirteen books including *Behind Bars: Surviving Prison*, *Convict Criminology*, *Special Problems in Corrections*, and *Beyond Bars: Rejoining Society After Prison*.

Greg Newbold, PhD, is an ex-convict and Professor of Sociology at the University of Canterbury, New Zealand. His MA, on the social organization of a maximum-security prison, was completed while he was serving a 7½ year sentence for drug dealing at New Zealand's maximum security prison at Paremoremo, Auckland. He studied for his PhD after he was released in 1980. Since then he has published seven books and more than 60 scholarly articles. Currently regarded as New Zealand's leading authority on corrections, he is frequently sought by media and government agencies for advice on matters relating to crime and criminal justice.

Michael Lenza, PhD, is an ex-convict who is now an Associate Professor of Criminal Justice at the University of Wisconsin-Oshkosh. He has published on the death penalty, research ethics, medical marijuana, a historical political view of the development of mass incarceration in the USA, as well as theory and research methods. He is currently working on the institutional foundations of violence in the American context, and utilizing postmodern autoethnograpic theory and methods to provide voice to prisoners.

Richard S. Jones, PhD, is an ex-convict now Professor of Sociology at Marquette University. He is the author of the books *Doing Time: Prison Experience and Identity* (with Tom Schmid) and *Global Perspectives on*

Re-entry (with Ikponwosa O. Ekunwe). He has also published in the areas of prison experience, social identity and the problems of reentry faced by previously incarcerated individuals.

Daniel S. Murphy, PhD, is an ex-convict now Associate Professor in the Department of Justice and Criminal Studies, Appalachian State University. He has published many peer-reviewed articles and a recent book delineating an expansion of Robert K. Merton's work on strain/anomie theory. He is an active member of the Convict Criminology group as well as co-chair of the Federal Citizens United for the Rehabilitation of Errants' (FedCURE) Legislative Action Committee. He also serves as a member of FedCURE's Board of Directors.

Bob Grigsby, BA, is an ex-convict and independent researcher and policy analyst who is currently working as the education and social policy director for the Center for Social Justice Policy in the United States. He is a lecturer, as well as a facilitator of workshops and seminars on contemporary issues of crime and criminology. Bob is the web administrator for the Convict Criminology Group, co-authoring a number of articles and book chapters with its members.

Convict Criminologists in the Classroom
John F. Frana, Michael Lenza and Ryan D. Schroeder

INTRODUCTION

The United States has the highest incarceration rate in the world, with now over seven million, or one in thirty-one Americans under correctional supervision (PEW, 2009). Every year over 600,000 individuals are released from prisons that need to reintegrate back into society (Petersilia, 2004). It is not unreasonable that some of these released prisoners will aspire to careers in academia (Ross and Richards, 2003). In previous research, studies have found that criminal justice (CJ) students hold negative attitudes towards ex-prisoners, which suggest that ex-convict professors may experience opposition to the idea of having them teach courses. This exploratory research derived from survey responses highlighted in this article that found the overwhelming majority of students surveyed expressed a positive interest in and support for having a Convict Criminologist (CC) teaching in their CJ program. Utilizing a CC Perspective (Richards and Ross, 2001; Ross and Richards, 2003) we will first briefly discuss the prejudice against prisoners and ex-prisoners that is held by some faculty in criminology and CJ programs, how bias can infect the validity and reliability of research, as well as other relevant critiques advanced by CCs. We will then review our findings and discuss their implications.

REVIEW OF RELEVANT
CONVICT CRIMINOLOGY CRITIQUES

The term *infect* reflects current social science research on cognitive triggers. Referencing prejudicial stereotypes can trip these triggers inadvertently or unintentionally. Once tripped, a person's orientation to information and how it is processed can change without a person being consciously aware of it, as they reproduce the prejudice or bias embedded in the stereotypes (Levinson, 2008/2009). We have no reason to believe social scientists have some special cognitive immunity, thus prejudice and bias may enter the research process unannounced and unnoticed, infecting survey questions and replies. We will return to a discussion of how these cognitive triggers may affect or infect previous studies after presentation of our research and outcomes.

In the U.S., the vast majority of university faculty employed full-time as penologists are sheltered middle-class men and women. They have doctorates, but little experience with prisons, beyond the occasional tour of institutions. Many of these so-called academic prison experts have never spent more than a few hours inside a prison or interacted with prisoners for any prolonged period. With no real lived experience with convicts, they do not understand the subjects of their studies (Irwin, 2003). Smaller groups of faculty are former employees of the criminal justice system, for example lawyers, police, or correctional officers that may have mixed opinions of prisoners.

Many academic criminologists do not value the perspective of prisoners, nor do they view prisoners as respectable people (Jones *et al.*, 2009). In addition, most prison research is motivated by political ideology, economics and/or government funding (Richards and Ross, 2001; Austin, 2003; Terry, 2003; Jones *et al.*, 2009; Lenza and Jones, 2011; see also Lenza, this issue). This research tends to focus upon generating new typologies or categorizations, surveillance technologies and the management of a vast but marginalized population of Americans under correctional control (Austin, 2003). There is a significant disconnect between academic literature and the realities prisoners experience in our nations prisons (Richards and Ross, 2001; Ross and Richards, 2003, Richards *et al.*, 2010).

Beginning in the 1970s with Law Enforcement Alliance of America (LEAA) grants for police training programs, law enforcement and CJ programs became popular majors at two-year community and technical colleges. These programs later spread to four-year universities. Today, criminology and CJ programs have expanded to offer master's and doctoral degrees. Nevertheless, as academic programs or departments they remain resource dependent on state and federal criminal justice budgets who provide the job market for their students, funding for research and agency publications of research, much of which is controlled by political agendas. It is not surprising that many criminal justice faculties either are wedded to or fail to question the political ideologies of the criminal justice agencies they prepare students for careers in, or that fund their research. To question the validity of the social identities CJ constructs and places people in threatens a system that maintains its validity through systematic exclusion of the voices of people under their control (Lenza, 2011).

Many universities, claiming to value diversity, regularly deny employment to convicted felons. In the past, the majority of academics with a criminal record stayed in the closet, choosing to keep their past secret (Jones *et al.*,

2009). Today, with the wide use of computer generated criminal background checks it is nearly impossible to conceal a criminal record in the hiring process. Eventually, the university will learn about felony convictions, even if they are old and not included in computer databases.

Most CJ students, like many of their professors, have never actually visited a prison, interacted with prisoners or been the victim of a felony. Their knowledge comes from a co-mingling of stereotypes presented in the simulated realities of mass media where movies, news, culture, and beliefs are constructed and presented carefully. Stereotypes are an element of mass media constructions and our consumption of them. They require no empirical grounding in lived reality. Stigmatizing stereotypes in particular gain their validity through cyclic repetitions stimulating fears and emotions. The meanings of these self-referential symbols often float in a netherworld, independent of knowledge or the lives of real people. In modern technologies of mass communications, all too much is in Baudrillard's (1993) term nothing more than mere "simulacra".

The stereotypical prisoner is a mixture of media representations of sensationalized crimes, political rhetoric, as well as academic studies of career criminals (Irwin and Austin, 1997). One of the best ways of defining what we are is by "pointing to what we are not" (Ericson *et al.*, 1987 cited in Greer and Jewkes, 2005, p. 29). This then creates a sense of otherness or that "they" commit crime because they are not like "us" (Garfinkel, 1956; Greer and Jewkes, 2005). This simulacra construction of "us" and "them" is false. Bohm (1986, pp. 200-201) points out that "over 90% of all Americans have committed some crime for which they could be incarcerated". There is little actual difference between the person labeled criminal and the average citizen (Becker, 1963; Lemert, 1967).

CC questions the validity of studies in CJ that exclude the perspective of the people placed under its control. Irwin (1987, p. 42) argues that "any approach not based firmly on qualitative or phenomenological ground is not only a distortion of the phenomenon but also is very likely a corruption". Academics that simply analyze secondary data collected or funded by correctional or government bureaucracies conduct most academic research on prisons or prisoners. The researchers sit in their university offices, far removed from the realities of the prison, and produce "statistical trivia" which is not relevant to prisoners or the underlying factors related to crime (Richards and Ross, 2001). The current research is a qualitative and statistical analysis of CJ students' attitudes towards having an ex-convict as a professor teaching in their program.

ATTITUDES OF STUDENTS CONCERNING PUNISHMENT AND PRISONS

In examining the academic acceptability of a CC in the classroom it is appropriate to explore the attitudes of CJ and criminology students themselves. This research is unique in that it is the first study of CJ student attitudes (n=186) on having ex-convicts as professors in the classroom that has a sufficient sample and methodology for valid and reliable analysis. Prior research on the academic acceptability of former prisoners as professors in the classroom has been limited at best (see Richards *et al.*, 2008).

Mackey and Courtright introduced CC John Irwin's book *The Jail* (1985) in several courses to provide students with an alternative view on relying on incarceration in dealing with crime. Irwin's book was met with open hostility by numerous students. Due to this experience the professors decided to examine if there were differences between CJ students and non-CJ students' attitudes towards punishment. They found compared to students in other majors, CJ majors, at all levels of student status, held more punitive attitudes (Mackey and Courtright, 2000).

In 2005, Courtright *et al.* (2005) hypothesized that CJ students were less able to empathize with disadvantaged populations, especially prisoners. Measuring "emotional empathy" of CJ majors to non-CJ majors they found CJ majors overall scored lower empathy scores than others students. In contrast, CJ majors enrolled at Catholic Universities, which often include a social justice perspective, displayed significantly higher levels of empathy than their public university peers.

Research conducted by Farnworth *et al.* (1998) examined students' attitudes in relation to the death penalty, alternatives to incarceration (e.g. probation), as well as attitudes towards the 'war on drugs'. They hypothesized that as students progressed in higher education it would lead to a less punitive orientation to punishment, with the exception of those with employment experience in the penal system and CJ majors. Their findings revealed that for all variables non-CJ majors were less likely to hold strongly punitive views than CJ majors. However, their analysis did not reveal any reduction in punitive views as students, both CJ and other majors, progressed in their education.

Utilizing a pretest-posttest design, Lane (1997) found that students enrolled in a corrections course about jail and prison at a California university emphasizing intermediate punishments or alternatives to incarceration (e.g. house arrest, probation or boot camp), would be increasingly likely to accept the less punitive punishments. This shift in belief to less punitive punishment only held for nonviolent offenders. Student support for a strong punitive emphasis for violent crimes did not change.

Research undertaken by Miller *et al.* (2004) concluded that most university students, CJ majors or not, commonly do not have an educated understanding of crime in America or comprehend many of the problems within the correctional system. Interestingly, they found CJ majors were just as misinformed and inaccurate in assessments of the reality of crime within prisons as non-CJ majors. They argued that if educators do not address this misinformation within the classroom, they "create a vacuum in which the students are never challenged to rethink the realities of crime compared to the myths" (Miller *et al.*, 2004, p. 314). From this review of research on CJ majors' attitudes on punishment and empathy for prisoners, we initially assumed that CJ university students would be resistant to having an ex-convict as a professor teaching in their program.

FINDINGS

To measure CJ majors' attitudes and perceptions of ex-convicts, a short survey of socio-economic questions and an open ended question was developed. "How would you react to a course being taught by a former convict?" Surveys were distributed to a random selection of upper level CJ courses, at a mid-sized, mid–western university. A total of 197 student surveys were distributed to sophomores, juniors and seniors enrolled in upper level CJ classes. Students were informed it was an attitudinal survey on having an ex-convict professor teaching classes. Participation was voluntary. A total of 186 valid surveys were returned.[1]

As part of a qualitative review (Glaser and Strauss, 1967) of responses by students to how they would react to a course taught by an ex-convict professor, the data was coded into three mutually exclusive dimensions: 1) not an issue; 2) hesitant; and 3) would drop the course. Surprisingly 67.7 percent reported no problems with an ex-convict professor teaching in their program. More surprising were the numerous responses received within this

___

large majority of CJ majors that expressed views that an ex-convict professor would enhance their understandings of the criminal justice system.

Within the 67.7 percent of CJ majors expressing no problem with an ex-convict professor teaching, 61 percent provided responses that expressed views that a former convict professor could bring a different perspective into the classroom that would enhance their understanding of the criminal justice system. In addition, some of these students believed there was ideological bias in the classes of traditional CJ academics that constricted learning. One student wrote: "They [the former convict] are probably more knowledgeable than some of the professors I have had in past experience. Teachers who seem to be cops are not open minded about ideas. More strict on what they believe to be right and wrong". Another student noted:"The ex-convict would have more experience and a better stand point then a regular prof [essor]". One student added: "I think it would be interesting to get a different perspective on things, other than what we are taught".

Overall, it is the firsthand experience a former convict would bring to the class that students believed would be most beneficial to them. One student wrote: "an ex-convict professor would have more insight [and] firsthand experience. [And could] teach us about prison culture [along with] reasons for recidivism that a "book" teacher couldn't provide". Another replied: "I would be interested in their teaching point of view. I think it would be a good window to some real world experience".

Other students added that they would receive a better education learning CJ from an ex-convict:

> ...[learning] from a person, who actually knows [firsthand] instead from a person who only knows through research and study.

> The ex convict would know both sides of the law.

> Firsthand knowledge is better than any textbook or college degree.

> To actually hear what goes on in a prison / jail, well I can't even imagine.

Another student expanded their remarks, noting: "I think there are things to be learned from these people [ex-convicts] as much as anyone else. A convict has inside knowledge of the system and can bring another perspective to research this student would have no problem enrolling in a class taught by an ex-convict. If the class is not too difficult then yes".

Another dominant theme was the belief students expressed in rehabilitative change, which are similar to findings by Richards *et al.* (2008). One student wrote:

> They might have made a bad decision but now reject that choice. I would enroll in that class because I would like to hear their side of the story and learn more about why they were in that position. [After all] everybody gets a second chance, but 3 strikes and your out. I want to hear everyone's story and try to learn from everyone I can.

A second student noted: "It would be different but interesting. I think it would be inspiring to see an ex-convict reformed enough to actually teach a class effectively". A third student stated: "Peoples [sic] past shouldn't carry to the future if they're changed [...] as long as he/she has received proper education, this student would welcome an ex-con as an instructor". A fourth student responded: "To grasp the ideas of why the person did what they did in their past and what caused them to change. It would be a little frightening because of their past but interesting as well".

Students, who expressed less enthusiastic views or were hesitant about an ex-convict professor, were coded into the hesitant category, which comprised 26.9 percent of the respondents. Their main concern was that an ex-convict professor might introduce too much bias into the classroom material or they could be hesitant having them teaching, dependent upon the nature of the crime they committed. One student wrote: "He'd probably be biased but would have good insight". A second student responded: "Depends on [the] crime & time served [a] murder[er] teaching after 5 years [I would be] pissed off, former drug abuser, cool, people change". A third student stated: "I'd be fine with [an ex-con teaching class] as long as he knew what he was talking about [...] No[t] so for some crimes (murder child molesting etc.)". A fourth student wrote: "It depends on his crime. I would find it ironic".

A small minority of students, comprising 5.4 percent of those who completed the survey, responded that they would immediately drop the course upon learning of a professor's status as a convict. One student wrote: "I would be shocked that the university was paying an ex-convict let alone hired one to teach me my education". A second student stated: "I wouldn't like it. Laws need to become harsher to where [...] ex-convict will loose the opportunity to become a teacher". A third student responded: "I would have a definite problem w/it [...] there is no such thing as an ex-convict".

In our statistical analyses of students responses to having an ex-convict professor, the following independent measures were included in both a one way analysis of variance (ANOVA) and a multinomial logistic regression (Aldrich and Nelson, 1985): age (1 = 18-21, 4 = 31 or older), gender (female = 1), race (minority = 1), self-reported socioeconomic status (1 = poor, 5 = wealthy), current or prior work in the criminal justice system (1 = yes), full time college enrollment (1 = yes), class standing in college (1 = junior, senior or graduate student), and a measure of political conservatism (1 = conservative).

Surprisingly, the strongest independent variable in our analysis was racial minorities, who were significantly more likely to place an ex-convict professor either in the "not an issue" category or "would drop course" category, compared to a response in the "hesitant" category. The other significant variable was students with upper class standing. Third and fourth year students were significantly less likely to report that an ex-convict professor is not an issue than indicating that they would drop the course. No other independent variables were significant in either statistical analysis.

DISCUSSION

This research clearly established that a large majority of the CJ majors sampled had no issues with a CC teaching in their program. Further, many of the CJ students surveyed expressed interest or even preference for the educational insight a formerly incarcerated professor could bring to their educational experience. As noted by Ross (2003) many of the portrayals of prisoners and prisons are often a distortion of reality. Students themselves seem to have an awareness of this distortion of reality prevalent in CJ and criminology courses. Our question clearly asked the students to provide their thoughts about a professor who was an ex-convict, teaching in their program. Yet, we did not receive many responses reflecting the predominant stereotyping of prisoners as less than others individuals. Why?

Our exploratory findings run directly counter to previous research indicating CJ students do not value or have empathy for the experience of prisoners (Mackey *et al.*, 2005) and that CJ students are hostile to the writing of an ex-convict criminologist like John Irwin, due to being blinded by their strong punitive attitudes (Mackey and Courtright, 2000). We have no reason to believe the CJ students sampled in this study are vastly different than the CJ students in previous studies completed at other universities.

What we do believe is that most CJ and criminology faculty are unaware of or have not considered how language and the use of stigmatizing stereotypes can trigger an auto-prejudicial framing and processing of information (Levinson, 2008/2009). In most CJ and criminology academic programs there is hardly a subject addressed that does not carry an assumptive categorization of prisoners as some form of degenerate other. Convicts endure profound degradation ceremonies (Garfinkel, 1956), as they are processed through courts, jails and prisons that have no common comparison in free society. Middle-class faculty, many born to economic and social privilege, have never experienced the degradation of their master identity or humiliation of living for years under the rule of authoritarian order and control. Even if they are theoretically empathetic to the plight of prisoners, they may still not have the insight, experience or awareness to represent that reality in a valid way to their students. For example, they do not appreciate or comprehend the intellectual life of prisoners, or how some convicts learn humility and then reach for books to educate themselves.

Instead, most university faculty teach textbook CJ, using literature that is loaded with prejudicial terms (see Richards, 2009, pp. 142-143). Faculty can reify these prejudicial terms in lectures and class discussions, and thereby reinforce the stereotypes learned from crime movies, and spark emotional resentment and distrust of felons and convicts (e.g. terrorist, serial killer, child molester, sex offender, murderer, rapist, drug addict and thief). Arguably, most CJ faculty never consider that the textbooks they use systematically reflect the same cultural stereotypes of prisoners projected in the mass media, such as the idea that criminals are necessarily dangerous and dishonest.

We know that individual and group attitudes have an element of reflexivity in their social expression. People reflect on who they were and who they want to be. Mead wrote (1934, p. 311): "he can undertake and effect intelligent reconstructions of that self or personality in terms of its relations to the given social order, whenever the exigencies of adaptation to his social environment demand such reconstructions". He later elaborated on this idea further, noting: "A past never was in the form in which it appears as a past. Its reality is in its interpretation of the present" (Mead, 1938, p. 616). Student attitudes in a classroom are not predetermined outcomes. Rather, faculty as teachers construct the social environment of the classroom and thereby create the exigencies in the construction of selfhood that students must adapt to through reflexive reconstructions of their selves in the asymmetrical power relations of teacher-student interactions.

Our research suggests that the problems of prejudice and bias in CJ student attitudes towards prisoners is not necessarily embedded within and arise from students. It is troubling to read the work of faculty and researchers who do not even question the validity of the prejudicial stereotypical framings of prisoners' social identities that have been institutionalized in their academic disciplines (criminology and CJ). This is consistent with faculty and department self-interest due to their resource dependency upon agencies of coercive social control. In effect, academics still think and write "cop shop", teaching the same to their students. This is the very language that inflicts and enforces stigmatization, as well as suffering upon the millions of men and women that are labeled as felons and criminals (Hulsman, 1986).

The simple wording of the research questions in this study, of an ex-convict as a professor teaching CJ or criminology classes, was a construct that avoided triggering prejudicial cognition in most students, and allowed them to consider the proposition on its own merits. Opening that doorway to critical reflection on the merits of such a professor for their education resulted in strong positive responses from CJ students. Our findings suggest that a large majority of CJ students are quite capable of rejecting the dominant stereotype of a prisoner as one committed to crime and unresponsive to rehabilitation. The overwhelming majority of CJ students sampled clearly valued the perspective and experiences an ex-convict professor would bring to the classroom. Such findings, if supported by additional empirical studies that come to similar conclusions, could influence hiring policies in colleges and universities.

A small minority of CJ students sampled, 5.4 percent, were totally against the idea of having an ex-convict as a teacher. By introducing ex-convicts into the classroom, this could help this minority of students to face their fear of stereotyped others and thereby possibly reconsider their preconceived ideas. University classrooms are an ideal setting to expose and dismiss stereotypes and myths surrounding ex-convicts. Well-educated students could help to transform social control agencies and eventually lead to a more humane criminal justice system (Lenza and Jones, 2011).

ENDNOTE

[1] The vast majority of the sample was between the ages of 18 and 26 (90 percent). Women and minorities comprised 43 percent and 24 percent of the sample respectively. Class standing was relatively evenly split, with 54.8 percent having junior or higher student status. A large majority of respondents were full-time students (88.2 percent) and 29 percent of subjects reported a conservative political viewpoint.

REFERENCES

Aldrich. J. H. and F. D. Nelson (1985) *Linear Probability, Logit, and Probit models: Quantitative Applications in the Social Sciences*, Thousand Oaks (CA): Sage Publications.

Austin, J. (2003) "The Use of Science to Justify the Imprisonment Binge", in J. I. Ross and S. C. Richards (eds.), *Convict Criminology*, Belmont (CA): Thompson/ Wadsworth, pp. 17-36.

Baudrillard, J. (1993[1976]) *Symbolic Exchange and Death*, London: Sage.

Becker, H. S. (1963) *Outsiders: Studies in the Sociology of Deviance*, New York: Free Press.

Berger, P. L. and T. Luckmann (1966) *The Social Construction of Reality: A Treatise in the Sociology of Knowledge*, Garden City (NY): Doubleday.

Bohm, R (1986) "Crime, Criminal and Crime Control Policy Myths", *Justice Quarterly*, 3(2): 193- 214.

Courtright, K. E., D. A. Mackey and S. H. Packard (2005) Empathy Among College Students and Criminal Justice Majors: Identifying Predisposition Traits and the Role of Education, *Journal of Criminal Justice Education*, 16(1): 125-144.

Debbs, E. V. (2000[1927]) *Walls & Bars: Prison & Prison Life in the "Land of the Free"*, Chicago: Charles H. Kerr Publishing Company.

Ericson, R., P. Baranek and J. Chan (1987) *Visualizing Deviance: A Study of News Organizations*, Buckingham (UK): Open University Press.

Farnworth, M., D. R. Longmire and V. M. West (1998) "College Students' Views on Criminal Justice", *Journal of Criminal Justice Education*, 9(1): 39-57.

Glaser, B. and A. Strauss (1967) *The Discovery of Grounded Theory: Strategies for Qualitative Research*, New Jersey: Aldine Transaction.

Garfinkel, H. (1956) "Conditions of a Successful Ceremony", *American Journal of Sociology*, 61(5): 420-424.

Goffman, E. (1963) *Stigma: Notes on the Management of Spoiled Identity*, Englewood Cliffs (NJ): Prentice-Hall.

Greer, C. and Y. Jewkes (2005) "Extremes of Otherness: Media Images of Social Exclusion", *Social Justice*, 32(1): 20-31.

Harding, S. (1991) *Whose Science? Whose Knowledge? Thinking from Women's Lives*, Ithaca (NY): Cornell University Press.

Hulsman, H.C. (1986) "Critical Criminology and the Concept of Crime", *Contemporary Crisis*, 10: 63-80.

Irwin, J. (2003) "Preface", in J. I. Ross and S. C. Richards (eds.), *Convict Criminology*, Belmont (CA): Thompson/Wadsworth, pp. xvii-xxii.

Irwin, J. (1987) "Reflections on Ethnography", *Journal of Contemporary Ethnography*, 16: 41-48.

Irwin, J. (1985) *The Jail*, Berkeley (CA): University of California Press.

Irwin, J. and J. Austin (1997) *It's About Time: Americas Imprisonment Binge* (second edition), Belmont (CA): Wadsworth Publishing.

Jones, R. S., J. I. Ross, S. C. Richards and D. S. Murphy (2009) "The First Dime: A Decade of Convict Criminology", *Prison Journal*, 89(2): 151-171.

Lane, J. S. (1997) "Can You Make a Horse Drink? The Effects of a Corrections Course on Attitudes Towards Criminal Punishment", *Crime & Delinquency*, 43(2): 186-202.

Lemert, E. M. (1967) *Human Deviance, Social Problems and Social Control*, Englewood Cliffs (NJ): Prentice-Hall.

Lenza, M. (2011) "The Importance of Postmodern Autoethnography and Ethnography in Criminal Justice Research and Policy Development", I. O. Ekunwe and R. S. Jones (eds.), *Global Perspectives on Re-Entry*, Tampere (FI): Tampere University Press.

Lenza, M. and R. S. Jones (2010) "Money, Criminology and Criminal Policies: The Impacts of Political Policies, Criminality, and Money on Criminal Justice in the United States", M. Herzog-Evans (ed.), *Transnational Criminology Manual* (volume 1), Netherlands: Wolf Legal Publishers, pp. 313-332.

Levinson, J. D. (2008/2009) "Race, Death, and the Complicitous Mind", *DePaul Law Review*, 58: 599-644.

Mackey, D. A. and K. E. Courtright (2000) "Assessing Punitiveness Among College Students: A Comparison of Criminal Justice Majors With Other Majors", *The Justice Professional*, 12: 423-441.

Mackey, D.A., K. E. Courtright and S. H. Packard (2006) "Testing the Rehabilitative Ideal Among College Students", *Criminal Justice Studies*, 19(2): 153-170.

Mead, G. H. (1938) *The Philosophy of the Act*, edited by C. Morris, J. Brewster, A. Dunham and D. Miller, Chicago: University of Chicago Press.

Mead, G. H. (1934) *Mind, Self, & Society from the Standpoint of a Social Behaviorist*, Chicago: University of Chicago Press.

Miller, A. J., R. Tewksbury and C. Hensley (2004) "College Students' Perceptions of Crime, Prison and Prisoners", *Criminal Justice Studies*, 17(3): 311-328.

Petersilia, J. (2004) "What Works in Prisoner Reentry? Reviewing and Questioning the Evidence", *Federal Probation*, 84: 4-8.

Pew Center on the States (2009) *One in 31: The Long Reach of American Corrections*. Retrieved from <http://www.pewcenteronthestates.org/uploadedFiles/PSPP_1in31_report_FINAL_WEB_pdf>.

Pew Center on the States (2008) *One in 100: Behind Bars in America*. Retrieved from <http://www.pewcenteronthestates.org/uploadedFiles/8015PCTS_ Prison08_ FINAL_2-1-1_FORW EB.pdf>.

Potter, G.W. and V. E. Kappeler (1998) *Constructing Crime: Perspectives on Making News and Social Problems*, Prospect Heights (IL): Waveland Press.

Richards, S. C. and J. I. Ross (2001) "Introducing the New School of Convict Criminology", *Social Justice*, 28(1): 177-190.

Richards, S. C., D. Faggiani, J. Roffers, R. Hendricksen and J. Krueger (2008) "Convict Criminology: Voices from Prison", *Race/Ethnicity: Multidisciplinary Global Context*, 2(1): 121-136.

Ross, J. I. and S. C. Richards (2003) "Introduction: What is the New School of Convict Criminology", in J. I. Ross and S. C. Richards (eds.), *Convict Criminology*, Belmont (CA): Thompson/Wadsworth, pp. 1-14.

Terry, C. M. (2003) "From C-block to Academia: You Can't Get There From Here", in J. I. Ross and S. C. Richards (eds.), *Convict Criminology*, Belmont (CA): Thompson/Wadsworth, pp. 95-119.

Wood, J. T. (2004) *Communication Theories in Action: An Introduction*, Belmont (CA): Thompson/Wadsworth.

ABOUT THE AUTHORS

John F. Frana, a former prisoner, is now a PhD student in the Department of Sociology at the University of Louisville.

Michael Lenza, PhD, is an ex-convict who is now an Associate Professor of Criminal Justice at the University of Wisconsin-Oshkosh. He has published on the death penalty, research ethics, medical marijuana, a historical political view of the development of mass incarceration in the USA, as well as theory and research methods. He is currently working on the institutional foundations of violence in the American context, and utilizing postmodern autoethnograpic theory and methods to provide voice to prisoners.

Ryan D. Schroeder is an Assistant Professor in the Department of Sociology at the University of Louisville.

Convict Criminology and Community Collaboration: Developing a Unique Program to Empower Vulnerable Youth in Idaho

James Burnett and D J Williams

INTRODUCTION

There has been a debate among those who work with the young adult criminal justice population about how best to serve them. There are various therapeutic programs, behavior modification techniques, and program interventions used to help shape and manage this young adult population.

Nearly four decades ago, Martinson (1974) proclaimed that nothing done in corrections has any meaningful impact on criminal behavior and recidivism. This influenced a defensive posture among juvenile justice practitioners attempting to provide safe and secure environments that young adults need to grow. In some communities, practitioners wanted to remove the at-risk young adults and punish them harshly for antisocial criminal behavior. This negative approach remains influential today in the form of 'tough on crime' policies (including among juveniles) and trying youthful offenders as adults. On the other hand, scholars have subsequently realized that there are principles of structured programming that can effectively reduce recidivism.

As part of our work we asked the following question: "Can at-risk young adults who are sentenced to an intensive supervised release program at the Bannock County Youth Development Center (BCYDC) in Idaho use an intervention program informed by the Convict Criminology (CC) Perspective to make a transition from corrections to college?" In this paper, we discuss how an intervention program – whose design, plan and organization is informed by CC – is merged with a traditional program. Following a brief discussion on Stan Cohen's (1985) concept of *community* from his work, *Visions of Social Control*, we reflect on how the program was conceived and implemented, including preliminary observations from various stakeholders involved in this project. While stakeholders' observations are overwhelmingly positive, a thorough program evaluation has been planned and we will not know its effectiveness until that evaluation has been completed. Nevertheless, the preliminary observations included later in the paper are noteworthy.

TRADITIONAL PROGRAM:
BANNOCK COUNTY YOUTH DEVELOPMENT CENTER

The BCYDC is a diversion program that provides a means to hold young adults accountable for their actions, offers a way for them to develop skills and ensures protection of the community through intensive supervision. This program is an alternative to youth being remanded to the custody of the Idaho State Department of Correction. The State of Idaho spends approximately $74,000 per year per youth offender in its standard institutions. In comparison, the total BCYDC program budget is only $100,000. The program includes approximately 20 youth clients at any given time who have been charged for either misdemeanors or felonies. Program participants are referred by the court or probation officer, may be male or female, and typically range between 12 and 18 years of age.

The program has a traditional design in that is has a point system to control conduct with four sequential phases: 1) orientation; 2) development; 3) competency; and 4) reintegration. Clients must complete tasks and develop skills in order to progress through the program. BCYDC includes educational, therapeutic, service-learning, job assignments and adventure activity components.

APPLYING CONVICT CRIMINOLOGY TO THE
DEVELOPMENT OF YOUTH PROGRAMS

While CC has included a number of prominent scholars who have successfully made the transition from incarceration to higher education, most notably John Irwin, there remains a salient need to help many youth progress from corrections to college. Stronger educational programming, social mentoring and opportunities to engage in pro-social activities can connect youth to community, thus facilitating a potential successful transition from juvenile corrections to higher education.

CC offers a humane and empowering approach to developing youth programs. It recognizes the legitimacy of diverse experiences and perspectives among multiple stakeholders, including youth. In other words, it gives youth a voice and encourages their participation in the broader corrections dialogue. CC promotes cooperation among youth, corrections, colleges and universities, and various community partners that can, by working together, create new and effective programs (see Richards and Ross, 2001; Ross and Richards, 2002, 2003, 2009; Richards *et al.*, 2008; Jones *et al.*, 2009; Rose *et al.*, 2010a, 2010b). Through this process, "juvenile delinquency" can be deconstructed and reconstructed, and intensive supervision can be modified to highlight growth-oriented experiences and youth development.

Burnett's Personal Statement of Purpose
For the first author of this article, CC has always meant that one should use his or her voice to address the problem where young people are removed from schools to be locked up in juvenile prisons. He asserts that it is better to process youth through the school system. Ross and Richards' (2003, pp. xvii-xxii) statement that "the failure of criminologists to recognize the dehumanizing conditions of the criminal justice system and the lives of those defined as criminal" motivated the author to want to make a difference. When released from prison in 2002, he realized that he was part of what Arditti and McClintock refer to in *Voices* as the disadvantaged and marginalized minorities controlled by the criminal justice system (see http://www.convictcriminology. org/voices.htm). He also realized that he was part of "soft-line" social control outlined in Stanley Cohen's (1985) *Visions of Social Control*.

Such a position is where the state roots social control in community-based approaches and conventional social boundaries. From his experience in community corrections, the first author had an inside view and decided early in reentry that his contribution would be to let his experience inform the design and critique, enlightenment and contribution to meaningful programming within the "soft-line" system. Within this context, he wanted to provide individuals with strategies of empowerment to break out of the cycle of "soft-line" control, namely an education strategy. CC taught him to challenge the idea that a person's personality traits, level of self-esteem, or moral character can be determined by referral to the fact that they have been convicted of a crime or spent time in prison.

Education, the insider perspective, and the use of ethnography all influenced the program described in this paper. Within the education context, CC encouraged the first author to reach out to and work with others the way that Steve Richards, Annette Kuhlmann, Chris Rose, Tracy Andrus, Rick Jones and others had worked with him. They instilled a desire to improve the conditions and opportunities of others in transition toward personal growth. As reflective of this desire that was cultivated through CC mentoring, the first author decided to train his students as mentors to help young adults transition from corrections to college.

Program Roots and Convict Criminology

Richards *et al.* (2008) depict the CC Perspective as a proposal of new and less costly strategies that are more humane, provocative and affective approaches to criminology. CC has influenced the research design and implementation of this program, as well as the analytical understanding of the juvenile justice system by: 1) providing an alternative approach to traditional juvenile justice; 2) providing an understanding of victimology and constitutive criminology; 3) drawing on theoretical developments in criminology; 4) making use of perspectives from the inside; and 5) emphasizing the centrality of ethnography.

At a time that the taxpayers are calling for tightening of governmental budgets, the Idaho State University (ISU) BCYDC partnership is working to reduce youth criminal recidivism and help them to become productive citizens in the community. ISU students use creativity and effort to provide services to the mentees that will give them the academic skills they will need to succeed in college.

Victimology and Constitutive Criminology

The authors recognize the importance of including multiple voices and nurturing compassion in the attempt to reach out to and empower the youth involved in the program. Early in the process, a site visit to the BCYDC was scheduled and the ISU representatives listened to the youth express their experiences, needs, hopes, goals and dreams. This opportunity was used to hear the message of this oppressed, marginalized and victimized group of youth to inform the program design (Richards and Jones, 1997, 2004). Acknowledging the importance of these messages allowed the ISU mentors to empower the mentees.

Theoretical Developments in Criminology

The authors seek to enlighten the public discourse on juvenile programs, deconstruct juvenile delinquency, reconstruct intensive supervision to highlight youth development, and to give voice to the people who have the best interests of growth-oriented experiences of youth at heart. The program is rooted in post-modernism and post-structuralism, in the sense that the participants are encouraged to think beyond the status quo cognitive-behavioral restructuring, which is based on the traditional assumptions of knowledge that look at youth through a deficit lens instead of through humanistic eyes. The program seeks to foster critical thinking and transformation so that new knowledge can inform new behavior.

Additionally, as a result of using a multiplicity of perspectives, the partnership brought in multiple voices, narratives and discourses (Ferrell, 1998). Post-modernism helps to situate the participants in a context that helps to understand these youth as products of the power that seeks to limit their behavior, exclude their voices and marginalize their hopes. Also, using post-modern theory helps them to overcome social inequality through developing human relationships to deal with the concepts of difference (Carrington, 1998).

Perspectives from the Inside
The first author's ex-con background fits into the program as an authentic voice from his experience and perspective. Based on his own standpoint merged with his academic background, he was determined to help these youth progress from corrections to college the way he did. At the same time, he sought to enlighten the public discourse about the current state of carceral issues of youth. This is important because in the world of the youthful offender, the definitions and treatment of delinquency are often informed and maintained by the self-interests of administrative criminologists, who directly benefit from dominant responses to crime and approaches to penality.

Centrality of Ethnography
Both the authors have a practical understanding of juveniles and comprehend their lived experiences, as well as abstract knowledge of the criminal justice machinery that informs what is missing from treating juveniles. Burnett and Williams employ the unique research method of giving voice to the juveniles and their ISU student-mentors, and by tapping into their creative expression through journal entries and visual ethnography. The authors meet the juveniles on their own turf (BCYDC) to observe, interact, serve, empower and to invest in the subjects' personal growth, and as Richards and Ross (2001, p. 185) say, "to get a little dirty by violating social distance and value-free sociology, which is committing an academic felony".

ISU Sociology Program
Despite its admirable purposes, the BCYDC program, like many such programs across North America, needed more resources. It was recognized that trained ISU student mentors could provide individualized vocational and personal counseling, tutoring, service-learning, and participation in social, cultural and artistic activities within the structure of BCYDC.

The first author developed an elective sociology course wherein ISU students could receive three credits for participating in the program. BCYDC staff provided classroom instruction on youth behavior, common legal issues, center rules and regulations, safety issues, substance abuse and violence. Because many youth at BCYDC may have psychological issues concerning abandonment (addressed in therapy), it was important that ISU students trained as mentors were committed to the partnership. The university students provide essential leadership and stability in the lives of youth who they mentor. ISU faculty and BCYDC administrators met regularly to resolve concerns as they occurred, and to make sure the partnership was functioning smoothly.

BCYDC PROGRAM TARGET AREAS

BCYDC targets four major areas for youth development: 1) accountability; 2) social competence; 3) citizenship; and 4) integrity. Client goals are set in each of these areas that will help youth transition to community reintegration and crime-free living. Accountability is fostered by using case management plans that provide individual learning experiences, as well as demonstrate care and concern for each client. An important objective of BCYDC is for youth to increase their capacity for adapting to change in healthy and flexible ways. A client code of conduct and service-learning projects are used to facilitate social competence. Social competence is viewed as the range of skills that help youth integrate their feelings, thoughts, and actions in order to achieve social and interpersonal goals (Caplan *et al.*, 1992; Weissberg *et al.*, 1989). Besides modeling these skills, ISU student mentors engage in the following actions: a) teach youth appropriate information and skills; b) foster pro-social and health enhancing values and beliefs; and c) create environmental supports to reinforce the real-world application of skills. BCYDC promotes citizenship through education, cognitive-behavioral therapy and pre-vocational programs. Youth develop skills concerning their self-talk and general self-awareness, reading and responding to social cues, making decisions and solving problems, understanding the perspectives of others, and acquiring a positive outlook toward life. The foundation for progression through the program phases noted in a previous section is integrity. In order to progress through the program youth must learn how to make good choices, as well as take responsibility for their decisions and actions. The partnership used three distinct group pairings to enhance programming. Student mentors were trained and assigned to assist youth with education, vocational experiences or service learning.

PRELIMINARY OBSERVATIONS AND PERSONAL REPORTS OF SUCCESS

The BCYDC and ISU have partnered for over a year now and feedback from all stakeholders is very positive. Bannock County judges and corrections officials, as well as BCYDC administrators and staff, have been delighted to have help and support from ISU students and faculty. Although a formal program evaluation is underway, BCYDC strongly believes that the partnership is helping youth make therapeutic progress faster and more thoroughly. If this observation proves to be correct, then we would expect the partnership to be effective in lowering costs due to both reductions in recidivism and the longer periods of time that youth would spend in typical programming. ISU faculty members are grateful to BCYDC for helping train university students for work in corrections and providing an important learning opportunity for students to gain experience in applied sociology.

BCYDC Youth

The BCYDC-ISU partnership now has its first youth client that successfully progressed from "crime to college". This client was originally court ordered to the BCYDC due to an aggravated battery charge stemming from stabbing a family member. The client progressed through the phases of the program, learned valuable life skills and completed a high school education. He is now enrolled as a university student at ISU, and based on an application and interview process is eligible for scholarships in his first academic year. He will work with the ISU Center for New Directions to develop a university education and career plan, and counselors and faculty will support this ISU student in achieving continued academic success. Regarding his youth program experience, this client reported:

> When I first came to BCYDC, I came out of the detention center with anger issues. I was thinking the whole time that I didn't want to be here [...] Four months later I acquired my GED by studying hard and following the goals that were given to me by my probation officer [...] While working on all of this, I was seeing a counselor for advice on helping me with my anger and family issues. A few months later, I decided to get enrolled in college [...] I want to start by getting my Bachelor of Arts and majoring in psychology to get a job as a counselor. YDC has changed my life.

A female participant in the BCYDC program recently completed her high school education. She reported:

> This program has helped me to be more assertive and self-driven toward my goals. Setting goals every week motivates me to complete each step, and by doing so, ultimately moving closer to the main goal itself [...] When I knew what I needed to do for that week, it made me work harder to achieve the goal because I knew exactly what I needed to do. Now that I have my GED, my biggest priority right now is getting a job [...] I'd like to eventually get a degree in something, but right now I want to be able to support myself and my son. All in all, this place has really helped me turn my life around. Thank you to all of the BCYDC staff and the interns [ISU student mentors].

ISU Student Mentors

Self-reports from ISU student mentors have also been positive. Several of these college students shared how they learned the value of individualized mentoring of youth in correctional programs. Many also discovered personal insights about themselves through the helping process. A non-traditional student majoring in childhood education reported: "I have learned how important community involvement can be. I also have learned the importance of giving our youth real-life experiences". A non-traditional student majoring in sociology added, "I have learned more about who I am and what I truly care about. I care about people. I care about bettering society. And, through this class I have learned that bettering society is an attainable goal, working one step at a time, one day at a time, one person at a time". A traditional student in the ISU Criminal Justice Program reported how the class impacted her:

> I have learned more about myself this past year than I have in my entire career as a student at ISU. I learned that just being there with the mentees makes a difference, whether we are sitting with them helping them to write a paper or helping them sew sock monkeys. Every ounce of our effort has been rewarded. I have learned patience and humbleness. I think that working with a diverse group of people has helped us all grow in a positive way.

CONCLUSION

CC welcomes and seeks to legitimize a variety of voices and perspectives, and promotes creativity and collaboration. It is connected with social justice and empowering individuals and communities. In our view CC is not only a critical, intellectual approach to criminology (a way of understanding), but it is a process of being actively involved in helping to make positive changes in people's lives, both individually and collectively as a way of practice. It seeks solutions that benefit all people.

The partnership that has been developed and described herein is rooted in a CC Perspective. There were significant challenges in developing the BCYDC-ISU partnership. Of course, all correctional systems function within existing policies, regulations and frameworks. These structures may vary from place to place in conduciveness to establishing potential partnerships, as well as the ability to develop innovative strategies and programming. Nevertheless, it is important to discuss possibilities for improved programming in terms of common needs and values. BCYDC leaders and staff were exceptional in their desire for considering creative new ways to promote positive changes in the lives of the youth in their custody and the community.

Another significant challenge in building the partnership involved helping ISU student-mentors understand the important needs of BCYDC youth and to help motivate them to become actively involved. Put differently, a major challenge was, and still is, changing the immediate college student culture from a place of observation and passivity to one of action and direct involvement. This is an important trade off in that it is easy to run a traditional program, but an initiative like this requires a lot of work, energy, effort and time. Also, getting the needed training, synchronicity and commitment requires a lot of encouragement, empowerment, and mediation. This process has taken considerable time and patience from ISU faculty, as well as BCYDC administrators and staff. Nevertheless, significant benefits are starting to be realized.

Although formal evaluation of this partnership is forthcoming, the primary contribution of this paper is providing a description of the development of a symbiotic partnership built from CC principles that can facilitate youth transition from "crime to college". Documenting this important process provides valuable practical insights into how such programming may be further developed. We applaud the CC approach and believe that there is a current need to expand its application within communities. Hopefully, our work described here is a positive example of how such expansion can be realized.

REFERENCES

Arditti, J. A. and C. McClintock (2001) "Drug Policy and Families: Casualties of War", *Marriage and Family Law Review*, 32(3): 11-33.
Caplan, M., R. P. Weissberg, J. S. Grober, P. J. Sivo, K. Grady and C. Jacoby (1992) "Social Competence Promotion With Inner-city and Suburban Young Adolescents: Effects on Social Adjustment and Alcohol Use", *Journal of Consulting and Clinical Psychology*, 60: 56-63.
Carrington, K. (1998) "Postmodernism and Feminist Criminologies: Fragmenting the Criminological Subject", in P. Walton and J. Young (eds.), *The New Criminology Revisited*, London: Macmillan.
Cohen, S. (1985) *Visions of Social Control: Crime, Punishment, and Classification*, Cambridge (UK): Polity Press.
Ferrell, J. (1998). "Stumbling Toward a Critical Criminology (and into an anarchy and imagery of postmodernism)", in J. I. Ross (ed.), *Cutting the Edge*, Westport (CT): Praeger, pp. 63-76.
Jones, R. S., J. I. Ross, S. C. Richards and D. S. Murphy (2009) "The First Dime: A Decade of Convict Criminology", *Prison Journal*, 89: 151-171.
Martinson, R. (1974) "What Works? Questions and Answers About Prison Reform", *The Public Interest*, 35: 22-54.
Richards, S. C., D. Faggiani, J. Roffers, R. Hendricksen and J. Krueger (2008) "Convict Criminology: Voices from Prison", *Race / Ethnicity*, 2: 121-136.
Richards, S. C. and R. S. Jones (2004) "Beating the Perpetual Incarceration Machine", in S. Maruna and R. Immarigeon (eds.), *After Crime and Punishment: Pathways to Offender Reintegration*, London: Willan Publishers, pp. 201-232.

Richards, S. C. and J. I. Ross (2001) "The New School of Convict Criminology", *Social Justice*, 28: 177-190.

Richards, S. C. and R. S. Jones (1997) "Perpetual Incarceration Machine: Structural Impediments to Post-prison Success", *Journal of Contemporary Criminal Justice*, 13: 4-22.

Rose, C. D., K. Reschenberg and S. C. Richards (2010a) "Inviting Convicts to College", *Journal of Offender Rehabilitation*, 49(4): 293-308.

Rose, C. D., K. Reschenberg and S. C. Richards (2010b) "Where Are We Now? An Update on the Evolution of the Inviting Convicts To College Program", *Offender Programs Report*, 14(3): 33-34, 43-45, 47.

Ross, J. I. and S. C. Richards (2009) *Beyond Bars: Rejoining Society After Prison*, New York: Alpha/Penguin Group.

Ross, J. I. and S. C. Richards (eds.) (2003) *Convict Criminology*, Belmont (CA): Wadsworth.

Ross, J. I., and S. C. Richards (2002) *Behind Bars: Surviving Prison*, New York: Alpha/Penguin.

Weissberg, R. P., M. Caplan and P. J. Sivo (1989) "A New Conceptual Framework for Establishing School-based Social Competence Promotion Programs", in L. A. Bond and B. E. Compas (eds.), *Primary Prevention and Promotion in the Schools*, Newbury Park (CA): Sage, pp. 255-296.

Welch, M. (1996) *Corrections: A Critical Approach*, New York: McGraw-Hill.

Williams, D J, G. J. Walker and W. B. Strean (2005) "Correctional Recreation on Death Row: Should Pardon be Granted?", *Journal of Offender Rehabilitation*, 42(2): 49-67.

ABOUT THE AUTHORS

James Burnett, PhD, is an ex-convict and Visiting Assistant Professor Department of Sociology, Social Work & Criminal Justice at Idaho State University. Dr. Burnett is a member of the Convict Criminology Group.

D J Williams, PhD, is an Assistant Professor in the Department of Sociology, Social Work & Criminal Justice at Idaho State University. He is an interdisciplinary scholar and has several years' experience as a forensic psychotherapist.

Fundamental Problems in Criminal Justice Knowledge Production
Michael Lenza

INTRODUCTION

Ex-prisoners, along with their children and families, are becoming a permanently managed underclass being cycled and recycled into the vast prison industrial complex of the United States (Clear, 2007; Richards, 1998, 2009a; Richards and Jones, 1997, 2004). In California alone, "the budget for the state's corrections administration has sprung from under $200 million in 1975 to over $4.3 billion in 1998 (no, that is not a typo: it is a 22-fold increase)" (Wacquant, 2002, p. 380). Historically, it was during the 1968 political campaign that Richard Nixon successfully politically reframed the tumultuous discord surrounding the civil rights and anti-Vietnam War movements into a 'law and order' policy solution. Preceding this historical moment incarceration rates in the United States had been stable for 50 years (Lenza and Jones, 2010). It was in this political shift from funding social programs to deal with structural inequalities to using institutions of coercive social control to maintain the order that criminal justice (CJ) as an academic paradigm took root and flourished. That was the beginning of what has become a 600 percent increase in incarceration rates in the USA.

In this article, I question the validity and reliability of knowledge produced in CJ and criminology. Further, I examine how this historically unprecedented expansion of the criminal justice system is changing the social structure of American society through internal colonization of its poorest and most vulnerable populations into a new caste system deprived of civil rights and economic opportunity. I meld the New School of Convict Criminology (CC) with postmodern insights on power and knowledge as an exemplar of why the voices of the human subjects held captive in CJ institutions must be heard to develop a valid and independent knowledge base to inform criminal justice policies. I will begin by briefly expanding the review of the institutional relationships between CJ academic programs and research with the expansion of coercive social control in American society.

THE TAUTOLOGICAL DANCE BETWEEN CJ ACADEMICS AND CJ SOCIAL CONTROL AGENCIES

Critical academics back in the 1970s raised concerns as the success of 'law and order' political campaign platforms, which translated into expansion of government funding for coercive social control. Quinney (1974) commented on American criminology's failure to examine crime within the larger socio-economic structural inequalities due to the economic system, arguing that the rising crime rates of the time were a consequence of disillusionment with the modes of production and distribution of goods. He pointed out that the economic elite use fear of crime as a way to cover over the inadequacies of 'official reality' through using a symptom of capitalistic structural inequalities – crime, as a way to hide the capitalist contradiction from which it arises. In addition, Quinney warned of the dangers lurking in the rapid development of a more centralized and rationalized policing power for the state that the Law Enforcement Assistance Administration (LEAA) funding was then constructing. He believed this would not solve any of the underlying social problems from which much crime arises, but would serve to expand police surveillance and classifications of our own citizenry as our enemies.

Similarly, Chambliss (1975) argued that criminal law was less about customs and beliefs of the people than it was state action protecting the interest of the ruling class. The continual elimination of workers through technologies or machines replacing them also created the dynamics reducing wages of those left. This grows the numbers of surplus workers and the impoverishment of the working class while increasing profits for the owners of production. Projecting causality of crime as deviant individual acts hides these underlying structural factors of crime, while simultaneously providing a rational justifying the use of coercive social control to manage the growing army of surplus labor it creates at public expense.

History has served to validate Quinney (1974) and Chambliss' (1975) critiques. Through the decades that followed these critiques, mass media and political campaigns continually focused the public's attention on 'fear of crime', and the need to keep expanding the power and scope of the criminal justice system. Meanwhile the economic elite's share of wealth concentrated as the working and middle class crumbled. Between 1979 and 2007, the richest 10 percent received 91.4 percent of all income gains, with the richest 1 percent receiving 59.9 percent of all income gains. Wealth concentration trends are similar with 94 percent of all wealth gains from 1983 to 2009 were accumulated in the top fifth of wealthiest households, with the wealthiest 5 percent capturing 82 percent of the wealth while the bottom 60 percent share of wealth in 2009 was negative, which is less than what they held back in 1983. Another way of seeing this is in 1983 the top 1 percent held 131 times more wealth than the median household and this grew to the top 1 percent holding 225 times more wealth than the median household in 2009 (Mishel and Bivens, 2010). For the poor, who have no accumulated wealth, incarceration rates in the U.S. increased 600 percent since the early 1970s. They got prisons (Reiman, 2009).

An element not addressed in the preceding argument that the economic elite can divert the public's attention away from their wealth and income concentration through transfixing the public on 'fear of crime' is that there is another significant player that needs to be in this model – CJ institutions. CJ coercive social control agencies have a self-interest in increasing their power and budgets, independent of the interest of the economic elite or of the American public. On economy of scale, the more social resources CJ consumes the more influence criminal justice exerts over society, while society's ability to meet its citizenry's needs is proportionately diminished due to CJ's over consumption of social resources. It is a destructive dialectic for the general welfare of any nation.

In this historical moment, there are over seven million Americans under criminal justice (CJ) supervision or one in thirty-one citizens (Pew Center, 2009). CJ policies in practice all too often reflect political exploitation of societal fears of crime cultivated by prejudicial media stereotypes of minority youth (Waymer, 2009). Young black males and increasing numbers of young black females are thrown, shackled, and belly chained into jails and prisons in numbers far exceeding the proportion of crime they commit (Tonry, 1999). Through this expansion of the CJ system's capacity and how it is being utilized, we are engaging in a vast internal colonization of legally 'stigmatized others' (Goffman, 1963, 1961), from our poorest and most vulnerable minority communities (Alexander, 2009; Hind, 1984; Staples 1975; Tatum, 2002).

Internal colonization refers to the tens of millions of Americans, who after completing their sentence for a conviction remain legally deprived of access to many areas of employment, professional licensing, housing, education and voting rights (Birnbaum and Taylor, 2000; Litwack, 1998; Mauer, 2009, 2010; Soss *et al.*, 2008). In essence, we have created a vast new caste system of citizenry for whom discrimination is allowed or even required regardless of how long they have lived law-abiding lives. This population of citizens can remain forever branded as degenerate felons and cast into roles of not quite human others (Garfinkel, 1956), undeserving of civil rights and social economic opportunities.

The racial threat aspect of public perceptions of crime, successfully cultivated into national politics by Nixon in 1968 (Yates and Fording, 2005) has become so pervasive and reified in the United States that black males with no criminal record now have much more difficulty finding employment than white males with a felony conviction (Clear, 2007). The growing social inequalities being exacerbated by our criminal justice policies in the United States (Lenza and Jones, 2011; Clear, 2010; Tonry, 2009; Soss *et al.*, 2008; Clear, 2007; Gottschalk, 2006; Western and Pettit, 2005; Irwin, 2005; Smith, 2004; Pettit and Western, 2004; Jacobs and Kleban, 2003; Uggen and Manza, 2002; Fording, 2001; Austin, 2001; Tonry, 1999; Western and Beckett, 1999; Jacobs and Helms, 1996) is the underlying foundation and impetus for this article.[1]

Criminology, as a sociological paradigm, began in the United States in 1893 when the University of Chicago began offering courses on the sociological study of crime. The "Chicago School" emphasized social causes of crime and the types of ecological social environments that could lead to criminal behaviors. CJ as an independent academic paradigm, which tends to have a different emphasis than criminology, did not begin gaining broad acceptance until the late 1960s. CJ focuses more on how our CJ institutions operate, the different functions of the procedural stages of the CJ system and how CJ practitioners work within the systems (Thistlethwaite and Wooldredge, 2010, p. xv).[2] As a paradigm, it is less oriented to the practice of social science than it is focused towards career training for employment in criminal justice agencies.

The major force behind establishing CJ as an academic paradigm came with the establishment of the LEAA whose funding grew 27-fold to $1.75 billion between 1968 and 1972. It was LEAA grants paying college tuition for the professional training of police officers that led to academia's quick development of CJ academic programs on campuses to gain this revenue source. The basic model for CJ undergraduate education can be traced to the police training programs developed in California (Morn,

1995). CJ programs jumped from just 50 in the nation in 1960 to 600 CJ programs by 1970, then doubling to 1200 higher educational programs by 1978. Now there are almost 2000 undergraduate CJ programs and 32 universities with doctorial degrees (Thistlethwaite and Wooldredge, 2010, p. xvi; see also Akers, 1992). Similarly, the growth of CJ's academic arm shadowed this expansion. The American Society of Criminology grew from a membership of about 300 in 1970 to 3,485 in 2000 (Savelsberg *et al.*, 2004, p. 1278).

Our other social sciences have had well over a century or more of academic development within which they have had to face and deal with many issues and problems within their knowledge production. One can examine most of the social sciences to see how the validity and reliability their knowledge has grown due to internal critical discourses involving challenges from feminist, minorities, non-heterosexuals, and indigenous postcolonial populations around the globe, as well as other critical standpoints.

The CJ academic paradigm has not demonstrated much interest in critically addressing what impacts their resource dependency on the state's coercive power agencies has on its knowledge production while it has prospered within the expansion. Nor has CJ shown interest in examining the impacts of the criminal justice system's growth upon the broader features of our society, or what role CJ knowledge production has played in the incredible expansion of costs and use of coercive social control, or how this growth has degraded other vital government functions. Much of CJ research is mere descriptive endeavors of existing social arrangements, of CJ policy initiatives, or focused upon on new ways of identifying, rationalizing, differentiating, and categorizing typologies of crime and offenders (Austin *et al.*, 2001, 2003; Taylor *et al.*, 1975). This managerial emphasis in CJ on identification, categorization, and management of subject populations is in many respects reminiscent of anthropology's research focus and utility to imperialistic nation states during colonialism.

ISSUES IN KNOWLEDGE PRODUCTION WHEN PARADIGMS ALIGN TO STATE POWER AND CONTROL

During colonialism, anthropology grew as an academic paradigm conducting ethnographic studies of indigenous populations and constructing categorical cultural identities of subjugated populations. These studies often proved useful to colonial administrators. Construction of categorical identities cleaves differences between the people in a society. Even when those social identity constructions were not based upon real differences within the population, they become very real when utilized in governance of the indigenous populations. Smith (1999, p. 1) explains that in post-colonial regions of the world the term "research" remains "inextricably linked to European imperialism and colonization" and "is probably one of the dirtiest words in the indigenous world's vocabulary" (also see Brown, 2005; Freire, 1970; Naples, 2003). How identity typologies are constructed and utilized is of particular importance to CC (Jones *et al.*, 2009). A brief examination of the inter-related roles of government and social scientists in the construction of official identities during colonialism is informative for understanding the internal colonization of poor and minority citizenry by CJ institutions. Scientific knowledge is not developed independent of the interests of those engaged in its social production (Clough, 2001). "Writing always involves what Roland Barthes calls 'the ownership of the means of enunciation'. A disclosure of writing practices is thus always a disclosure of forms of power (Derrida, 1982)" (in Richardson, 1991, p. 174).

Michel Foucault's (1977) concept of modern social control theorizes individuals are inscribed with identities. This occurs through particular dominant standards that permeate one's social world, particularly official identities. These identity constructs coercively applied through a myriad of governmental, institutional, and ideological techniques that officially define the meaning, identity, and competence of individuals or social groups to which they are applied. "The soul is the effect and instrument of a political anatomy; the soul is the prison of the body" (Foucault, 1977, p. 30).

When identity categories are constructed and authenticated, however weakly, or even wrongly, by science, the state, or both, power is exercised over the identity production of the people placed in these identity constructs. These official identities begin replicating themselves throughout a social system as they are reapplied throughout the interlocking social institutions of a society. They take on lives of their own. Many of the errors within social science research from colonialism to today are due to researcher's neglect of listening to or understanding the self-definitions of their subjects (Jenkins, 2003). Postmodernism gives voice to previously silenced groups whose social lives and meaning have been colonized by social science research, as it provides a necessary corrective to knowledge production (e.g. Allen and Chung, 2000; Andersson, 2002; Bayly, 1995, 1999; Dirlik, 1996; Guhu, 1998; Staples 1975).

Jenken (2003) reviews British anthropology's role in constructing castes in India. British anthropologists identified castes that had not existed in India prior to their projection of their imaginations upon the peoples of India and discovering them. She notes that it was not until after the 1857 rebellion against British rule that colonial administrators began systematic studies of caste identities, both to tighten administrative control and to identify certain groups as criminal castes prone to rebellion against British colonization. Once colonial administrators adopted the new social castes created by their own state sponsored research, they became enforced prejudicial social identities for human populations they placed in them, restructuring the culture and society in India (Jenkins, 2003, p. 1146).

Rather than producing objective knowledge researchers can reproduce unacknowledged ideological bias in constructions of social identity independent of the actuality of their subjects' lives. This is particularly true if it serves the needs of the state. Often in state sponsored research, the researcher's 'objective' interpretations of acts or meanings come to stand in place of the actual meanings experienced by their subjects in their lives. These state sponsored interpretations then become officially validated substitutions for the actual human experiences of the subjects without their review or approval. Subjects have occasionally used these tools of their masters to turn the table.

Brown (1993) makes this point in his review of Jomo Kenyatta, leader of Kenya's independence movement. Kenyatta studied anthropology attending Malinowski's seminars in London in the 1930s and then used the anthropological objective voice to present an Afrocentric record of facts to a British white audience. For an African to speak in an academic voice for Africans in the 1930s was a revolutionary act:

> Kenyatta: My chief object is not to enter into controversial discussion [...] but to let the truths speak for itself. I am well aware that I could not do justice to the subject without offending those "professional friends of the African" who are prepared to maintain their friendship for eternity as a sacred duty, provided only that the African will continue to play the part of an ignorant savage so that they can monopolize the office of interpreting his mind and speaking for him. To such people, an African who writes a

study of this kind is encroaching on their preserves. He is a rabbit turned poacher (Brown, 1993, p. 672).

This brief review shows how easily significant problems in knowledge production occurs when social science research is uncritically conducted in close association with the power of the state, particularly in constructing social identities of subject populations. Anthropology has taken a postmodern turn to repair its status as a valid independent paradigm in the social sciences. Voloder (2008, p. 34) explains one of the newer approaches to field studies in anthropology:

> Anthropology argued in favor of the objectification of the researcher, whereby the researcher's self and their relationship to the subject of study became an object of exploration (Bourdieu, 2003). This approach to reflexivity required the ethnographer to reflect on their own trajectory and identifications with the aim to disclose how these positions impact on the analysis of the ethnographic material. The focus is on the 'situatedness' (Abu-Lughod, 1999, p. 141) of knowledge, the recognition that the ethnographers' personal history plays a significant role in enabling or inhibiting particular kinds of analytic insights or oversights (Hastrup, 1992).

The lack of reflexivity in most CJ and criminology research raises the issue of whether much of this research can be accurately described as social science when its questions, focus and findings can be so easily constrained or empowered by the political and ideological interests of funding institutions:

> ...competitive pressure in the United States results in academics' attempting to increase salaries, social status, and their market value by gaining outside funding from academically governed funding agencies as well as from policy-making institutions. When research is funded by political agencies, which to a large degree is the case in criminology and CJ studies, then it is rather likely that academically produced knowledge will follow political knowledge. This underlying resource-dependency theory has been exemplified (Savelsberg, 1994, p. 934; see also Denzin, 2009).

Similarly, Schutz's (1967) critique of Weber's ideal type for understanding another's behavior is also relevant in statistical and qualitative studies, as when we construct categories to code people for analysis, whether we acknowledge it or not, we are constructing an ideal type. In this constructed category:

> ...the personal ideal type is always determined by the interpreter's point of view. It is a function of the very question it seeks to answer [...] The illusion consists in regarding the ideal type as a real person, whereas actually it is only a shadow person. It "lives" in a never-never temporal dimension that no one could ever experience (Schutz, 1967, pp. 190-191).

CJ research all too often creates distortions of the human identities of individuals and populations subjected to coercive management by CJ institutions. Any human being's life carries a vast number of meanings and roles beyond institutionally derived categories of alleged personal attributes dependent upon their classification by offense or sentence. This juxtaposition of objectified classifications of imposed identities with the lived reality of human life can awaken Dorothy Smith's concept of bifurcation of consciousness. Individuals and social groups, whose material embodied reality has been systematically objectified by systems or structures of power, can awaken to see the diverse forms of oppression under which they live (Smith 1987, pp. 88, 107, 154). Through reflexive ethnographic and autoethnographic methods, they can speak with their own human voices to shatter these objectifications and regain their biographies.

The predominant research on prisoners today is similar to earlier eras of research on race, gender and sexual orientation when the field was dominated by heterosexual, male, middle class, white academics. Being other than heterosexual in one's sexual orientation in the recent past could serve for being diagnosed as mentally ill or a felon. Patriarchy deprived women of full citizenship: voting rights, educational opportunities, careers, as well as ownership and control of their own bodies. In racial and ethnic studies knowledge production was the exclusive reserve of white academics, often serving to rationalize minority's social and economic subjugation. As women, minorities, and non-heterosexuals gained public and academic voices they became able to challenge the stereotypes and beliefs underlying their legal subjugation to homophobic, patriarchal, and racist beliefs that pervaded our laws, policies, and social practices.

Hulsman's (1986) insightful critique on the ontology and epistemologies institutionalized in criminal justice system's concept of crime argues these are constructed to serve the organizational interests of CJ systems and are devoid of input by the human beings that actually experienced the events. More importantly, if social scientists do not problematise the concept of crime, they are stuck within a "catascopic view of social reality, based upon the definitional activities of the system which is the subject of study" (Hulsman, 1986, p. 74). Researchers become imprisoned themselves within a tautological circle preventing them from developing an exterior view of the reality of their subject – crime. "Crime has no ontological reality. Crime is not the *object* but the *product* of criminal policy" (ibid, original emphasis). Understanding this irreconcilable problematic in developing valid knowledge in CJ research requires researchers to take an anascopic standpoint on reality.

Certainly American history carries within it centuries of racial oppression wherein it was a criminal act for an African American to claim a human identity during slavery or Jim Crow, or the legal and cultural rights of whites to use brutal violence against any African American that dared to challenge that status quo. This is but one example. It would take a very large book to review all the human acts defined as crime without substantive evidence that these acts caused harm to innocent others or acts that caused harm to innocent others that were not criminal acts. The weight of human history and our present gives great credibility to Hulsman's position.

(One way out of this political, ideological, and academic quagmire in the study of CJ is for the academic field to recognize it must incorporate the voices and experiences of its subjects as an essential counter-weight to the institutional tautologies inherent in the study of crime. Research that does not ground itself in the actual thinking, understandings and material conditions of life of the subjects is in John Irwin's words, "not only a distortion of the phenomenon but also is very likely a corruption" (Irwin, 1987, p. 42; also see Jones, 1995, p. 108; Richards, 2009b).

A significant problem with CJ research is that a primary component of the system – prisons – are total institutions. It all too easy for researchers who have never experienced having the meaning of their lives categorically objectified by hostile others while living in a total institution that operates through constant threats of violent repression to misinterpret the lives of prisoners (Jones *et al.*, 2009). Wallace (2002, p. 53) discusses importance of developing effective language to frame the discourse:

> Because their (researchers) experiences with discourse have not
> consistently placed them in positions in which they needed to speak
> back to cultural values that defined them in problematic ways, they have
> difficulty understanding why others must do so. Thus, for many people,
> the ideologies of culture and discourse appear neutral and their sense
> of agency as relatively unencumbered [...] a person or group must find
> language and actions that expose the ideologies of dominant culture and
> engage those who espouse these ideologies in substantive discourse.

In the gay rights movement development, the use of term 'homophobia'
exposed the unwarranted fear within the dominant ideology, while opening
the frame so voices of gays could be heard. Part of the challenge for
prisoners and ex-prisoners is to expose the stigmatizing labels placed on
them are not representative of any actual human being. They represent the
imaginative projected fears and ignorance of those using them. We need to
expose these stereotypes for what they are, shatter them and into the breach
bring forward the reality that prisoners are mostly just people: mothers,
fathers, sons and daughters, friends and neighbors, who love and care, and
have hopes and dreams like everyone else. No human being is just a thing.
All human beings are much more than that.

The New School of Convict Criminology's research on prisons and
prisoners provides a bridge between prisoners' experiences and much
of the existing academic research. Our research combines substantive
experience within the CJ system with our traditional academic training.
This allows us to view our subjects and issues through more reflexive
lenses due to our familiarity with both worlds (Richards and Ross,
2001). The CC theoretical perspective encourages development of a
new synthesis of critical theory with postmodern theories and methods
to restore a measure of balance and social justice within the knowledge
productions of CJ and criminology. As ex-convict academic researchers
we have lived the experience of prisoners, had the meaning of our lives
stripped away and replaced by reified categorical constructions as we
descended into the depths of prisons, and in varying degrees survived to
tell the tale. Yet, even having completed our sentences, and then gained
doctorates, we remain tainted by the stigma of fears projected upon us,
and in many states discriminatory laws and policies constrain who and
what we can be with their self serving foolish little minds and hearts.

Reflexive autoethnographic (and ethnographic) research done by academics that embeds the subject's voice within their conditions of life, by its very nature does critical theory (Ellis and Bochner, 2000; see also Reed-Danahay, 2000). Gready (1993) discusses the importance of prisoner narratives:

> The pain of imprisonment is made visible from the viewpoint of the prisoner thereby enabling it to be acknowledged for what it is (p. 522).

> The crucible of incarceration with its textures of violence, pain and suffering seems universally to demand 'factually insistent' narratives (p. 490).

> Autobiography serves to restore elemental political ground to the prisoner, and is the most sophisticated articulation of the oppositional 'power of writing' (p. 493).

As a paradigm CJ is long overdue to open its eyes to the incredible costs of our current policies, most of which are founded on ignorance and fear. Meanwhile, the extraordinary cost of the expansion of the criminal justice system is compromising the state's ability to provide essential needs and services to communities (Lenza and Jones, 2010). Recently, the New York Times discussed the United States Department of Agriculture's reports that the number of children facing food insecurity in 2009 rose to nearly one in four. Undernurition in young children is linked to delayed growth and motor development, behavioral problems and learning deficits. The recent Children Defense Fund Report informs us that presently the U.S. spends almost two and a half times as much per prisoner as per public school pupil (Blow, 2011). At present, governments across the United States are laying off thousands of teachers and essential civil servants, cutting services to our most needy, as our infrastructure crumbles, while CJ greadily consumes more and more public resources by incarcerating over one million non-violent offenders within our prisons that pose little to no threat to anyone (Irwin *et al.*, 1999).

CJ and criminology have played a significant role in creating the stigmatized identity constructions, rationalizations, justifications and management tools utilized in our current mass incarceration of our fellow citizens. Studies examining the impact of mass incarceration policies on crime rates, show modest impacts at best. A recent study found only a 7 percent reduction in crime rates due to mass incarceration of offenders (Western, 2005). In the near tripling of the prison population just from 1980 to 1996, crime itself explained only 12 percent of the prison rise, while changes in sentencing policy accounted for 88 percent of the increase (Blumstein and Beck, 1999).

Further, we need to be constantly aware that the CJ system and the prison industrial complex it has spawned, grows through failure and bad policies (Davis, 2003). Longer prison terms, more parole violations for minor rule violations, the systematic incarceration of nonviolent offenders, excessive use of coercive social repression upon our most vulnerable populations, prison overcrowding, and much more translates to more employees, more prisons, and increased correctional budgets as it feeds on other people's children.

THE ELEMENTARY NECESSITY AND SUFFICIENT CONDITIONS FOR ESTABLISHING CAUSALITY

Reviewing the elementary necessary and sufficient conditions for establishing causality is required because these basic preconditions are often set aside in CJ and criminology's reliance on categorical variables to identify populations for enhanced punishments, surveillance, and coercive bureaucratic management. In the physical sciences, one can take oxygen gas and hydrogen gas, bring them together under controlled conditions and produce water (H_2O). From this type of scientific research in the physical sciences, one could then state the necessary and sufficient conditions that will always produce water from these two gases. Our social realities are much more complex.

In statistical analysis, showing the independent variable preceded the dependant variable and the independent variable is significantly related to changes in the dependant variable in a data set, establishes a variable's significance in the model constructed. However, that alone does not establish causality. We must also establish that this cannot be due to other unmeasured or unexamined variables acting on them both before we can claim that a measure of causality has been established (Babbie, 1992, pp. 67-84; Maxfield and Babbie, 2008, pp. 85-98). This vital point is all too often omitted in too many statistical textbooks and research publications.

In other words, causality is established when we can prove that when variable 'A' is present then crime 'B' will occur. This is rarely a causal statement CJ can advance. Yet causality claims are implied when claims of statistical significance between independent and dependant variables are stressed along with the implications of the findings, without clear warnings of the limitations of the findings. In the social sciences, proving causality is a quite difficult task.

In addition, CJ and criminology in particular need to avoid reliance upon closed, self-serving, ideologically driven knowledge production. The complex realities of the social worlds in which people's lives are actually lived needs to inform our research. If other research creates counterfactuals to a research finding, or plausible alternative explanations exist from other paradigms, we cannot claim a particular interpretation has established a valid causality claim.

It does not take even a majority of subject's coded into category 'X' to act in a particular way for a variable to be significant in relation to a dependant variable (Tabachnick and Fidell, 1996). Yet significant findings in CJ often stigmatize and implicate everyone coded into category 'X', when it may not even apply to the majority of individuals coded as 'X'. This is particularly problematic in development of statistical scales used to guide security level decisions on prisoners, parole and probation decisions, and even sentencing guidelines. Even if the researchers understood the difference between correlations, causation and attributes, when these statistical tools are picked up and used in CJ institutions to determine outcomes in the criminal justice system they are applied as if they carry within them independent causal proof when in statistical reality "[i]t is epistemological nonsense to talk about one trait of an individual causing or determining another trait of the individual" (Kempthorne, 1978, p. 15).

At best, probabilistic models approximately measure but do not define causation (Cat, 2006). In addition, with probabilistic modeling or theoretical constructs, only statistical regularities are observed, while causation on the ontic level may well not be probabilistic at all (Salmon, 1980). CJ agencies through grant funding requirements can, and often do, create deterministic research through specifying the data to be used or by providing the data and requiring that particular questions are examined. Criminal justice agencies funding of CJ academic research has influenced the scope, amount of research, as well as what research tends to be published in CJ and criminology (Savelsberg *et al.*, 2004). In addition, there are serious problems with claims of objectivity in data analysis or experimental models.

Lynch and Woolgar (1990) trace the recognition that scientific objectivity is in part a literary style of writing that avoids acknowledgement of the interpretive

"I" within the act. Philosophers and historians Thomas Kuhn, Ludwig Fleck, Michael Polanyi, Imre Lakatos and Paul Feyerabend all suggested that scientific knowledge is socially produced. Thus, the claimed purity of scientific objectivity fell and scientific or positivist methodologies hold no special relationship to truth or understandings of reality. Scientific production is now open to the same types of critiques used for other forms of human production of information or products: what is seen is relative to one's point of view and/or methods used (Lynch and Woolgar, 1990; Gusfield, 1976; Goffman, 1974).

Most social science paradigms have accepted that knowledge production is bound within historical, cultural, and socioeconomic contexts that influence how researchers see and interpret the world. "Postmodern social theory has helped attuned us to the fact that no single perspective can possibly grasp the complexity and diversity of the social world" (Ritzer, 1997, p. 205). CJ and much current criminology fail to recognize that social science claims of objectivity are questionable at best. Until CJ comes to terms with the interpretive, cultural, and historical nature of knowledge production, which is also influenced by funding sources, it will continue to produce mere descriptive research and ideology than valid knowledge production (Crank and Proulx, 2009; also see Habermas, 1971).

CONCLUSION

Yates and Fording (2005) review a convincing series of studies on how the Republican Party and their candidates in the late 1960s and early 1970s courted new constituencies within the backlash against the gains made in the turbulent civil rights movement. Through utilizing racially charged code words within the 'law and order' political discourse, officials from the Nixon administration acknowledged that they intentionally used such rhetoric to gain political traction with the traditional democratic voting working class with anti-minority sentiments. The successful use of such discourses as a political wedge issue soon led to the 'tough on crime' politics and policies that have continued unabated to the present. For the resulting 600 percent increase in use of incarceration that followed the U.S. has gained is very modest reductions in crime at an incredible financial and social cost (Lenza and Jones, 2011; also see Clear, 2007).

CJ, which was an intrinsic facet of this political shift, is long overdue in learning the lessons of anthropology when it comes to constructing categorical identities from our own perspective or that of our funding agencies. Anthropologists, from the perspective of many post-colonial populations around the globe, were not so much social scientists as they were deceiving informants, gaining the trust of indigenous populations and then replacing the meaning of their lives with objectified abstractions, stealing their souls as they stuffed them into categorical boxes from which they are still trying to escape. CJ is currently replicating these same errors and whether intentional or not, is playing a major role in creating the knowledge claims that may well further widen the internal colonization of our own citizenry through criminal justice institutions of social control.

Within CJ and criminology in North America, the *Journal of Prisoners on Prisons* published by the University of Ottawa Press remains the only peer-reviewed journal that actively brings forth prisoner's voices on the realities of our criminal justice system. That is not enough. The voice of the subjects must have a presence in mainstream CJ research methodologies if we are going to move beyond stigmatizing stereotypes and unrecognized bias in studies of crime and our criminal justice system, and move towards valid knowledge production.

ENDNOTES

[1]   References have been placed in order by year instead of alphabetical order to provide the reader with a clearer view of the consistency of findings through time.

[2]   By citing this book, I am not endorsing it. One of numerous critiques I found is that the authors favorably cite the Wisconsin Risk Assessment System (298) when its most salient and decisive risk factor, "assaultive offense in last 5 years", was found to have no predictive value for acts of violence, while adding great cost to parole supervision (Eisenberg *et al.*, 2009, p. iv).

REFERENCES

Akers, R. (1992) "Linking Sociology and Its Specialties: The Case of Criminology", *Social Forces*, 71: 1-16.

Alexander, M. (2009) *The New Jim Crow: Mass Incarceration in the Age of Colorblindness*, New York: The New Press.

Allen, W. R. and A. R. Chung (2000) ""Your Blues Ain't Like My Blues": Race, Ethnicity, and Social Inequality in America", *Contemporary Sociology*, 29(6): 796-805.

Andersson, J. A. (2002) "Administrators' Knowledge and State Control in Colonial Zimbabwe: The Invention of the Rural-urban Divide in Buhera District, 1912-80", *Journal of African History*, 43(1): 119-143.

Austin, J. (2003) "The Use of Science to Justify the Imprisonment Binge", in J. I. Ross and S. C. Richards (eds.), *Convict Criminology*, Belmont (CA): Thompson/ Wadsworth, pp. 17-36.

Austin, J., M. A. Bruce, L. Carroll, P. L. McCall and S. C. Richards (2001) "The Use of Incarceration in the United States: ASC National Policy Committee White Paper", *Critical Criminology*, 10(1): 17-41.

Babbie, E. (1992) *The Practice of Social Research* (sixth edition), Belmont (CA): Wadsworth.

Bayly, S. (1999) *Caste, Society and Politics in India from the Eighteenth Century to the Modern Age*, Cambridge: Cambridge University Press.

Bayly, S. (1995) "Caste and 'Race' in the Colonial Ethnography of India", in P. Robb (ed.), *The Concept of Race in South Asia*, Delhi: Oxford University Press

Birnbaum, J. and C. Taylor (eds.) (2000) *Civil Rights Since 1787: A Reader on the Black Struggle*, New York: New York University Press.

Blow, C., M. (2011) "Falling forward", *New York Times* – August 26. Retrieved from <http:// www.nytimes.com/2011/08/27/opinion/blow-failing forward.html?ref=opinion>.

Blumstein, A. and A. J. Beck (1999) "Population Growth in USA Prisons, 1980-1996", in M. Tonry and J. Petersilia (eds.), *Prisons: Crime and Justice - A Review of Research*, Chicago: University of Chicago Press.

Brown, L. and S. Strega (eds.) (2005) *Research as Resistance: Critical, Indigenous and Anti-oppressive Approaches*", Toronto: Canadian Scholars' Press / Women's Press.

Brown, R. H. (2000) "Rhetoric, Textuality, and the Postmodern Turn in Sociological Theory", *Sociological Theory*, 8(2): 188-197.

Brown, R. H. (1993) "Cultural Representation and Ideological Domination", *Social Forces*, 71(3): 657-676.

Cat, J. (2006) "Fuzzy Empiricism and Fuzzy-set Causality", *Philosophy of Science*, 73(1): 26-41.

Chambliss, W. (1975) "Toward a Political Economy of Crime", *Theory and Society*, 2(2): 149-170.

Chambliss, W. (1973) "The Saints and the Roughnecks", in J. M. Henslin (ed.), *Down to Earth Sociology*, New York: The Free Press/Macmillan, pp. 180-194.

Clough, P. T. (2001) "On the Relationship of the Criticism of Ethnographic Writing and the Cultural Studies of Science", *Cultural Studies: Critical Methodologies*, l(2): 240-270.

Crank, J. P. and B. B. Proulx (2010) "Toward an Interpretive Criminal Justice", *Critical Criminology*, 18: 147–167.

Clear, T. (2010) "Policy and Evidence: The Challenge to the American Society of Criminology – 2009 Presidential Address to the American Society of Criminology", *Criminology*, 48(1): 1-25.

Clear, T. (2007) *Imprisoning Communities: How Mass Incarceration Makes Disadvantaged Neighborhoods Worse*, New York: Oxford University Press.

Davis, A. Y. (2003) *Are Prisons Obsolete?*, New York: Seven Stories Press.

Denzin, N. K. (2009) "The Elephant in the Living Room: Or Extending the Conversation About the Politics of Evidence", *Qualitative Research,* 9: 139-160.

Derrida, J. (1982) *Margin of Philosophy* (translated by Alan Bass), Chicago: Chicago University Press.

Dirks, N. B. (2001) *Castes of Mind: Colonialism and the Making of Modern India*, Princeton (NJ): Princeton University Press.

Dirlik, A. (1996) "The Past as Legacy and Project: Postcolonial Criticism in the Perspective of Indigenous Historicism", *American Indian Culture & Research Journal*, 2 (2): 1-31.

Eisenberg, M., J. Bryl, T. Fabelo (2009) "Validation of the Wisconsin Department of Corrections Risk Assessment Instrument", Lexington (KY): Council of State Governments Justice Center. Retrieved from <http://www.wi-doc.com/>.

Ellis, C. and A. Bochner (2000) "Autoethnography, Personal Narrative, Reflexivity: Researcher as Subject", in N. Denzin and Y. Lincoln (eds.), *The Handbook of Qualitative Research* (second edition), Newbury Park (CA): Sage, pp. 733-768.

Freire, P. (1972) *Pedagogy of the Oppressed*, Harmondsworth: Penguin

Fording, R. C. (2001) "The Political Response to Black Insurgency: A Critical Test of Competing Theories of the State", *American Political Science Review*, 95: 115-130.

Foucault, M. (1977) *Discipline and Punish: The Birth of the Prison*, New York: Random House.

Garfinkel, H. (1956) "Conditions of Successful Degradation Ceremonies", *American Journal of Sociology*, 61(5): 420-424.

Goffman, E. (1974) *Frame Analysis: An Essay on the Organization of Experience*, Cambridge (MA): Harvard University Press.

Goffman, E. (1963) *Stigma: Notes on the Management of a Spoiled Identity*, Englewood Cliffs (NJ): Prentice-Hall.

Goffman, E. (1961) *Asylums: Essays on the Social Situation of Mental Patients and Other Inmates*, Garden City (NY): Anchor Books.

Gottschalk, M. (2006) *The Prison and the Gallows: The Politics of Mass Incarceration in America*, New York: Cambridge University Press.

Gready P. (1993) "Autobiography and the 'Power of Writing': Political Prison Writing in the Apartheid Era", *Journal of Southern African Studies*, 19(3): 489-523.

Guhu, S. (1998) "Lower Strata, Older Races, and Aboriginal Peoples: Racial Anthropology and Mythical History Past and Present", *Journal of Asian Studies* 57(2): 423-441.

Gusfield, J. (1976). "The Literary Rhetoric of Science: Comedy and Pathos in Drinking Driver Research", *American Sociological Review*, 41(1): 16-34.

Habermas, J. (1971) "Technology and Science as 'Ideology'", in *Toward a Rational Society*, Boston: Beacon, pp. 81-122

Hind, R. J. (1984) The Internal Colonial Concept", *Comparative Studies in Society and History*, 26(3): 543-568.

Hulsman, L. (1986) "Critical Criminology and the Concept of Crime", *Contemporary Crisis*, 10: 63-80.

Irwin, J. (2005) *The Warehouse Prison: Disposal of the New Dangerous Class*", Los Angeles: Roxbury.

Irwin, J. (1987) "Reflections on Ethnography", *Journal of Contemporary Ethnography*, 16: 41-48.

Irwin, J., V. Schiraldi and J. Ziedenberg (1999) "America's One Million Nonviolent Prisoners", Washington (D.C.): Justice Policy Institute. Retrieved from <www. justicepolicy.org/.../99-03_REP_OneMillionNonviolentPrisoners_AC .pdf>.

Jacobs, D. and R. E. Helms (1996) "Toward a Political Model of Incarceration: A Time-series Examination of Multiple Explanations for Prison Admission Rates", *American Journal of Sociology*, 102: 323-357.

Jacobs, D. and R. Kleban (2003) "Political Institutions, Minorities, and Punishment: A Pooled Cross-national Analysis of Imprisonment Rates", *Social Forces*, 82: 725-755.

Jenkins, L. D. (2003) "Another "People of India" Project: Colonial and National Anthropology", *Journal of Asian Studies*, 62(4): 1143-1170.

Jones, R. S. (1995) "Uncovering the Hidden Social World: Insider Research in Prison", *Journal of Contemporary Criminal Justice*, 11(2): 106-118.

Jones, R. S., J. I. Ross, S. C. Richards and D. S. Murphy (2009) "The First Dime: A Decade of Convict Criminology", *Prison Journal*, 89: 151-171.

Kempthorne, 0. (1978) "Logical, Epistemological and Statistical Aspects of Nature-nurture Data Interpretation", *Biometrics*, 34: 1-24.

Lenza, M. and R. S. Jones (2011) "Money, Criminology and Criminal Policies: The Impacts of Political Policies, Criminality, and Money on the Criminal Justice in the United", in M. Herzog-Evans (ed.), *Transnational Criminology Manual* (volume 1), Netherlands: Wolf Legal Publishers, pp. 313-332.

Litwack, L. F. (1998) *Trouble in Mind: Black Southerners in the Age of Jim Crow*, New York: Alfred A. Knopf.

Lynch, M. and S. Woolgar (1990) "Introduction: Sociological Orientations to Representational Practice in Science", in M. Lynch and S. Woolgar (eds.), *Representation in Scientific Practice*, Cambridge (MA): MIT Press, pp. 1-18.

Massey, D. and N. Denton (1998) *American Aparthied: Segragation and the Making of the Underclass*, Cambridge (MA): Harvard University Press.

Mauer, M. (2010) *The Two-tiered Justice, Race, Class and Crime Policy*, New York: Routledge.

Mauer, M. (2009) Racial Disparities in the Criminal Justice System, Washington (D.C.): The Sentencing Project. Retrieved from <http://www.sentencingproject.org/template/page.cfm?id=120>.

Maxfield, M. J. and E. R. Babbie (2008) *Research Methods for Crimnal Justice and Criminology* (sixth edition), Belmont (CA): Wadsworth.

Mishel, L.and J. Bivens (2011) "EPI Briefing Paper #331", *Economic Policy Institute* – October 26. Retrived from <http://www.epi.org/files/2011/BriefingPaper331.pdf>.

Morn, F. (1995) *Academic Politics and the History of Criminal Justice Education*, Westport (CT): Greenwood Press.

Naples, N. (2003) *Feminism and Method: Ethnography, Discourse Analysis and Activist Research*, New York: Routledge.

Pew Center on the States (2009) *One in 31: The Long Reach of American Corrections*, Washington (D.C.): The Pew Charitable Trusts – March.

Pettit, B. and B. Western (2004) "Mass Imprisonment and the Life Course: Race and Class Inequality in USA Incarceration", *American Sociological Review*, 69: 151-169.

Quinney, R. (1974) "Critique of Legal Order: Crime Control in Capitalist Society", Boston: Little Brown.

Reed-Danahay, D. (ed.) (1997) *Auto/Ethnography: Rewriting the Self and the Social*, New York: Berg, pp. 1-17.

Reiman, J. (2009) *The Rich Get Richer and the Poor Get Prison: Ideology, Class, and Criminal Justice*, Upper Saddle River (NY): Prentice Hall.

Richards, S. C. (2009a) "A Convict Perspective on Community Punishment: Further Lessons from the Darkness of Prison", in J. I. Ross (ed.), *Cutting the Edge: Current Perspectives in Radical/Critical Criminology and Criminal Justice* (second edition), Edison (NJ): Transaction, pp. 122-144.

Richards, S. C. (2009b) "John Irwin", in K. Hayward, S. Maruna and J. Mooney (eds.), *Fifty Key Thinkers in Criminology*, London: Routledge, pp. 173-217.

Richards, S. C. (1998) "Critical and Radical Perspectives on Community Punishment: Lessons from the Darkness", in J. I. Ross (ed.), *Cutting the Edge: Current Perspectives in Radical/Critical Criminology and Criminal Justice* (first edition), New York: Praeger, pp. 122-144.

Richards, S. C. and R. S. Jones (2004) "Beating the Perpetual Incarceration Machine", in S. Maruna and R. Immarigeon (eds.), *After Crime and Punishment: Pathways to Offender Reintegration*, London: Willan, pp. 201-232.

Richards, S. C. and R. S. Jones (1997) "Perpetual Incarceration Machine: Structural Impediments to Post-prison Success", *Journal of Contemporary Criminal Justice*, 13(1): 4-22.

Richardson, L. (1991) "Postmodern Social Theory: Representational Practices", *Sociological Theory*, 9(2): 173-179.

Ritzer, G. (1997) *Postmodern Social Theory*, New York: McGraw Hill.

Salmon, W. (1980) "Causality: Production and Propagation", in *Proceedings of the Biennial Meeting of the Philosophy of Science Association*.

Savelsberg, J. J. (1994) "Knowledge, Domination, and Criminal Punishment", *American Journal of Sociology*, 99: 911-943.

Savelsberg, J. J., L. L. Cleveland and R. D. King (2004) "Institutional Environments and Scholarly Work: American Criminology – 1951-1993", *Social Forces*, 82(4):1275-1302.

Schutz, A. (1967) *The Phenomenology of the Social World*, Boston: Northeastern University Press.

Sheldon, S. (2001) *Controlling the Dangerous Classes*, Boston: Allyn & Bacon.

Smith, K. B. (2004) "The Politics of Punishment: Evaluating Political Explanations of Incarceration Rates", *Journal of Politics*, 66: 925-938.

Smith, L.T. (1999) *Decolonizing Methodologies, Research and Indigenous Peoples*, New York: Zed Books.

Smith, D. (1987) *The Everyday World as Problematic*, Boston: Northeastern University Press.

Soss, J., R. C. Fording and S. F. Schram (2008) "The Color of Devolution: Race, Federalism, and the Politics of Social Control", *American Journal of Political Science*, 52(3): 536-553.

Staples, R. (1975) "White Racism, Black Crime, and American Justice: An Application of the Colonial Model to Explain Crime and Race", *Phylon*, 36(1): 14-22

Tabachnick, B. and L. Fidell (2006) *Using Multivariate Statistics* (fifth edition), Needham Heights (MA): Allyn & Bacon.

Tatum, B. (2002) "The Colonial Model as a Theoretical Explanation of Crime and Delinquency", in S. L. Gabbidon, H. T. Greene and V. D. Young (eds.), *African*

American Classics in Criminology & Criminal Justice, Thousand Oaks (CA): Sage, pp. 307-322.

Taylor, I., P. Walton and J. Young (1975) *The New Criminology*, Boston: Routledge.

Tonry, M. (2009) "Explanations of American Punishment Policies: A National History", *Punishment & Society*, 11(3): 377-394.

Tonry, M. (1999) "Why Are USA Incarceration Rates So High?", *Crime & Delinquency*, 45: 419-437.

Thistlethwaite, A. B. and J. D. Wooldredge (2010) *Forty Studies That Changed CK: Explorations Into the History of Criminal Justice Research*, New Jersey: Prentice Hall.

Uggen, C. and J. Manza (2002) "Democratic Contraction? Political Consequences of Felon Disenfranchisement in the United States", *American Sociological Review*, 67: 777-803.

Voloder, L. (2008) "Autoethnographic Challenges: Confronting Self, Field and Home", *Australian Journal of Anthropology*, 19(1): 27-40.

Wacquant, L. (2002) "The Curious Eclipse of Prison Ethnography in the Age of Mass Incarceration", *Ethnography*, 3(4): 371-397.

Wallace, D. L. (2002) "Out in the Academy: Heterosexism, Invisibility, and Double Consciousness", *College English*, 65(1): 53-66.

Waymer, Damion (2009) "Walking in Fear: An Autoethnographic Account of Media Framing of Inner-city Crime", *Journal of Communication Inquiry*, 33(2): 169-184.

Western, B. (2005) *Punishment and Inequality in America*, New York: Russell Sage.

Western, B. and K. Beckett (1999) "How Unregulated is the USA Labor Market? The Penal System as a Labor Market Institution", *American Journal of Sociology*, 104: 1030-1060.

Western, B. and B. Pettit (2005) "Black-white Wage Inequality, Employment Rates, and Incarceration", *American Journal of Sociology*, 111: 553-578.

Yates, J. and R. Fording (2005) "Politics and State Punitiveness in Black and White", *Journal of Politics*, 67: 1099-1121.

ABOUT THE AUTHOR

Michael Lenza, PhD, is an ex-convict who is now an Associate Professor of Criminal Justice at the University of Wisconsin-Oshkosh. He has published on the death penalty, research ethics, medical marijuana, a historical political view of the development of mass incarceration in the USA, as well as theory and research methods. He is currently working on the institutional foundations of violence in the American context, and utilizing postmodern autoethnograpic theory and methods to provide voice to prisoners.

Convict Criminology and Social Justice Advocacy: Toward Radical Change
Robert S. Grigsby

INTRODUCTION

My name is Bob Grigsby, and I am a twenty-year veteran of California's prison system. My prison education includes doing time in San Quentin, Folsom, Soledad and gladiator arenas less known by name but just as educationally impressive. One of the major reasons for sharing my voice with you is to discuss the significance Convict Criminology (CC) has for those who have been, and continue to be, marginalized by the policies and practices of the current criminal justice system long after they have fulfilled their debt to society. As others in the discipline have sought to generate a discussion in journals such as *Theoretical Criminology* (see Chancer and McLaughlin, 2007) and *Criminology & Public Policy* (see Clear, 2010) on what roles criminologists can play to affect change beyond academia, I hope to cultivate and nourish a call for a radical change in how CC currently approaches social justice advocacy and practice.

Personally, as an ex-convict that pursued higher education, I know that the ability to point to our college degrees and the growing list of CC publications is socially and politically empowering. While I am an ex-convict, I am also a social scientist, criminologist, policy analyst and professional researcher. My professional resume lists my work as a violence suppression specialist, gang intervention counselor, cognitive-behavioral program coordinator, rehabilitation program developer inside and outside prison, and research analyst serving the institutional research and planning department needs for a community college. I have also served numerous community human service agencies and organizations as subject matter expert, policy analyst, advocate, consultant, and educator.

This article seeks to explore how CC can help to build a community of social justice advocates. I will discuss my personal background, the continued growth, acceptance and effectiveness of CC, along with my experience counseling former prisoners in Iowa. From there I advance a call to action in lieu of CC's marginalized public voice. I conclude with a discussion on what the future of CC may look like if those who adopt this perspective make space for a larger role for public engagement.

CONTINUED GROWTH, ACCEPTANCE
AND EFFECTIVENESS OF CC

As a member of the CC Group, I have witnessed with enthusiasm the continued growth, acceptance and effectiveness of the perspective (Richards and Ross, 2001, 2004; Ross and Richards, 2003; Jones *et al.*, 2009; Ross *et al.*, 2010; Richards *et al.*, 2011) as a platform for change. In pointing to the growth and acceptance of CC first, I am referring to both the book *Convict Criminology* (Ross and Richards, 2003) and the concept of theoretical criminology from the perspective of a Convict Criminologist.

As people who have been incarcerated our voices and views have not always been heard or understood. There have been moments when a dialogue is attainable, where ideology merges and opportunities are possible to discuss what "works". As prisoners and former prisoners, we have consistently been confronted with "what qualifies you" to speak on such matters. Unfortunately, our experiential understanding of the criminal justice system is not always accepted as legitimate by academics and policy makers.

As felons we have been summarily dismissed as being irrelevant to the process, yet we are the very subjects of observation and scrutiny. There is a deep appreciation for the opportunity CC offers to those seeking to orchestrate change in the social policy that maintains our current state of criminal justice administration. CC validates our jailhouse experiential learning degrees, helping to qualify us to speak on such issues related to criminal justice and corrections.

As a former prisoner, I know that our criminal justice system is terribly offensive and sick. Still, our voices are few and our dialogue is fractured in many places. Nevertheless, through our exchange of ideas we must seek to find coordination that directs our efforts to move such a coalition forward. We have a unique responsibility to describe what we have directly observed about the atrocities of prisons and a criminal justice system that is failing miserably. We are a voice that speaks for the many men and women who cannot speak. We are among their representatives and hope. We must speak clearly, with conviction, and as a collective voice if we are to be among their advocates.

In stating this, I have arrived at that point where a more "public voice" and "direct social engagement" is required, where the focus of the discussion centers on seeking to establish a platform for change. While CC has moved

our voices forward, a more public voice – in face and presence – must seek
to bring the discourse out of the dark. We must capture the attention of
mainstream society for CC to become a more effective platform for change.
This means we must actively engage society and become proactive change-
agents in the public's understanding of crime, criminals, victimization,
reentry, reintegration, and social policy practices.

MY EXPERIENCE COUNSELLING
FORMER PRISONERS IN IOWA

I want to share a few observations and a couple of thoughts with regards
to my experience researching and interviewing ex-felon individuals and
families as they transitioned from prison to communities in Iowa (Richards,
1995; Richards and Jones, 1998, 2004) over the past few months. Such an
endeavor provided an opportunity to actively engage with an ever-growing
number of men and women who rely on 'hand-outs' and 'volunteers' to assist
them with their personal and socio-economic needs for every day living
and survival. Much of this engagement centered on performing assistance
with locating social services that provide food, clothing and shelter to these
marginalized families. However, an equal amount of my time was devoted
to listening to the concerns voiced by the men and women concerning their
struggles with homelessness, unemployment, drug addiction, mental health,
and reintegration into society after years of incarceration.

What I found during my discussions with these viable, capable men and
women is an undeniable desire to succeed, to right themselves and their
families by changing their current circumstances to reach their personal
intentions. Many of the women I talked with shared their distrust of others,
their fears of being victimized "again" by those they once trusted, vowing
to never allow themselves to be so vulnerable that others could or would
take advantage of them or use them. Paradoxically, they expressed these
concerns, yet ventured into situations and relationships that have all the
elements of them being once more victimized.

Many others voiced their fear, anxiety and apprehension of what the future
holds for them, especially for those who are transitioning from prison to the
community with little to no resources. Discussion also evolved around the
frustrations with managing a "spoiled identity" (Murphy *et al.*, 2010), that of
being labeled an ex-felon. Their concerns gravitated to how they are viewed

by others, which causes them to feel that they somehow have the words "ex-con" emblazed or tattooed on their forehead, rendering them as worthless, and generating emotions of low self-worth, emptiness, insignificance, and uselessness contaminating their decision-making process.

I also found that some of these men and women were living on the street, in parks or under bridges. They face many roads of uncertainty, with many obstacles and detours to overcome. Many of them are confronted with medical issues, which require professional caregiver involvement to address emotional or psychological pain, severe trauma, or chronic physical disabilities. Most have financial difficulties that contribute to their problems.

The emotional despair these men and women feel continues to be unresolved, long after the circumstances that brought them about have occurred. For most, they still face issues of unemployment, court proceedings and government intrusion into their personal lives, while confronting difficulties with psychological health and instability, which has further jeopardized and alienated their recovery and reintegration. Some suffer from loneliness and alienation, as they cannot learn to trust other people for fear of being victimized again, which may lead to experiencing deeper isolation and depression. Often times, they have shared with me personal histories of family violence and abuse, the emotional pain and suffering of which is so great that some have retreated to a psychological state by which they are unable to function. Some find comfort in medication or street drugs to ease their suffering.

For the men and women I have talked with at length, they are confronted with enormous difficulties in maintaining relationships, parenting, socializing and with continuing employment. Their inability to provide emotional and financial support for themselves and their families has spiraled them into greater hardships. Still, there are others who revealed they are hungry for alternative ways to deal with their current situation, are enthusiastic about developing stronger relationships, and networking with individuals and groups that share experience with their circumstance.

They need mentoring and networks that offer opportunities for hope and opportunities to feel safe, when voicing their feelings and thoughts. Role models offer advising and guidance as they strive to make sense of their lives. Their lives are characterized by paradoxes: they strive for closeness, yet they also fear intimacy and often avoid it; they rebel against control, while at the same time they want direction and structure; although they push and test limits imposed on them, they see some limits as a sign of caring; they are not given complete autonomy, but they are often expected to act as though they have control over their own lives; they are typically highly self-centered, self-conscious, and preoccupied with their own world, yet they are expected to cope with societal demands, and go outside of themselves and expand their horizons often without the pro-social living skills to accomplish it; they are asked to face and accept reality, and at the same time they are tempted by many avenues of escape; and they are exhorted to think of the future, although they have strong urges to live for the moment just to survive. With all these polarities it is easy to understand that transitioning from prison or treatment programs into communities is typically a turbulent and fast-moving period that can be marked by stress, isolation, and despair.

Thus, there is a great need for convicts transitioning from prison to the community to form relationships with mentors who share their common experience. These should be ex-convicts with college degrees that have successfully navigated the transition, and can serve as qualified advisors and counselors, who assist them with reaching their personal and professional goals. Unfortunately, most community reentry programs are heavy on rhetoric and slim on services, and employ people at best that may have good intentions, but very little appreciation of the difficulties their clients face. In fact, we know there are many service program providers who do more damage than good. Yet, we continue to ignore our personal, social, and professional responsibility to change the narrative and commentary of such practice. We must provide realistic solutions for rehabilitating and restoring the lives of individuals, and reintegrating people back into our communities or face our own complicity in their failures.

A CALL TO ACTION

As social scientists, we must shed the value-free myth that we are to remain neutral that the mainstream in our discipline has invoked to choke us into silence. Our research and our findings must reflect our conclusions in a personal way, endeavoring to place our humanity into our scholarship and emotionally stamp the discourse with our personal approval or negation.

As criminologists, we must become active participants in formulating solutions to the social problems we encounter in our research. We must become change-agents through endeavoring to establish an applied and practical criminology that advocates for the development and implementation of sound social policy and practice. We must become *activist criminologists*, decoders for the public interest, which serve to inform and educate citizens, and thereby provide the impetus for social mobilization within the political domain.

As educators, we must embrace the desires of university students whose motivations are to change the world and who seek to bring passion for change. We must encourage them to challenge the social world and to let no one silence their voice. We must cultivate and nourish students to seek who and what they want to be, not what others require them to be.

As service providers, we must endeavor to ensure that we are providing and performing the services that produce results beneficial to those being served. This includes marshalling our efforts to help prisoners and former prisoners overcome the many barriers and impediments they encounter. We must help the men and women we work with to free themselves from correctional custody.

As citizens, we must study current research as a means to understand what really needs to be accomplished in providing for the safety of our families, our neighborhoods and our communities. We must seek to be all these things, if we want to be effective in our profession and as human beings.

CONVICT CRIMINOLOGY'S PUBLIC VOICE

As a social scientist, criminologist and an ex-convict, my voice speaks to the need for a different course for our society and our criminal justice philosophy, one that CC is well suited for – a course of radical change and activism, embodied in the legitimacy and authenticity of criminology that has a public face. I would like to see CC develop and establish an activist collective voice and presence that is more "public". This should be a collective group that socially, politically, and academically challenges what we know to be fraudulent in our present-day approach to criminal justice issues, policy and practice. Regardless of our discipline, specialization or profession, we must collectively voice a common theme: our current criminal justice system does not work. We must continuously emphasize this point in all we say and do.

More "public" means decoding the language of the criminal justice debate, the research literature, the double-speak of politicians and those within our discipline to educate mainstream society so that they can readily understand and grasp the deceptiveness of our current criminal justice policies and practice. More "public" means applying a greater emphasis on "public" in our social justice research efforts within criminology.

Academic discourse between student and professor, between colleagues, as well as university institutions may well promote a heightened sense of awareness among these bodies that endeavors to lead to further research, journal articles and debate, but these types of dialogue and dissertation are not reaching the "public" of mainstream America. There are also many advocacy organizations that seek to reform the criminal justice system that are astonished to learn that research literature is available, and has existed for many years, that supports their organization's specific arguments that policy change is necessary and required within the criminal justice domain. They have voiced anger that such knowledge has been "hidden" from their review.

We must make this literature more accessible and understandable for advocates and mainstream America. At the same time, we should address our own writing to the mainstream public audience so that they can grasp the significance of our research findings in a personal way; how it affects them, why it affects them, and what can be accomplished through policy options and alternatives (see Ross and Richards, 2002, 2009).

We must become public social justice advocates that are "explainers" and "interpreters" in educating the public audience, so that they can "touch" the mechanics of the political issues that must be confronted. When doing so, we must become more "public" in face and presence, individually and collectively. Such an endeavor requires an activist collective built on the CC paradigm – one that brings alternative dialogues, experiences, and scholarship to mainstream America with an activist voice and presence. It is time for mainstream America to hear these voices that seek to critically challenge the illusions of the criminal justice system, its administration and crime control policies of the status quo.

CONCLUSION:
LOOKING AT THE FUTURE OF
CONVICT CRIMINOLOGY

As a man that survived twenty years behind bars in some of America's worst prisons and who has also been free from the pain of confinement for just as much time, I witnessed prison conditions that prove we are not a civilized nation. It is time that people with firsthand knowledge and understanding of our politicized criminal justice system to speak and be heard on the poignant effects of social policy and practice that condones or applauds disproportionate minority confinement, civil and human rights abuses, that accepts prisoner rape, torture and murder, that criminalizes mental illness and chemical addiction, and that excludes and disenfranchises millions in this country. Only through a critical paradigm that does not silence scholarship and voice, censor critical thoughts or questions, seek to ridicule, reject or de-legitimize experience, can such an endeavor succeed in facilitating change of social policy and politics of injustice and inequality.

The very essence of CC is to use the many experiences of current and former prisoners to create a critical discourse to examine and reveal, not conceal, the prejudicial bias within our criminal justice system and our own traditional criminology practice. We can no longer accept that anything will change if our voices remain silent. As with any endeavor, it begins with the birth of an idea, a notion, of what could or should be. At the moment we are in our infancy, looking at the future and what we will become.

REFERENCES

Chancer, L. and E. McLaughlin (2007) "Public Criminologies: Diverse Perspectives on Academia and Policy", *Theoretical Criminology*, 11(2): 155-173.

Clear, T. (2010) "Editorial Introduction to "Public Criminologies"", *Criminology & Public Policy*, 9(4): 721-724.

Jones, R. S., J. I. Ross, S. C. Richards and D. S. Murphy (2009) "The First Dime: A Decade of Convict Criminology", *Prison Journal*, 89(2): 151-171.

Murphy, D. S., B. Fuleihan, S. C. Richards and R. S. Jones (2010) "The Electronic "Scarlet Letter": Criminal Backgrounding and a Perpetual Spoiled Identity", *Journal of Offender Rehabilitation*, 50(3): 101-118.

Richards, S. C. (1995) *The Structure of Prison Release: An Extended Case Study of Prison Release, Work Release, and Parole*, New York: McGraw-Hill.

Richards, S. C. and J. I. Ross (2004) "The New School of Convict Criminology", *Journal of Prisoners on Prisons*, 13: 11-26.

Richards, S. C. and J. I. Ross (2001) "The New School of Convict Criminology", *Social Justice*, 28(1): 177-190.

Richards, S. C., M. Lenza, G. Newbold, R. S. Jones, D. S. Murphy and R. S. Grigsby (2010) "Prison As Seen By Convict Criminologists", in M. Herzog-Evans (ed.), *Transnational Criminology Manual* (volume 3), Nijmegen (Netherlands): Wolf Legal Publishers, pp. 343-360.

Richards, S. C., J. I. Ross, G. Newbold, M. Lenza, R. S. Jones, D. S. Murphy and R. S. Grigsby (2011) "Convict Criminology: Prisoner Re-entry Policy Recommendations",

in I. O. Ekunwe and R. S. Jones (eds.), *Global Perspectives on Re-entry*, Tampere (FI): University of Tampere Press, pp. 198-222.

Ross, J. I., and S. C. Richards (2009) *Beyond Bars: Rejoining Society After Prison*, New York: Alpha/Penguin Group.

Ross, J. I. and S. C. Richards (2003) *Convict Criminology*, Belmont (CA): Wadsworth.

Ross, J. I. and S. C. Richards (2002) *Behind Bars: Surviving Prison*, New York: Alpha/ Penguin Group.

Ross, J. I., S. C. Richards, G. Newbold, M. Lenza and R. S. Grigsby (2010) "Convict Criminology", in W. DeKeseredy and M. Dragiewicz (eds.), *The Handbook of Critical Criminology*, London: Routledge, pp. 160-171.

ABOUT THE AUTHOR

Bob Grigsby, BA, is an ex-convict and independent researcher and policy analyst who is currently working as the education and social policy director for the Center for Social Justice Policy in the United States. He is a lecturer, as well as a facilitator of workshops and seminars on contemporary issues of crime and criminology. Bob is the web administrator for the Convict Criminology Group, co-authoring a number of articles and book chapters with its members. Contact: bobgrigsby@convictcriminology.org

PART II:

PRISONERS IN THE COMMUNITY

Policy Options to Mitigate the Criminal Record Barrier to Employment

Daniel S. Murphy, Stephen C. Richards and Brian Fuleihan

INTRODUCTION

Since the Great Depression, the principle of least eligibility, which posits that criminals should be last in line when competing with regular citizens for jobs and resources, has often restricted large-scale policy measures geared toward assisting ex-cons in the United States. Today, we know that employers use criminal records to exclude millions of men and women from the prospect of earning an adequate living. The systematic exclusion of people with criminal convictions from the labor market has far-reaching effects on people, communities and American society.

The sheer numbers of people who cycle in and out of jail and prison does concern policymakers. The domino effect of mass incarceration, increased availability of criminal records, and institutional-level blacklisting of people with criminal convictions has drawn attention of both criminal justice researchers and policy makers. This article discusses how criminal records are used to deny employment and then explores several policy options to address this growing problem.

THE SOCIAL CONSTRUCTION OF CRIMINALS

American society typically relegates criminals to the bottom of the political and social power structure where they are typically considered ineligible or deemed the least deserving of most social benefits (Ingram *et al.*, 2007), and receive a disproportionate share of burdens and sanctions. The widespread growth of criminal history repositories and their low-cost access have further eroded possible opportunities or avenues for persons convicted of crimes for personal and social empowerment, even when they have changed their ways. Criminals are labeled as incorrigible deviants. The public would like to think that they are a separate species, persons unlike themselves, different and damaged.

The social construction of criminals is accomplished through criminal law, criminal records, and the need to define and control individual behavior. Durkheim considered the criminal to be a functional element of all normal societies (see Simpson, 1963). They serve as a scapegoat for indignation and outrage, and as a measuring rod for defining what society deems as "bad" or "immoral" behavior. The criminal helps to reinforce the bonds among law-abiding citizens as the punishment of the criminal demonstrates the solidarity among the people as to what is defined as bad. In fact, society uses the bad to define the good.

THE ELECTRONIC PANOPTICON

Twenty-five years ago, Gordon (1987) warned of the burgeoning dangers surrounding the accumulation of personal information in the interest of law enforcement. Richards (1998, p. 130) wrote:

> Gordon (1990) named this technological surveillance the "electronic panopticon" which extends the reach of criminal justice sanctions beyond prison walls into the community. Computer generated criminal justice data are used to systematically redefine the opportunity structure and create a permanent underclass of leveled aspirations. For example, while it is illegal to discriminate on the basis of race, it is legal to discriminate on the basis of criminal record, constructing biographical barriers to viable employment; the most apparent to felons, particularly the poor and minorities.

Gordon questioned the Federal Bureau of Investigation's need to build a national criminal records system, largely because of its foreseeable reach beyond the margins of law enforcement purposes. It is doubtful that policymakers could have anticipated the exacerbating effect that widespread availability and exchange of criminal histories would have on mass incarceration and its social consequences.

Nevertheless, Gordon (1987, p. 506) anticipated the quandary we face today, during a time when the Internet barely existed:

> Because the effects on individuals of the Panopticon are as yet either potential or unmeasured in any systematic way, it is easy to dismiss it as a minor civil liberties issue unrelated to structural problems. But the continuing extension of record checks goes beyond the right to be *let alone* or the right to speak up. Those who have records in the system – disproportionately poor and darker-skinned – run the risk of more or less

permanent unemployability. As more employers, landlords, and insurers gain access to the system on a national basis, and as more investigative files are included within it, the system may become a hidden stratifier of social and economic power, channeling many millions of Americans away from jobs and services because they have been arrested at some time for something other than a traffic offense.

Still, even Gordon's remarkable insights could not predict the explosion the Internet has created in instant access to immeasurable storehouses of digitalized information, including both criminal and civil courts.

THE GROWING UNDERCLASS OF FELONS AND FORMER PRISONERS

Punitive crime-control policies, along with the public's easy access to criminal records, have created a permanent underclass of stigmatized persons. In the United States it is estimated that 9 to 25 percent of working-aged males have some form of criminal history for arrest or conviction available for public access (Freeman, 2008, p. 409; Stoll and Bushway, 2008). At any given time, over two million people are incarcerated in American prisons and jails, while approximately five million persons are under some form of community corrections supervision, and in excess of 700,000 prisoners are being released from prison each year (U.S. Department of Justice, 2009).[1]

Every year the number of people with criminal or prison records grows. For example, at the current rate of release, in five years approximately three and a half million prisoners will exit prison returning to the community. Furthermore, at least fourteen million individuals are arrested every year – a figure that has fluctuated, but remained fairly constant for the last two decades. There are over two hundred and twenty eight million arrest cycles contained within the National Criminal History Record File (Federal Bureau of Investigation, 2008). Approximately eighty one million criminal records were stored in state databases in 2006 (Bureau of Justice Statistics, 2006), an estimated seventy one million Americans presently have at least one arrest record (Legal Action Center, 2009), and sixty five million working-age citizens have some type of criminal history (Rodriguez and Emsellem, 2011). Researchers estimate that 40 to 80 percent of employers conduct background checks (Burke, 2004; Holzer *et al.*, 2004; Stoll and Bushway,

2008), and persons with criminal records, no matter how trivial, are more likely to be denied employment (Schmitt and Warner, 2010).

The American prison system is releasing record numbers of ex-convicts into the labor force (Finlay, 2008; Schmitt and Warner, 2010). Those recently released join millions of convicted felons already living in American communities. Many employers are reluctant to hire people with criminal records (Pager, 2003; Holzer *et al.*, 2004; Stoll and Bushway, 2008; Schmitt and Warner, 2010; Ross *et al.*, 2010; Murphy *et al.*, 2011), precisely because criminal records are so easily accessed on the Internet, the public fear of victimization, and the misinformed idea that all or most ex-convicts are dishonest and/or violent. These strictures coalesce, forming a mounting impasse between cautious employers, a growing number of people with criminal records – the vast majority of which need jobs – and the communities who must safely absorb an influx of stigmatized individuals. The use of criminal records to deny employment is contributing to a growing underclass in the United States. This underclass of homeless, unemployed and underemployed people is disproportionately minority. Every large American city now has a felony ghetto.

THE ELECTRONIC SCARLETT LETTER

Criminal labels are now instantly circulated in the form of an "electronic scarlet letter" (Murphy *et al.*, 2011). People "marked" with a criminal record (Pager, 2003, p. 937) must now reckon with widely accessible Internet search engines. The routine dissemination of electronic criminal records has now become entrenched in American society (Murphy *et al.*, 2011) and the availability of computerized records to employers has increased 83 percent since 1985 (Ramker, 2006). A report by SEARCH (2005) referred to this trend as the "criminal backgrounding of America" through the commercial sale of criminal justice information. The report states that criminal backgrounding has become "a necessary, even if not always welcome, rite of passage for almost every adult American" (SEARCH, 2005, pp. 1-2). Hundreds of companies now engage in the selling of criminal histories over the Internet through daily downloading, storing both arrest and conviction records from court systems, as well as developing repositories around the country.

Following an arrest or conviction, the criminal label is immediately propelled to an institutional plane, transmitted electronically among countless interested parties, including employers, landlords, schools, public assistance entities, state and federal agencies, commercial criminal history repositories, and the Internet in general. A fast and inexpensive mechanism for screening and evaluating a person's worth, the electronic scarlet letter has permeated so many social domains that criminal offenders encounter a formidable barrier to self-efficacy or what is best described as institutional stigma. Add to this the fact that the public may now simply Google or Yahoo a person's name and access newspaper, radio or TV stories stored on Internet servers. Many of these media stories convey false or misleading information about arrests, convictions and/or court proceedings. These accounts can then be printed out and distributed at work sites ruining a person's professional career or occupational status. Unfortunately, many people may accept what they read as truth without reference to all the facts in the case as they pass judgment, which may contribute to conspiracies, slander and libel.

THE RELATIONSHIP BETWEEN
THE RATE OF UNEMPLOYMENT AND
THE RATE OF INCARCERATION

Is government sending more people to prison as a means of artificially reducing the rate of unemployment? What would be the rate of unemployment without the 'war on drugs'? Marxist criminologists might assert that during a decline in economic conditions, when the rate of unemployment goes up, the government might decide to reduce the pool of surplus labor by increasing the rate of incarceration by sending more people to prison and keeping them for longer. We could argue that the 'war on drugs' has been used to artificially reduce the rate of unemployment.

Conversely, although the current economic crisis is forcing some states to consider reducing the costs associated with the incarceration binge by reducing prison populations, this has only added more former prisoners to the army of unemployed workers (Austin and Irwin, 2001). Thus, mass incarceration (Rose *et al.*, 2010) has produced a substantial reallocation of labor, whereby at any given time, at least two million persons are not being counted among the unemployed (U.S. Department of Labor, 2010). Therefore, while high incarceration rates might lower "conventional measures of unemployment in the short run by concealing joblessness among able-bodied, working age men" (Western and Beckett, 1999, p. 1031), it raises unemployment rates over time as the labor market is flooded with ever-growing numbers of released prisoners whose job prospects are dismal at best.

A FRESH START OR A SECOND CHANCE

"As President Bush has said, 'America is the land of second chances, and when the gates of the prison open, the path ahead should lead to a better life'" (U.S. Attorney General, 2004). The opportunity for a fresh start is an important concept in American culture. There remains a long-standing tradition, perhaps lingering from early Americans' distaste for religious and political oppression of the "social benefits of forgetfulness" (Blanchett and Johnson, 2002, p. 33). It is an ideal that "once a debt has been paid to society, it is forgotten [...] However, with the mass of easily accessible files, one's past is always present [...] This can create a class of permanently stigmatized persons" (Marx, 1988, p. 223).

Blumstein and Nakamura (2009) introduce the notion of "redemption" in their analysis of electronic criminal records and their proposed regulation. The idea of a second chance for persons convicted of crimes has become a compelling reason for reintegrating these citizens into society. The combination of punitive crime control policies and the expansion of the criminal record archives have intensified punishments to disproportionate levels when compared to the overall harms incurred to society (Maruna, 2001; Uggen, 2006; Austin, 2010).

A modern criminal record can be used to deny persons convicted of crimes fair access to economic resources and opportunities, regardless of the offense or the individual's credit score. Richards (1998, p. 130) wrote:

> We live in a computer age where social security numbers trace criminal records, credit histories, and insurance records. Exconvicts are denied bank loans, credit cards, student loans, welfare assistance, as well as fair market insurance rates. Without credit, exconvicts may be unable to purchase homes or a car, provide for their families, or pay for education. Prisoners, upon release from prison, may encounter an opportunity structure limited by the rule of law that denies them access to employment resources, legitimate opportunities and conventional social structure.

In effect, felons and ex-convicts may find they are not welcome at banks and pay more for all types of insurance, and may not understand why. Denied employment they are unable to open their own small businesses.

Surprisingly, federal regulations governing credit have been employing the idea of second chances for decades. For instance, over 40 years ago, credit reporting agencies began taking advantage of accessible personal information on individuals, the gathering and use of which had no established time limits. The resulting abuses prompted regulation of the credit reporting industry through the *Fair Credit Reporting Act* (FCRA, 1971, 1991). Not only did the FCRA imposed time limits on adverse credit history, it offered people a second chance. For example, adverse credit information is deleted from credit reports after statutory time expires. Under federal law, the bankruptcy reporting period for Chapter 7 is 10 years, while Chapter 13 is only 7 years.

FEDERAL POLICY ALTERNATIVES FOR MITIGATING THE EFFECTS OF CRIMINAL RECORDS

In the early 1970s, the public seized upon 'get tough' policies as a means for solving the crime problem and the stream of politics, irrespective of party affiliation, has been guided by this ideology ever since (Austin, 2010). The policy course sustaining this approach is now being reexamined given budgetary constraints, an increasingly expensive correctional system, the unrelenting "revolving door" of our prison system, a falling crime rate, and America's unbecoming reputation for incarcerating more of its citizens than any other country in the world (Pew Center on the States, 2008). Below are three federal policy alternatives that we suggest could mitigate the effect of criminal records as more individuals are released from prison.

Imposing Time Limits on the Use of Criminal Records
One policy alternative would impose time limits on availability of criminal history to employers and the general public, similar to the length of time credit information is retained by credit bureaus. Several researchers have found that the odds of recidivism declines over time (Kurleychek *et al.*, 2006; Blumstein and Nakamura, 2009). This research suggests that once a person desists from crime for a period of about seven years, the likelihood of committing another crime, or what is termed the *hazard rate*,

becomes almost indistinguishable from that of the comparable non-offender population. The rationale holds that once a man or woman reaches a certain point in years, beyond the last criminal offense, then that person should be "redeemed" for employment purposes since there is no longer a substantial risk for recidivism (Blumstein and Nakamura, 2009).

The question of whether or not the removal of "stale" records will increase employment prospects for persons with criminal records will require future study. This stated, by comparing to information contained within credit reports, if an individual makes a serious attempt to improve a poor credit score and does not accumulate any negative credit information for seven years, then that person is rewarded with a clean slate. In parallel, such a policy may provide people an incentive to function within the realm of legitimate opportunity rather than return to crime. If such a policy was combined with enforced compliance that limited the use of outdated records, more former prisoners might successfully reintegrate into the fabric of society.

Expanding the Scope of Criminal History Information

Another policy option, that we do not support, assumes that electronic criminal history is here to stay – in other words, what has been done cannot be undone. From a political and public safety point of view, the citizenry is quite comfortable with more, rather than less, criminal history information. Therefore, it may benefit both employers and the general public if more detailed information were made available, by which better-informed appraisals and hiring decisions may be made when considering ex-offenders. This position has at its roots in the assumption that more detailed records may establish a hierarchy of criminal activity for consideration in the hiring process.

Not only do prisons send over seven hundred thousand prisoners per year back into the community, national expenditures in corrections alone reach $70 billion annually (Austin, 2010). Corrections agencies should begin to shoulder more responsibility for meeting the needs of public safety and offender reentry, moving beyond custodial duties to proactive efforts or rehabilitation. Under this model, corrections officials would implement a scoring system, providing interested parties with a risk assessment score that included not only past criminal events and convictions, but also accounts of a person's behavior in prison, on community supervision, or his or her continued work at self-improvement and efforts directed toward rehabilitation. Constructive efforts toward a crime-free lifestyle would influence the score in a positive way, yet continued risky behavior, criminal associations, substance use or marginal compliance with supervision restrictions would impact the score negatively. This "panoptic-like" policy may increase the deterrent effect on individuals who otherwise are contemplating a return to criminal behavior (Freeman, 2008).

Reduce Employer Risk When Hiring Ex-Offenders

Changes to negligent hiring laws would ease the due diligence burden imposed upon employers and help ease their fears when they are considering an ex-offender for a job (Holzer *et al.*, 2003; Williams, 2008). A policy that would enable employers to reduce their risk of violating negligent hiring laws when considering felons for jobs, coupled with federally subsidized programs like the Federal Bonding Program and tax breaks for employers who hire, might result in lower unemployment rates for workers with a criminal history.

The Federal Bonding Program provides employers with insurance benefits up to $25,000 if an insured person steals, embezzles, or otherwise causes a financial harm to a business or employer. It does not insure against incidents of violence. Alone, the benefits of the Federal Bonding Program, including an additional tax break for hiring felons, is often insufficient in persuading an employer to hire. Relaxing the current negligent hiring laws, particularly in the case of persons under correctional supervision, coupled with the insurance bonding program and tax incentives, would provide employers motivation to hire.

The Work Opportunity Tax Credit is available to employers who hire, but is often under-utilized and may not be considered strong motivation (Holzer *et al.*, 2003). Whether or not the tax credit in itself generates any new employment for felons and former prisoners is unclear, but some evidence suggests that the credit might be better utilized if employers were not only made aware of the advantages, but were provided assistance by an intermediary who could help them understand how to access the tax credit (ibid).

STATE-LEVEL POLICY CHANGES

Beyond the role the federal government can play in helping to mitigate the impacts of criminal records on the ability of former prisoners to obtain employment, state governments can also put in place policies to this end. Three such policy alternatives are outlined below.

Banning the "Box"

From job applications to housing applications, it is common practice to include a "box" to check if one has been arrested for or convicted of a crime. Unfortunately, many employers may discount or reject an applicant based on the checking of this box. A national movement to "ban the box" has actually gained momentum in many states (All of Us or None of Us, 2010). It is suggested that if people are not required to disclose criminal history during the initial application process by checking the box or listing criminal convictions they have a better chance at getting through the screening process and can then explain their criminal history in a face-to-face interview. Although two states, Minnesota and Massachusetts, have recently passed legislation prohibiting the box, there has been little research conducted that demonstrates how absence of the box might actually affect an employer's hiring decision beyond the application stage of the hiring process, thus further analysis is warranted. This said, it appears reasonable to assume that some people might enhance their likelihood of employment if they could get an interview.

Standards for Hiring People with Criminal Records

Continuing to allow broad sweeping discrimination by employers against the hiring of people with criminal records will only worsen the situation over time, again, since employment is a key indicator of reduced recidivism. Legislation is needed that encourages employers to make individualized assessments for people with criminal records, or at the very least, prohibit employers from preemptively excluding applicants solely because of criminal history.

At the time of writing, fourteen states require government agencies to look beyond the actual record and make an individual determination in the hiring process (Legal Action Center, 2009). In fact, twenty-one states require a substantial reason for the denial of a professional license beyond the existence of a criminal record, while all other states allow denials based solely on an applicant's criminal record. Moreover, thirty-six states still allow employers and occupational licensing boards to consider arrests that never led to a conviction (ibid).

Expunging or Sealing Arrest / Conviction Records

In the absence of regulation controlling the use of arrest history many citizens who have never been convicted of a crime are being denied housing, employment and other forms of public assistance. Legislation needs to be proffered allowing individuals with arrest only records to have those records expunged. Certain types of conviction records need to be sealed after a reasonable period of time. Records of first time non-violent offenses, for example, should only be obtainable by law enforcement agencies, thereby mitigating stigma associated with the ex-con label and thus fostering successful reintegration into society (Legal Action Center, 2009).

At this time, only Nevada allows the sealing of felony convictions after certain waiting periods determined by the offense class. Illinois provides for the sealing of misdemeanor convictions four years after completion of the sentence if no intervening convictions occur. These laws provide a model for other states as a mechanism to offset the long reach of current unrestricted access to criminal records.

CONCLUSION

If an additional ten percent of the almost fifteen million felons were able to secure steady employment, which means one and a half million men and women with jobs, considerable costs could be saved. Using an average yearly conservative imprisonment cost of $30,000 – which builds in other economic costs, such as lost tax revenue, law enforcement expenditures, court costs, additional public assistance burden, and victim costs – this would result in a savings of $4.5 billion. Whereas these figures are extrapolations, yet not unreasonable for evaluating any program's effectiveness, this would result in a net gain for employees and employers, along with a significant reduction in the economic burden society currently absorbs.

While it is difficult to predict what universal criminal record access will have on the future labor market, the consequences for felons and former prisons are obvious unless policies change. It should be abundantly clear, that when fourteen million arrests are being made each year, the correctional population continues to number around seven million persons and almost sixty-five million Americans have criminal records, that a tipping point will be reached at some point in the future. In light of these figures, the continued reliance upon criminal records to exclude persons from employment in our society will deplete the pool of eligible workers and create more poverty.

Compare this situation to the plight of African Americans almost fifty years ago. In 1960, about one hundred and eighty million persons lived in the United States. Approximately twenty million were non-white or approximately 11 percent of the total population (U.S. Census Bureau, 1960). Blacks were being systematically denied opportunities in a myriad of ways and this continual state of inequality was perpetuated through institutional discrimination. Their plight became so egregious and unfair that this rather small minority of Americans managed to capture the nation's attention. In this context, the *Civil Rights Act* of 1964 was passed, mainly as a measure of relief to Blacks by legislating equal treatment under the law.

Today, the majority of those incarcerated, and thus the majority of those released, are African-American (Pew Center on the States, 2008). The ubiquitous presence of "criminal backgrounding" by a few strokes of a keyboard, disproportionately effects Black men and women who now suffer under another form of institutional discrimination, one that currently overrides many of their former gains against racial inequality. The use of criminal records to deny employment is contributing to a growing underclass in the United States. Minorities disproportionately represent this underclass of homeless, unemployed and underemployed people. Every large American city now has a felony ghetto. The United States needs a new civil rights movement to limit the use of criminal records.

There is a new slavery in this country predicated on the widespread public access to criminal records that is systematically eliminating people from economic competition. We need a new civil rights movement to remove the electronic bondage – the mark and brand of stigma that locks us away in felony ghettos, jails and penitentiaries. We should never forget that many of the founding fathers of America, Gandhi, Martin Luther King and Nelson Mandela were ex-convicts, and that today they would be denied employment in America due to criminal records. We suggest that all criminal records should be subject to privacy laws, the same as medical records, and only available for law enforcement and courts, as they are in France and many other European countries.

ENDNOTE

[1]   See Richards (1997, pp. 125-126; 2004, pp. 122-144) for a discussion of how even these figures underestimate the number of people with criminal records or "in custody" of correctional authorities.

REFERENCES

All of Us or None (2010) Ban the Box Campaign. Retrieved from <http://www. allofusornone.org/campaigns/ban-the-box>.

Austin, J. (2010) "Reducing America's Correctional Populations: A Strategic Plan", *Justice Research and Policy*, 12(1): 9-40.

Austin, J. and J. Irwin (2001) *It's About Time*, Belmont (CA): Wadsworth.

Blanchette, J. and D. Johnson (2002) "Data Retention and the Panoptic Society: The Social Benefits of Forgiveness", *The Information Society*, 18: 33-45.

Blumstein, A. and K. Nakamura (2009) "Redemption in the Presence of Widespread Criminal Background Checks", *Criminology*, 47: 327-359.

Bureau of Justice Statistics (2006) *Survey of State Criminal History Information, 2003.* Washington (D.C.).

Bureau of Justice Statistics (2009) *Prisoners Released*, Washington (D.C.). Retrieved June from <http://bjs.ojp.usdoj.gov/content/pub/pdf/p08.pdf>.

Burke, M. (2004) *Reference and Background Checking Survey Report: A Study by the Society for Human Resource Management*, Alexandria (VA): Society for Human Resource Management.

FedCure News (2010) "DOJ announces $110 million for reentry programs", p. 2 – October 14. Retrieved from <www.fedcure.org>.

Federal Bureau of Investigation (2008) *Crime in the United States, 2007*, Washington (D.C.): Federal Bureau of Investigation.

Finlay, K. (2008) "The Effect of Employer Access to Criminal History Data on the Labor Market Outcomes of Ex-offenders and Non-offenders, *NBER Working Paper No. 13935)*, Cambridge (MA): National Bureau of Economic Research.

Gordon, D. R. (1990) *The Justice Juggernaut: Fighting Street Crimes, Controlling Citizens*, New Brunswick (NJ): Rutgers University Press.

Gordon, D. R. (1987) "The Electronic Panopticon: A Case Study on the Development of the National Criminal Records System", *Politics & Society*,15: 483-511.

Holzer, H., S. Raphael and M. Stoll (2004). "How Willing Are Employers To Hire Ex-offenders?, *Focus*, 23: 40-43.

Holzer, H., S. Raphael and M. Stoll (2003) *Employment Barriers Facing Ex-offenders*, New York: Urban Institute Reentry Roundtable.

Ingram, H., A. Schneider and P. deLeon (2007) "Social Construction and Policy Design", in P. Sabatier (ed.), *Theories of the Policy Process*, Boulder (CO): Westview Press, pp. 93-126.

Kurleychek, M., R. Brame and S. Bushway (2006) "Enduring Risk? Old Criminal Records and Short-term Predictions of Criminal Involvement", *Crime and Delinquency*, 53: 1-24.

Legal Action Center (2009) *After Prison: Roadblocks to Reentry*, New York: Legal Action Center.

Maruna, S. (2001) *Making Good*, Washington (D.C.): American Psychological Association.

Marx, G. (1988) *Undercover: Police Surveillance in America*, Berkeley (CA): University of California Press.

Murphy, D., B. Fuleihan, S. C. Richards and R. S. Jones (2011) "The "Electronic Scarlet Letter": Criminal Backgrounding and a Perpetual Spoiled Identity", *Journal of Offender Rehabilitation*, 50(3): 101-118.

Pager, D. (2003) "The Mark of a Criminal Record", *American Journal of Sociology*, 108: 937-975.

Ramker, G. F. (2006) *Improving Criminal Records for Background Checks, 2005*, Bureau of Justice Statistics Program Report, Office of Justice Programs. Retrieved from <http://www.ojp.usdoj.gov/bjs/pub/ascii/ichrbc05.txt>.

Richards, S. C. (2009) "A Convict Perspective on Community Punishment: Further Lessons from the Darkness of Prison", in J. I. Ross (ed.), *Cutting the Edge: Current Perspectives in Radical/Critical Criminology and Criminal Justice* (second edition), Edison (NJ): Transaction, pp. 122-144.

Richards, S. C. (1998) "Critical and Radical Perspectives on Community Punishment: Lessons from the Darkness", in J. I. Ross (ed.), *Cutting the Edge: Current Perspectives in Radical/Critical Criminology and Criminal Justice* (first edition), New York: Praeger, pp. 122-144.

Rodriguez, M. and M. Emsellem (2011) *65 Million "Need Not Apply": The Case for Reforming Criminal Background Checks for Employment*, New York: National Employment Law Project.

Rose, C. D., V. Beck and S. C. Richards (2010) "The Mass Incarceration Movement in the USA", in M. Herzog-Evans (ed.), *Transnational Criminology Manual* (volume 2), Nijmegen, Netherlands: Wolf Legal Publishers, pp. 533-551.

Ross, J. I., S. C. Richards, G. Newbold, R. S. Jones, M. Lenza, D. S. Murphy, R. G. Hogan and G. D. Curry (2010) "Knocking on the Ivory Towers' Door: The Experience of Ex-convicts Applying for Tenure-track University Positions", *Journal of Criminal Justice Education*, 21(3): 1-19.

Sampson, R. and J. Laub (1993) *Crime in the Making: Pathways and Turning Points Through Life*, Cambridge (MA): Harvard University Press.

SEARCH (2005) *Report of the National Task Force on the Criminal Backgrounding of America*, Sacramento (CA): SEARCH, The National Consortium for Justice Information and Statistics.

Schmitt, J. and K. Warner (2010) *Ex-offenders and the Labor Market*, Washington (D.C.): Center for Economic and Policy Research.

Simpson, G. (1963) *Emile Durkheim: Selections from his Work*, New York: Cromwell, pp. 61-64.

Stoll, M. and S. Bushway (2008) "The Effect of Criminal Background Checks on Hiring Ex-offenders", *Criminology & Public Policy*, 7: 371-404.

The Pew Center on the States (2008) *One in 100: Behind Bars in America 2008*, Washington (D.C.): The Pew Charitable Trusts.

Uggen, C. (2006) "The Effect of Criminal Background Checks on Hiring Ex-offenders", *Criminology & Public Policy*, 7(3), 367-370.

Uggen, C. (2000) "Work as a Turning Point in the Life Course of Criminals: A Duration Model of Age, Employment, and Recidivism", *American Sociological Review*, 67: 529-546.

United States Attorney General (2004) "Prepared Remarks of Attorney General John Ashcroft – Department of Justice Re-Entry Conference", Cleveland (OH). Retrieved from <http://www.justice.gov/archive/ag/speeches/2004/ag092004_reentry.htm>.

United States Census Bureau (1960) *Characteristics of the Population*, Washington (D.C.).

United States Department of Justice (2009) *Crime in the United States*, Washington (D.C.).

United States Department of Labor (2010) *Bureau of Labor Statistics*, Washington (D.C.).

Western, B. (2006) *Punishment and Inequality in America*, New York: Russell Sage Foundation.

Western, B. and K. Beckett (1999) "How Unregulated is the US Labor Market? The Penal System as a Labor Market Institution", *American Journal of Sociology*, 104(4): 1030-1060.

Williams, K. (2008) "Employing Ex-offenders: Shifting the Evaluation of Workplace Risks and Opportunities From Employers to Corrections", *UCLA Law Review*, 55: 521-558.

ABOUT THE AUTHORS

Daniel S. Murphy, PhD, is an ex-convict now Associate Professor in the Department of Justice and Criminal Studies, Appalachian State University. He has published many peer-reviewed articles and a recent book delineating an expansion of Robert K. Merton's work on strain/anomie theory. He is an active member of the Convict Criminology group as well as co-chair of the Federal Citizens United for the Rehabilitation of Errants' (FedCURE) Legislative Action Committee. He also serves as a member of FedCURE's Board of Directors.

Stephen C. Richards, PhD, is an ex-convict now Professor of Criminal Justice at the University of Wisconsin-Oshkosh. His work has appeared in numerous academic journals. The author of five books, his most recent books include *Behind Bars: Surviving Prison* (2002), *Convict Criminology* (2003) and *Beyond Bars* (with Jeffrey Ian Ross) (2009). Richards is a Soros Senior Justice Fellow and member of the American Society of Criminology National Policy Committee. He is lead organizer of the Convict Criminology Group.

Brian Fuleihan is an ex-convict doctoral student at the University of South Carolina. He has co-authored one article on the stigmatizing effects of electronic criminal records and is currently researching the net effect of drug treatment courts on incarceration rates.

A Tale of Two Convicts:
A Reentry Story About the Impacts of Ethnicity and Social Class
Richard Hendricksen and Alan Mobley

INTRODUCTION

Why do the disciplines of criminal justice and criminology persist in denying the harm caused by imprisonment? On a general level, perhaps one answer lies in the production of knowledge concerning penality (see Austin, 2003; Austin *et al.* 2007). There are no shortages of surveys and quantitative studies on imprisonment and its aftermath. This information, often presented mostly in numeric form, in large part comprises the penal knowledge base. Here, we present knowledge of a different kind.

Convict Criminology (CC) highlights the importance of direct experience. It does so mostly because first-person accounts remain rare in criminology. Convict Criminologists understand that crime and the societal response to crime are complex phenomena. We aim to contribute to knowledge using our rare ability to draw from our own life experiences within criminal justice systems, and draw upon the ample and often enlightening academic literature (see Jones *et al.*, 2009). It is our hope that this combined approach, which could be called our preferred method, might lead to furthering social goals of creating safer, more just societies (see Richards and Ross, 2001; Ross and Richards, 2003; Mobley, 2011).

Ethnographers, such as anthropologists, study the lives of others. They do so by attempting to record and interpret experience. Autoethnographers do the same thing, but with the crucial difference that the experience they study is their own (Irwin, 1987; Ellis and Bochner, 2000). Autoethnography shares some characteristics with memoir, but an important distinction is that autoethnographers are using their experience to inform more general topics of interest. In other words, whereas in memoir the end goal may be the skillful telling of the tale, autoethnography tells a more general story that may shed light on broader social concerns (see Lenza, 2011; Leyva and Bickel, 2010). In this autoethnographic narrative, the more general concern we address is the difficulty of prisoner reentry.

TWO CONVICTS RETURN HOME

Prisoner reentry has become a major topic in criminology and public policy (Petersilia, 2003; Mobley, 2005; Ross and Richards, 2009; Richards *et al.*, 2011). Neither of these academic forums, however, receives much information in the way of direct experience (Ross and Richards, 2002, 2003; Irwin, 2005, 2009; Richards *et al.*, 2010). In what follows, one of us (Richard) will tell of his own recent reentry and compare it with what he knows about the reentry of another felon (Josh). The two outcomes are very different, with one embodying something of a best-case scenario. The other outcome, sadly, is as predictable as it is unfortunate.

The point here is that the prison experience harms human beings (Mauer and Chesney-Lind, 2002). Sending someone to prison will nearly always lessen his or her ability to lead a productive contributing life (Clear, 2007). Although Richard uses his prison experience to propel a new life as a scholar, part of the poignancy in his recital is his earnest desire to succeed. However, in another sad twist, penologists are beginning to report that many "best-case" reentry scenarios also end badly (Mobley, 2008; Braun, 2011).

Reentry scholarship informs us that incarceration disproportionately affects the lives of racial minorities and the poor (Alexander, 2010; Bernstein, 2007; Mauer, 2006; Western, 2006). In this paper, the reentry experiences of a young white working class man whose working family can provide him with basic shelter and modest support (i.e. a roof over his head, meals and a few dollars until he gets on his feet) is juxtaposed with the experience of a young Latino man without access to such basic resources. We encourage readers to consider issues of race, class and relative disadvantage in the United States. We also invite readers to become involved in the emotional information conveyed in these accounts. These are the lives of real people. They celebrate their successes and grieve over failures. If prisons harm, which they most surely do, these are the people they hurt.

Richard's Story:
Zero Days and a Wake-Up Call
Walking out of Racine Correctional Institution in Wisconsin was a surreal experience that I think to this day I am still processing. I remember waking up late and missing breakfast because I had so much to do. I had to go to the Prison Laundry to turn in my linens, then to the Property Room and sign off on everything I had packed up the night before, and then verify that it was on the cart ready to be sent to the Gate House. After going back to my Housing Unit to have my cell inspected for damages that I would be billed for later if any were found, I went to the courtyard to socialize for the last

time with my friends before saying goodbye. Not surprisingly, only a few of them were out there. This is not uncommon. It is very hard to say goodbye to someone who is leaving when you are staying. I do not blame them.

I was sentenced to two years initial confinement and five years on extended supervision. I had fourteen months left until I would be discharged completely at the expiry of my sentence. Making it this far is something I always tried not to think about. Even though on the surface I am doing well, my time involved with the Wisconsin Department of Corrections (WDOC) has left me a bit cynical. Most people coming out of prison do not have the advantages I did. I had a few things in my favor getting out: I am white, do not reside in an urban area, have a high school diploma and most of all I had social connections.

"Hendricksen you're out!" Finally, they called my name. I walk to the Segregation Unit to be handcuffed before being escorted to the Gate House. That is where the surrealness starts. I remember being in a tiny little room and someone yelling at me to hurry up and change into street clothes. I am thinking, "All this time trying to keep me in and now they're pushing me out the door". Walking out into the waiting room to my crying mother was almost too much. She is crying tears of joy today. I am so scared of the parole system that I do not have the heart to tell her that if the current state corrections trend holds, there is a very good chance that I am going back to prison within one year.

We go out to the car and it dawns on me that after spending two years here this is the first time I have seen the prison from the outside. This is also the first time in two years that I will leave an area the size of a few blocks. I got carsick on the way home. I rode in front, my mom slept in the backseat after the conversation died down. I was in a prison about three hours from my hometown and my mom could not make it to see me often, so we did have a lot to talk about. We stopped at a nice restaurant to eat lunch. The colors and taste of the food was an experience that I had often thought about. However, now that I had a menu in front of me, I could not decide what to order from the menu. My widowed mother had become engaged while I was in prison. Because of prison rules regarding how many times you can add people to your prisoner visitors list – you are allowed 12 family members and you can only change them twice a year – I had not met my new father figure before the car ride home. What a way to meet someone for the first time! Fortunately, this man who I will call "Dane" was very trusting and invited me to live at his house.

After checking in with my P.O. (parole officer) I arrived at my new home, a ranch style house in the country. It was a serious step up. It was quiet and surrounded by trees. I had not seen a tree or heard birds in a long time, so I relished it right away. I fell asleep in my room that night a bit uneasily though – maybe it was just because it was a new surrounding or perhaps it was because I was still a bit nervous and excited. I think it was because for the first time in a few years the room was dark. There were no suicide lights on in every cell and no light from the security towers streaming in through my window. I had not slept in the dark in two years.

Josh's Story

Josh is Mexican-American who grew up in the urban area of Milwaukee and was raised by a single mother. His father had never been in the picture and was assumed in prison dead or deported back to Mexico. He joined the Army and was sent to Iraq after graduating from an alternative high school. Josh got up on his last day in prison and had less to do. No one was coming to pick him up so there was no rush. Josh lived on the north side of Milwaukee, which is populated by a diverse working-class population. He had no family home that met the standards of the state of Wisconsin's Division of Community Corrections as a suitable living environment, so he was being released to a Temporary Living Placement (TLP) facility. He left prison in his state issued garb, which he was charged for, and taken by bus to his new home. He then hit the streets the first day to look for a job in his prison uniform. The TLP charges weekly rent and if not paid he could be re-incarcerated by his P.O. He had no luck finding employment his first day out. Josh wanted to eat a late dinner with his mother, but because his brother who is also an ex-con was living with her he was not allowed to go to her house. Since there were sex offenders in the TLP there were lights on at night, so Josh did not get to sleep in the dark.

THE FIRST FEW WEEKS:
TRYING TO PICK UP THE PIECES AND FINDING
THEY ARE NOT WHERE YOU LEFT THEM

Richard

One of the hardest things emotionally about getting out is realizing that no one put their life on hold while you were in there. The house I left had new occupants. My job was gone. My wife moved on. The house that I grew up in was gone, and my mother and I lived with Dane. It seemed like there was nothing now that connected me with my old life – there were no constants. I remember the first week I was home I bought a pint of ice cream that me and my wife used to enjoy. I went to a bench that overlooked the Lemonwier River where we used to picnic to eat it. That was the first time I felt like myself and even then I knew it was temporary. Even with the few friends I had left the general consensus among them was that I was not the same person. I had to learn to manage my "spoiled identity" (Jones, 2003). I cannot think about it now though. First things first, I need a job.

I was lucky. I got a job the first week. I got an entry-level job and slightly above minimum-wage compensation. I was a machine operator for a plastic injection-molding factory. It was not the American dream, but it was an honest paycheck. It also was not enough to support myself, pay my supervision fees and go to school, but Dane said I could stay with him for as long as I needed. I enrolled part time at the community college and took classes.

Josh

Josh finally got some proper clothes through a church. After a few weeks of no luck finding employment he got a job as a cook. It was not the classiest restaurant so the compensation was barely enough to live on. He had only ninety days total in the TLP and he was already nearing the end of the first month. The TLP takes about one-third of his paycheck. The rest he uses for food, clothing (he has almost none), the cost of his court appointed drug counseling and his supervision fees. Josh has to find a way to save enough money to pay a security deposit and first month's rent on a place within two months. If he cannot the TLP will kick him out as they have limited space and usually have someone waiting for the bed. His P.O. has threatened to revoke him if he cannot find a way to "pay his own way in life". He is contacting every church, social program, and charity organization available to try and come up with something. Unfortunately, we are in a recession. Our tax dollars are tight and with our current economic climate social programs are limited. Josh eats at the Salvation Army when he can to save money.

THE FIRST FEW MONTHS:
TRYING TO GET IN THE GROOVE

Richard

The first few months were in some ways the time I realized how many advantages I had compared with most ex-cons. I had a stable and free place to live. I also had food that I did not have to buy. My mother had dropped out of high school pregnant with me, but between her job as a waitress and Dane's income as a factory manager, I had all I needed physically. I knew I had the basics. I was taking classes at a community college and it seemed like I was in good with my P.O. I had a plan to attend university as soon as I could, and with the help of the University of Wisconsin – Oshkosh (UWO) professors (Dr. Stephen Richards, Dr. Chris Rose, Dr. Michael Lenza) and all the others in the CC network, I had a support system to help nurture my goals into fruition. Soon after my release I was accepted into the UWO. I was with my mother in the car when I opened the letter. I was going to a real university. I would become the first of my family to get a degree past high school.

Josh

Josh reunited with his child's mother and between them they raised enough money for an efficiency apartment within walking distance from his job. His girlfriend, who we will call "Jane", works as a housekeeper, a full time but low paying job. Among the challenges Jane is facing is that she is recovering from cocaine dependency. She has been clean for three years. It is at first a good living arrangement. Between their collective incomes their budget is tight, but they are managing. They have food with the help of community assistance. The apartment is in her name because they get rent vouchers, although the lease states a felon cannot occupy the dwelling. His P.O. does not know about this arrangement. It is technically unlawful, but they are left with little choice. He feels that as long as he is maintaining his obligations his P.O. will overlook the infraction if it is discovered. His girlfriend agrees to try and get the County to remove the garnishment of his wages for child support, since they are living together and sharing the expenses of the child. The process is initiated, but never makes it all the way through the bureaucratic red tape.

Josh is having a hard time with the people at work. They are mostly only a few years younger than him, but they are in high school and find a kind of novelty in knowing someone who has been to prison. One of these kids asks him to buy him beer after work one night. Josh says no. Two days later Josh is arrested at work and jailed. It seems an anonymous tip was made about his living arrangement. After three days of pleading his case to his P.O. Josh is released from jail. He comes home to find that he and his girlfriend have been evicted, and that he has been fired from his job for getting arrested on company property and for missing work. He reports this to his P.O. and is given orders to find full employment as soon as possible. He has no extra money to pay his monthly supervision fees. After not finding a job for the better part of a month he is placed on electronic monitoring. An ankle bracelet is connected to his phone line. He is allowed to leave his home from 8:00 a.m. till 7:00 p.m. Monday through Friday, and until 9:00 p.m. on weekends. He has no job and again needs to find a place to live. Eventually Josh finds a job doing landscaping and lawn maintenance. He makes less than he did as a cook, but even worse is the job environment. He works mainly with other people who also work there as a result of few options. Many of them are ex-cons and active drug users.

When Christmas comes he is excited at the prospect of seeing his family. His P.O. agrees to let him attend the family dinner as long as there are no alcohol or drugs present and no other felons in attendance. Because of this Josh was still not allowed to see his brother. That night when he got home he was arrested. His P.O. had agreed to let him out until 11:00 p.m., but she had forgotten to inform the people who monitor his electronic surveillance. When he did not register as "in" at the preprogrammed time of 8:00 p.m. an electronic arrest warrant was automatically issued. Josh was release from jail the next day. He was told that it officially "never happened". I wonder if his son will not-remember the Christmas when his father was officially not arrested while tucking him into bed.

Josh is living in a studio apartment with his girlfriend and child again. His P.O. now looks more closely at where he lives and as such they are no longer able to get rent vouchers. To save money the family eats more often at the Salvation Army. Josh and his girlfriend have also started selling blood plasma for about fifty extras dollars apiece each week.

Josh is working first shift and his girlfriend works second. The child is kindergarten age and at a phase where unanticipated expenses are frequent. The child, who we will call "Jack", is also showing signs of a learning impairment. They have some insurance benefits through her job, and between that and assistance from charitable organizations the child's problem is assessed. The affliction turns out to be controllable by medication and behavior therapy, which adds an expense. Josh and Jane usually do not have the money, time, or energy to do much besides work and care for Jack. Jane, though, is about to find out she is pregnant. Josh is about to find out that he is not the father of the child.

SECOND YEAR OUT

Richard
I collected my final paycheck from my job hoping it would be enough to make it until my first student financial aid check comes. I leave for UWO in three days. Nearly my whole family gathers to take me out to dinner that night. I remember the feeling of pride as they all wished me luck. I was the first to go away to university, as well as the least likely. They expressed how proud they were that someone was finally going to bring our family name into the educated world. Finally, one of us is going to have a career not a job – someone in our family is going to live a dream that everyone else could not. I was so touched that even in this rough economy my working-class family gave me almost a thousand dollars to help me get by until I could find a part time job.

My first night in the university dorm I was by myself. My roommate, whom I had not met yet, was not due to arrive until the next morning. I went to the student union and tried to buy dinner with my student ID. It did not work so I had to pay cash. I did not realize that the cards had to be activated. I spent that cold January evening alone walking around campus, figuring out where my classes the next day were located. I felt a bit isolated. I was on average five years older then everyone in my dorm. It does not seem much, but the gap between eighteen and twenty-four is a big one in terms of maturity and the unique experiences of my life. I longed for the morning when I would meet Dr. Richards in his office for a tour and a familiar reassuring face.

I soon found that for a person in my position part of succeeding is directly related to the people you have in your support network. So I had to figure out who I was going to surround myself with socially to increase my odds of making it. I looked at student leaders and campus organizations. I deliberated on what kind of student I wanted to be and how I could make friends. I found acceptance in an organization that measures itself in terms of scholarship, community service, and a collective set of high standards and ideals.

I had an opportunity to make friends with people who were student leaders. They maintained high grades and lived a day-to-day that was structured to ensure success. They lived up to ideals by participating at campus functions and volunteering to help at university events. They included regular community service projects into their lives. The best thing of all was they accepted me knowing my flaws and past. They encouraged me to follow my dreams and not be discouraged by setbacks. The help I got from my professors and the other faculty was great, but without the friendships with other students I do not know if I would have made it. I managed to finish the first semester working part time in the dish room and pulled off a decent GPA. I think I can make it now.

Josh

Josh started his second year out in a menial job with no real prospects for improvement. He lived with his son Jack, who has a learning disability, and his son's mother, who is carrying a child by a new boyfriend. It turns out the new boyfriend is a cocaine dealer. Jane has been using again since the last time Josh was arrested. The pregnancy was eventually terminated, but there was a tremendous amount of stress put on Josh's life. He figured he had no option but to continue living with his drug addict girlfriend and avoid altercations with her drug dealer / new boyfriend. They live on the agreement that they will not use drugs in the home.

Jane soon finds herself no longer employed. Being an active drug addict with a scattered employment history and few skills means legitimate income is in short supply. She starts working for her boyfriend who we will call "John". The small apartment soon becomes a base of operations for two drug dealers and a hang out for users. When Josh comes home from work one day he finds his drug dealer roommates, along with three people very much intoxicated on drugs and acting incoherently. The child is unattended in the bathroom. He takes his son to his mother's house and stays there. He calls his P.O. and leaves a message explaining the situation, in effect admitting to violating the terms of his release due to his living companions and their lifestyle.

When he returns home later that night an electronic warrant is issued for his address. He comes into the apartment where he is immediately accosted by John and his cohorts and beaten severely. When the police show up they find only Josh unconscious on the floor. They take him into custody and call an ambulance. As other officers arrive they conduct a search of the residence and find drug paraphernalia and residue. Josh is now facing revocation charges for violations of his parole because of his living arrangements and charges of drug paraphernalia and drug possession.

His son Jack is turned over to the child welfare agency. Josh's mother tries to get custody, but because her other felon son lives with her she is not deemed suitable. Because he has a job, Josh is allowed to serve time in a work release program. Things do not go well for him there and within a short time he is sent back to a Wisconsin prison where he is still a prisoner.

In my conversations with people and in my ongoing education I am finding that Josh's story is not entirely unique. In fact, it is alarmingly similar to the greater population of convicts and parolees, who are victims of poverty, failed educational systems, incompetent correctional authorities, and bad luck. Josh is still in the same position as the first time he went to prison. His street time will not count toward discharge, which effectively lengthens his sentence. He has no support system or place to go when he gets out of prison the next time, and no employment prospects. Josh is getting no programming while in prison, although he is over a year into a waiting list for a work release program, but it is like the one he was in before. He has lost most of the possessions he acquired and what little money he had went to court obligated fees. Josh has not seen his son Jack since he was arrested.

Maybe the worst thing about Josh's situation is that in the eyes of the state he has already failed. He made his best attempt and sacrificed much, and it was still not good enough. He will again be released and no doubt will realize that the deck is stacked against him. Besides issues with employment and living arrangements, Josh will have a P.O. that already locked him away once and he knows what a minefield parole can be. How difficult must it be to live knowing all that?

IN CLOSING
(RICHARD)

I had a lot of advantages compared to the majority of people getting out of prison. The difference in the outcomes for Josh and I was not that I worked harder and struggled to succeed more valiantly than he did. The opposite is much closer to the truth. Without any resources Josh faced difficulties every day securing a roof over his head and food to keep himself alive. Yet, he did not steal, cheat or commit crimes. He kept trying. When we regularly talked on the phone and he would tell me what was happening in his life, I often felt a mixture of unearned security and guilt for simply having a room, a roof over my head, food in the kitchen, or that my mother could lend me ten or twenty dollars when I needed it from her the tips she brought home from work until I found a job.

The resources had created enough security in my life that I could find my way towards a future, whereas Josh, for trying to protect his son and being honest with his parole officer about what his drug addicted girlfriend was doing, was beaten unconscious by her drug dealer boyfriend, only to awake to be handcuffed and charged with drug crimes he never committed. With parole revoked he was placed in chains and returned to prison. No one gave him the slightest consideration. He was just another poor Latino going back to prison.

Around $30,000 a year is spent to further stigmatize and punish Josh. That is more than it costs me to get my four-year degree at a University. It makes no sense to me. The American public is being taken for a ride through the politics of fear and difference. Here in Wisconsin we spend upward towards $700,000,000 more each and every year on corrections than our neighbor Minnesota (Lenza and Jones, 2010). Why? Demographically, we are very similar states and have almost identical crime rates. The difference is Minnesota saves prison for dangerous offenders. Nonviolent prisoners serve their time in the community so they may make restitution, get treatment, and so they and their families do not suffer unnecessary harms that exceed the harm they did. In Wisconsin we imprison individuals and as a consequence inflict damage on their families. How many teachers, housing spaces and food for our poor could be bought with those hundreds of millions of dollars? All of this money and funds spent in other states could be spent helping others and doing some good.

Using unnecessary violence against our own citizens is not only morally questionable, but it is also robbing us of our ability to provide essential services to our communities. Putting Josh back in prison for three years costs over $90,000. His little boy being placed in foster care, instead of with Josh or his mother, and the psychological damage children suffer from parents being incarcerated, that costs us too. Not just now, but long into the future. Brutal social repression of our poor minorities is not making us safer. Instead, it is robbing us of scarce public resources while harming children, families and communities.

Just think about the money we would have saved by providing Josh with a little assistance for housing, food and childcare for his son. As a father, when he saw probable harm surrounding his son, he did what a parent should do. He acted to protect his son. So what was done in our name? We rewarded that selfless act with re-imprisoning him and placing his son in foster care.

Treating other human beings with just a little consideration does not make us weak. It is an investment in our own citizenry and our future that would strengthen our communities, provide a better future for our children, and help families. In 1998, the United States had over one million nonviolent offenders incarcerated. In a comparative perspective, just this nonviolent prison population was then three times the total prison population of the European Union, which had one-hundred million more people than the United States. American taxpayers spent about $24 billion to incarcerate these nonviolent offenders in 1998, that is 50 percent more than what was spent for social welfare expenditures for eight and a half million poor Americans (Lenza and Jones, 2010, p. 323; also see Irwin *et al.*, 1999).

Next time a politician proclaims we should vote for him or her because they are 'tough on crime', ask them how sending a nonviolent offender to prison for five to seven years at $30,000 a year is a reasonable public investment? How will this impact his or her children? How is taking a hundred to two hundred thousand dollars or more out of our public coffers for each nonviolent offender we imprison providing a positive benefit to our communities?

You do not need to think very long, hard or deep to recognize this is bad policy that only benefits the prison industrial complex, not you or I.

REFERENCES

Alexander, M. (2010) *The New Jim Crow*, New York: New Press.

Austin, J. (2003) "The Use of Science to Justify the Imprison Binge", in J. I. Ross and S. C. Richards (eds.), *Convict Criminology*, Belmont (CA): Wadsworth, pp. 17-34.

Austin, J., T. Clear, T. Duster, D. Greenberg, J. Irwin, M. Jacobson, C. McCoy, A. Mobley, B. Owen and J. Page (2007) *Unlocking America: A Blueprint for Sentencing Reform*, Washington (D.C.): JFA Institute – Spring.

Bernstein, N. (2007) *All Alone in the World*, New York: New Press.

Braun, M. (2011) *Falling Stars*, Unpublished Doctoral Dissertation, Irvine (CA): University of California – Irvine.

Clear, T. (2007) *Imprisoning Communities*, Oxford (UK): Oxford University Press.

Ellis, C. and A. P. Bochner (2000) "Autoethnography, Personal Narrative, Reflexivity: Researcher as Subject", in N. Denzin and Y. Lincoln (eds.), *The Handbook of Qualitative Research* (second edition), Thousand Oaks (CA): Sage.

Irwin, J. (2009) *Lifers: Seeking Redemption in Prison*, New York: Routledge.

Irwin, J. (2005) *The Warehouse Prison*, Los Angeles: Roxbury.

Irwin, J. (1987) "Reflections on Ethnography", *Journal of Contemporary Ethnography*, 16: 41-48.

Irwin, J., V. Schiraldi and J. Ziedenberg (1999) America's One Million Nonviolent Prisoners, Washington (D.C.): Justice Policy Institute.

Jones, R. S. (2004) "Excon Managing a Spoiled Identity", in J. I. Ross and S. C. Richards (eds.), *Convict Criminology*, Belmont (CA): Wadsworth, pp. 191-208.

Jones, R. S., J. I. Ross, S. C. Richards and D. S. Murphy (2009) "The First Dime: A Decade of Convict Criminology", *Prison Journal*, 89(2): 151-171.

Lenza, M. (2011). "The Importance of Postmodern Autoethnography and Ethnography in Criminal Justice Research and Policy Development", in I. O. Ekunwe and R. S. Jones (eds.), *Global Perspectives on Re-entry*, Tampere (FI): University of Tampere Press, pp. 146-172.

Lenza, M. and R. S. Jones (2010) "Money, Criminology and Criminal Justice Policies: The Impacts of Political Policies, Criminality, and Money on the Criminal Justice in the United States", in M. Herzog-Evans (ed.), *Transnational Criminology Manual* (volume 1), Netherlands: Wolf Legal Publishers, pp. 313-332.

Leyva, M. and C. Bickel (2010) "From Corrections to College: The Value of a Convicts Voice", *Western Criminology Review*, 11(1): 50-60.

Mauer, M. (2006) *Race to Incarcerate*, New York: New Press.

Mauer, M. and M. Chesney-Lind (eds.) (2002) *Invisible Punishment*, New York: New Press.

Mobley, A. (2011) "Resuscitating Justice", in A. Leonard and K. Lawrence (eds.), *Rethinking Justice for the 21ˢᵗ Century*, New York: Aspen Institute Center for Community Change.

Mobley, A. (2008). "Falling Stars: Prisoner Reentry, Success Stories, and Recidivism – Implications for the Field", paper presented at the *Annual Meetings of the American Society of Criminology*, Atlanta (GA).

Mobley, A. (2005) "From Weeds to Seeds", *Journal of International and Applied Criminal Justice*, 38(1): 145-167.

Petersilia, J. (2003) *When Prisoners Come Home*, Oxford (UK): Oxford University Press.

Richards, S. C., D. Faggiani, J. Roffers, R. Hendricksen and J. A. Krueger (2008a) "Convict Criminology Courses at the University and in Prison", *Journal of Prisoners on Prisons*, 17(1): 43-60.

Richards, S. C., D. Faggiani, J. Roffers, R. Hendricksen and J. A. Krueger (2008b) "Convict Criminology: Voices from Prison", *Race/Ethnicity: Multidisciplinary Global Context*, 2(1): 121-136.

Richards, S. C. and J. I. Ross (2001) "The New School of Convict Criminology", *Social Justice*, 28: 177-190.

Richards, S. C., J. I. Ross, G. Newbold, M. Lenza, R. S. Jones, D. S. Murphy and R. S. Grigsby (2011) "Convict Criminology: Prisoner Re-entry Policy Recommendations",

in I. O. Ekunwe and R. S. Jones (eds.), *Global Perspectives on Re-entry*, Tampere (FI): University of Tampere Press, pp. 198-222.

Richards, S. C., M. Lenza, G. Newbold, R. S. Jones, D. Murphy and R. S. Grigsby (2010) "Prison as Seen by Convict Criminologists", in M. Herzog-Evans (ed.) *Transnational Criminology Manual* (volume 3), Nijmegen (Netherlands): Wolf Legal Publishers, pp. 343-360.

Rose, C. D., K. Reschenberg and S. C. Richards (2010) "Inviting Convicts to College", *Journal of Offender Rehabilitation*, 49(4): 293-308.

Ross, J. I. and S. C. Richard (2009) *Beyond Bars: Rejoining Society Prison*, New York: Alpha/Penguin Group.

Ross, J. I., and S. C. Richards (2003) *Convict Criminology*, Belmont (CA): Wadsworth.

Ross, J. I. and S. C. Richards (2002) *Behind Bars: Surviving Prison*, New York: Alpha/Penguin Group.

Western, B. (2006) *Punishment and Inequality in America*, New York: Russell Sage.

ABOUT THE AUTHORS

Richard Hendricksen is an ex-convict. Richard was one of the first prisoners to complete the Inviting Convicts to College Program taught by University of Wisconsin-Oshkosh students inside prison. He is now an undergraduate student studying Sociology and Criminal Justice at the University of Wisconsin-Oshkosh.

Alan Mobley is an ex-convict and Assistant Professor of Public Affairs at San Diego State University.

A Convict Criminology Perspective on Sex Offender Laws: America's "War against Sex Offenders"
Brian E. Oliver

INTRODUCTION

Over the past twenty years there has been a shift in the 'tough on crime' movement within the United States. While the 'war on drugs' began in the 1970s, in the 1990s America found a new 'enemy' to fight – the sex offender. In 2006, former President George W. Bush signed the *Adam Walsh Act* into law, escalating the war waged against sex offenders.

My name is Brian Oliver and I have just completed a PhD in Criminology and Criminal Justice at the University of Missouri – St. Louis. I am also a convicted sex offender, having served six years and three months in prison in the 1990s for non-violent sex offenses committed against minors while I was an adolescent and young adult. I have experienced firsthand the effects of America's punitive war towards those who have committed sexual crimes. This war has branded virtually every sex offender as a potential monster – a sociopath capable of kidnapping, raping, and murdering innocent women and children.

America's war against sex offenders shows little compassion for those people who have been convicted of a sex offense. As a result, many sex offenders experience a shortage of housing options, as well as additional isolation from employment opportunities, social support, social services and mental health treatment (Levenson, 2005). The number of sex offenders who find themselves homeless has increased dramatically in some places as a result of this war (Loving *et al.*, 2008). This war has not only affected those with sex offense convictions, but also has had destructive consequences for non-offending family members (Levenson and Tewksbury, 2009; Tewksbury and Levenson, 2009). In spite of these negative consequences, the war is raging and has only intensified in recent years.

This article will discuss the effects of this war. The first section will begin with a discussion of why America's war against sex offenders is misguided. The second section will show how 'tough' sex offender laws are harsher than other 'tough on crime' laws. The third section will review research findings relating to the effect of these laws and will discuss why the research indicates that these measures do not make American society safer. The fourth section will detail specific reasons why America's war against sex offenders actually does more harm than good. In the fifth section, specific attention will be given to the sex offender registry and how its very existence is punitive in nature. The sixth section will give a Convict Criminology (CC) Perspective, whereby it will be argued that America's war against sex offenders needs to end and that sex offenders need to stop being treated more harshly than other forms of criminal offenders. The seventh, and concluding section will argue that, instead of having laws in place which restrict where sex offenders can live, work, and travel, and require them to register with police for the remainder of their lives, the day sex offenders complete their full sentence is the day their punishment should end.

WHY AMERICA'S WAR AGAINST SEX OFFENDERS IS MISGUIDED

What is so tragic about America's war against sex offenders is that it runs counter to the findings of numerous, well-designed research studies that indicate that convicted sex offenders are not more dangerous than other classes of persons convicted of crime (Richards and Ross, 2003). For instance, two large, multi-state studies conducted by the Bureau of Justice Statistics found that convicted sex offenders who served time in prison had lower re-arrest rates than almost any other type of offender (Beck and Shipley, 1989; Langan and Levin, 2002). Several studies have found that most convicted sex offenders do not go on to commit new sex crimes (Bureau of Justice Statistics, 2003; Hanson and Morton-Bourgon, 2004, 2005; Harris and Hanson, 2004). In another study, Sandler *et al.* (2008) looked at people arrested for sex offenses in New York between 1986 and 2006 and found only 4.1 percent of arrested rapists and 5.9 percent of arrested child molesters involved repeat sex offenders. A study by Sample (2006) found that sex offenders were less likely to subsequently be arrested on a homicide charge than most other types of offenders.

Despite these fairly consistent findings, which show that convicted sex offenders are not more dangerous than other types of offenders, heavy media coverage following horrific, yet very rare, rapes and murders of women and children by previously convicted sex offenders have left the public with the perception that these individuals are very dangerous and have extremely high sexual recidivism rates (Levenson *et al.*, 2007; Katz-Schiavone *et al.*, 2008). These cases, along with intense lobbying for 'tougher' sex offender laws by certain groups whose members include sexual abuse survivors and parents of children who have been murdered in horrific manners, have left both state and federal legislators quite willing to pass a series of increasingly punitive laws limiting the rights of those convicted of sex offenses.

Researchers within the CC movement have made statements that the American criminal justice system provides many obstacles for ex-offenders to succeed once they are released from prison (see Richards and Jones, 1997, 2004; Richards, 2009; Ross *et al.*, 2010; Murphy *et al.*, 2010; Richards *et al.*, 2011) and about the harm caused to individuals who go through the criminal justice system (see Richards and Ross, 2001). However, there has not been much specific discussion about the extra barriers faced by offenders and by academics, like myself, who have been convicted of sexual offenses to date. Moreover, while the works of CC movement authors (Richards and Jones, 1997, 2004; Richards and Ross, 2001) and other scholars (Petersilia, 2003; Travis, 2005) clearly document the damage caused by collateral consequences convicted felons face, what they fail to note, and what this paper will address, is how these punitive laws affect convicted sex offenders more broadly and severely than any other category of convicted persons. Whereas other classes of felony offenders encounter many problems when they attempt to reenter the community, the extra consequences faced by sex offenders make their lives even after their sentences are over similar in many aspects to those who are still on parole. In essence, if you are a convicted sex offender in America, you will end up serving a sentence, complete with multiple restrictions and reporting requirements, for the rest of your life.

HOW SEX OFFENDER LAWS ARE HARSHER THAN OTHER 'TOUGH ON CRIME' LAWS

America's 'tough on crime' movement has limited the prospects of those with felony records in many ways, including limiting access former prisoners have to employment opportunities, public assistance, education loans, driving privileges, public housing, food stamps and the like (Petersilia, 2003; Travis, 2005). I would argue, however, that the laws are a lot harder and limit the rights of sex offenders much more than any other class of criminal in America. In many ways, sex offenders are viewed by the public and by the politicians they represent as being incurably lost, evil and completely depraved. Thus, while there may have been resistance if an attempt had been made to enact such laws for other classes of offenders, many of the sex offender laws currently in place were enacted with virtually no resistance because sex offenders are not viewed as deserving full human rights (Spencer, 2009).

For evidence in support of this proposition, I need to go no further than examining some of the laws currently in effect in states across America. A close look at these laws will show that lawmakers have deliberately and intentionally decided to limit the rights of sex offenders in a variety of fashions that do not affect other types of offenders (Mustaine and Tewksbury, 2011). While many will claim that these laws were put in place in a desire to make the United States a safer place, a closer look at the laws will show that what they actually do is continue to punish sex offenders long after their sentences are over.

Before discussing these restrictions, in light of my earlier statement that sex offenders in America are in essence on a form of lifetime parole, it is noteworthy to point out that many of these laws have also been common conditions of probation or parole for sex offenders for decades. Having conditions while on probation or parole is commonplace in America. What is different about the conditions as they pertain to sex offenders, however, is that laws make many of these conditions exist for the rest of a sex offender's life. These types of laws really do not exist for any other type of offender. While other felons still suffer some limitations once they have completed their parole (e.g. voting, firearms and occupational / professional prohibitions), they no longer have to report to parole authorities or register with law enforcement. This, however, does not hold true for male or female sex offenders.

A brief review of statutes from Missouri and Iowa exemplify some of these laws. Laws in Missouri have been passed in recent years making it illegal for sex offenders to live within 1,000 feet of a school, from being present or loitering within 500 feet of an elementary, middle or high school or licensed day care center (unless sex offender is the parent of a student there), from being present or loitering within 500 feet of a public park or swimming pool, and from participating in activities or being allowed outside their house on Halloween evening. Laws in Iowa include some of these same prohibitions, but also prohibit a sex offender from going to a public library, unless he or she has the written permission of the library administrator, and further prohibits sex offenders from being present on public beaches if a person under eighteen is present at the beach. It is again important to point out many of these laws apply to all registered sex offenders, not just those on probation or parole. While state legislators may argue that these laws are necessary to protect society, studies have not found evidence to support this proposition.

WHAT RESEARCH HAS FOUND: WHY THESE LAWS DO NOT MAKE SOCIETY SAFER

As far as residency restrictions go, for example, studies have not found evidence that limiting where sex offenders can live in proximity to schools enhances public safety. The Minnesota Department of Corrections (2003) examined the cases of 239 high-risk sex offenders living in the state to determine if where they lived in proximity to a school or park was related to the chances that they would commit a new sexual offense. This study reported, "there is no evidence in Minnesota that residential proximity to schools or parks affects reoffense. Thirteen level three offenders released between 1997 and 1999 have been rearrested for a new sex offense since their release from prison, and in none of the cases has residential proximity to schools or parks been a factor in their reoffense" (MDOC, 2003, p. 11). A second study conducted by the Colorado Department of Public Safety (2004) compared the cases of sex offenders who reoffended versus those who did not. This study found that "placing restrictions on the location of correctionally supervised sex offender residences may not deter the sex offender from re-offending and should not be considered as a method to control sexual offending recidivism" (CDPS, 2004, p. 4). A more recent study by Zandbergen *et al.* (2010) used a matched sample of 165 sexual recidivists and 165 non-recidivists from Florida for the period 2004 to 2006 to investigate if there was a relationship between where a sex offender resided and whether he reoffended. Like the two prior studies, "[t]he results of this study indicate no empirical association between where a sex offender lives and whether he reoffends sexually against a minor [...] Sex offenders who lived in closer proximity to schools and daycares were not more likely to reoffend than those who lived farther away" (p. 498).

Additionally, although there have not been many studies regarding laws that place limits on the activities convicted sex offenders are allowed to participate in, a study by Chaffin *et al.* (2009) nevertheless cast doubt on the benefit of restricting convicted sex offenders from engaging in Halloween activities. What the study found was that such laws had little impact on offending rates because sex offenders were not more likely to reoffend on Halloween than on other dates.

ADDITIONAL REASONS WHY HARSHER SEX OFFENDER LAWS DO MORE HARM THAN GOOD

Beyond the fact that many of these laws have not been found to increase public safety, there are additional factors that legislators fail to take into consideration in passing these laws. The first is that, although many of these laws were passed with the intent of protecting children, what state lawmakers fail to consider is that many convicted sex offenders later become law abiding parents with very legitimate reasons for engaging in some of these prohibited activities. Regarding the Halloween restriction, there are many convicted sex offenders who are no longer under supervision but who have children and who want the ability to supervise their children while trick or treating on Halloween.

Another legitimate use concerns parks. While sex offenders who have young children would certainly have a legitimate reason to want to appropriately supervise their children's activities at parks when the children are young, especially if they are single parents, another thing that lawmakers have neglected to take into consideration in passing these park restriction laws is that these milieus are also places where exclusively adult activities take place. I used to walk regularly on the walking trail at a park near where I lived. That was a legitimate use and had nothing to do with children. Additionally, from the time I was in my early thirties up until I turned forty, I was actively and regularly involved in church related volleyball. These events were healthy, safe ways for me to get exercise by being involved in sports activities with other adults. A few years back, after the park restriction laws went into effect, I started playing volleyball with a church group that would every once in a while schedule an outdoor volleyball event held at a public park. Even though this event was a legitimate adult activity, I was not permitted to go because of the law making my presence in a park a criminal offense.

While lawmakers may truly desire to make society safer by prohibiting the activities those formerly convicted of sex offenses engage in, the legal restrictions they have passed have been based on emotion and not scientific fact. What lawmakers fail to consider is that the vast majority of sex offenders are not high-risk offenders. Many are low risk offenders who do not pose a threat to reoffend. As a result, for many convicted sex offenders, these laws end up being little more than continued punishments after their court-imposed sentences are completed.

HOW THE SEX OFFENDER REGISTRY SERVES AS FURTHER PUNISHMENT

As bad as many of these harsher sex offender laws may be, perhaps the most destructive law passed in America related to this group are sex offender registries. Under these types of law, sex offenders are required to register on a regular basis with the police in the areas where they live, work or go to school. Although specific laws vary from state to state, the law in effect in Missouri in 2011, required sex offenders to register in person with the police between two and four times a year depending on the offense. While the law allowed a few exceptions, for many sex offenders, this was a lifetime requirement. In addition to registering, the Missouri Highway Patrol maintained an Internet based sex offender registry, which allowed anyone access to the following:

(1) The name and any known aliases of the offender; (2) The date of birth and any known alias dates of birth of the offender; (3) A physical description of the offender; (4) The residence, temporary, work, and school addresses of the offender, including the street address, city, county, state, and zip code; (5) Any photographs of the offender; (6) A physical description of the offender's vehicles, including the year, make, model, color, and license plate number; (7) The nature and dates of all offenses qualifying the offender to register; [and] (8) The date on which the offender was released from the department of mental health, prison, or jail, or placed on parole, supervised release, or probation for the offenses qualifying the offender to register" (Missouri Statute 589.402, subsection 3, 2011).

One problem with sex offender registration is that, similar to the findings of studies that looked at other forms of sex offender specific legislation, there is currently little empirical evidence that such measures have had a significant impact on offender sexual recidivism rates (Fitch, 2006). Schram and Milloy (1995) compared one group of 125 adult sex offenders released in Washington following the implementation of the community notification law against a second group of 90 adult sex offenders released in Washington prior to the implementation of this law. They found that at the end of fifty-four months at risk, the notification group had a slightly lower, yet statistically insignificant, estimated rate of sexual recidivism (19 percent) than the comparison group (22 percent). Adkins *et al.* (2000) further compared a group of 201 convicted sex offenders in Iowa released from supervision before the registration requirement with 233 convicted sex offenders released immediately following the implementation of this measure. Results showed that registered sex offenders had only slightly lower, yet not statistically significant, rates of recidivism for sexual offenses (3.0 percent versus 3.5 percent).

A second problem with the registry is that research has shown that sex offender registration can lead to counterproductive collateral consequences. Research conducted with 183 registered sex offenders in Florida (Levenson and Cotter, 2005), with 121 registered sex offenders in Kentucky (Tewksbury, 2005), and with 40 female registrants in Indiana and Kentucky (Tewksbury, 2004), indicates that such individuals may experience social stigmatization and incidents of harassment, along with difficulties securing housing and finding or maintaining employment as a result of sex offender registration.

I personally experienced negative collateral consequences as a result of being listed on the Missouri Sex Offender Registry on two separate occasions while in graduate school. The first occurred in May 2007, when the Director of Student Housing at the University of Missouri – St. Louis refused to renew my lease for an on-campus apartment after a student who lived in campus housing with his or her children complained about my presence there. This one student believed that my presence represented a danger to his or her children, even though I had done nothing inappropriate during the two and a half years I had lived in student housing.

The second problem occurred in February 2010, when the interim vice president at a private university where I had been hired as an adjunct lecturer terminated my employment after the parent of one of the adult students in the class I was teaching found out that I was registered sex offender and demanded that I not be allowed to continue to teach. My understanding from talking to various sources is that shortly after I began teaching, one of the students in the class found my name through a sex offender registry search and told other students. The word started to spread and eventually some of the students told their parents. Although I had told the department chair that I was a convicted felon when interviewed for the position, this fact did not allow me to keep my job. Instead, the threat of having the parent withdraw both his children from the university and take the story to the press was more than the university was willing to risk.

Once again, individuals meant well, but acted out of emotion and not scientific fact. What the information from the previously mentioned studies, along with the two personal experiences I discuss above where I lost both housing and employment as a result of being listed on the sex offender registry, show is that sex offender registries, in reality, do very little to make society a safer place. They do, however, make successfully reintegrating back into society a lot harder for those men and women who have been convicted of a sex offense.

A CONVICT CRIMINOLOGY PERSPECTIVE
ON SEX OFFENDERS

December 11, 2000, was supposed to be a day of joy and celebration for me. After spending six years and three months in prison, three months in a halfway house and seventeen months on parole, this was the date I successfully discharged my parole. I had completed my sentence. The days of having to regularly check in with my parole officer and being limited in where I could live, work, and hang out were supposed to be over. Or that is what I thought was going to happen that evening as I tore up my parole papers and threw them in the trash dumpster of the apartment complex where I lived.

It turns out that I was wrong. Fast forward to 2011. Although I have not been arrested for any felony or misdemeanor offense since my official discharge from parole, law enforcement still has me living with conditions quite similar to those I was required to live under while on parole. Even though I no longer have to check in with a parole officer every month, the law nevertheless currently requires me to register with the police every three months. From August 28, 2006 – the date the law went into effect – up until February 19, 2008, when the Missouri Supreme Court ruled that state residency restrictions could not apply to offenders convicted before the enactment date of the law, I was limited in where I could live. By being prohibited from living within 1,000 feet of an elementary, middle or high school, or day care center in Missouri, I was unable to temporarily move in with family after I was told I had to move out of student housing. This resulted in a frantic search for an alternative place to live. While the residency restriction law no longer affects my residency options in Missouri, I am nevertheless limited in where I can live in a large number of states. To this day, I would further be risking arrest if I travelled to a public park or swimming pool in Missouri, even if I had a legitimate reason for being there.

Such laws should be unconstitutional. When I pled guilty in the 1990s, I was given sentences that were supposed to have definite end dates. I pled guilty understanding that I would be punished for several years. However, I was not given a sentence that required me to register with the police and further placed restrictions on my activities for the remainder of my life. I was not given a life sentence and, as such, it is wrong to effectively give me one after the fact. This is wrong because this is not what I was sentenced to in the 1990s. The fact that I am a convicted sex offender should not matter because none of these laws were in effect when I committed my crimes. Adding additional conditions to my sentence after the fact is, in my opinion, a violation of the *ex post facto* clause of the Constitution and should not be allowed.

CONCLUSION

A common CC Perspective on sex offenders is that they should be treated the same as people convicted of non-sexual crimes. They should be given reasonable sentences of community treatment, probation, jail or prison. When the court ordered sentence has been completed it should be over. They should be permitted back into society and provided a fair opportunity to resume their lives in peace. As Dr. Stephen Richards, an ex-convict who served federal prison time on a drug conviction and now a professor of criminal justice, wrote me in an e-mail:

> I think all criminal records should be protected by privacy laws, like medical records, as is the case in many European countries. I do not think any person that has completed their sentence of incarceration and parole should have to register or report to police or anybody else, once their sentence is completed. Sex Offender Laws that require registration with

the police remind me of what the Nazi required of Jews in the 1930-40's. As a German Jew, I find the way we treat sex offenders in the USA to be a crime, a violation of human rights, and a frightening step towards fascism.

REFERENCES

Adkins, G., D. Huff and P. Stageberg (2000) *The Iowa Sex Offender Registry and Recidivism*, Des Moines (IA): Iowa Department of Human Rights.

Beck, A. J. and B. E. Shipley (1989) *Recidivism of Prisoners Released in 1983*, Washington (D.C.): Bureau of Justice Statistics.

Bureau of Justice Statistics (2003) *Recidivism of Sex Offenders Released from Prison in 1994*, Washington (D.C.): U.S. Department of Justice.

Chaffin, M., J. S. Levenson, E. J. Letourneau and P. Stern (2009) "How Safe Are Trick-or-treaters? An Analysis of Child Sex Crime Rates on Halloween", *Sexual Abuse: A Journal of Research and Treatment*, 21: 363-374.

Colorado Department of Public Safety (2004) *Report on Safety Issues Raised by Living Arrangements for and Location of Sex Offenders in the Community*, Denver (CO): Sex Offender Management Board.

Fitch, K. (2006) *Megan's Law: Does It Protect Children?*, London: NSPCC.

Hanson, R. K. and K. Morton-Bourgon (2005) "The Characteristics of Persistent Sexual Offenders: A Meta-analysis of Recidivism Studies", *Journal of Consulting and Clinical Psychology*, 73: 1154-1163.

Hanson, R. K. and K. Morton-Bourgon (2004) *Predictors of Sexual Recidivism: An Updated Meta-Analysis*, Ottawa: Public Works and Government Services.

Harris, A. J. R. and R. K. Hanson (2004) *Sex Offender Recidivism: A Simple Question*, Ottawa: Solicitor General of Canada.

Katz-Schiavone, S., J. S. Levenson and A. R. Ackerman (2008) "Myths and Facts About Sexual Violence: Public Perceptions and Implication for Prevention", *Journal of Criminal Justice and Popular Culture*, 15: 291-311.

Langan, P. A. and D. J. Levin (2002) *Recidivism of Prisoners Released in 1994*, Washington (D.C.): Bureau of Justice Statistics.

Levenson, J. S. (2005) "Sex Offender Residence Restrictions", *Sex Offender Law Report*, Kingston (NJ): Civil Research Institute.

Levenson, J. S., Y. Brannon, T. Fortney and J. Baker (2007) "Public Perceptions About Sex Offenders and Community Protection Policies", *Analyses of Social Issues and Public Policy*, 7: 1-25.

Levenson, J. S. and L. P. Cotter (2005) "The Impact of Sex Offender Residence Restrictions: 1,000 Feet From Danger or One Step From Absurd?", *International Journal of Offender Therapy and Comparative Criminology*, 49: 168-178.

Levenson, J. and R. Tewksbury (2009) "Collateral Damage: Family Members of Registered Sex Offenders", *American Journal of Criminal Justice*, 34: 54-68.

Loving, R., J. K. Singer and M. Maguire (2008) *Homelessness among Registered Sex Offenders in California: The Numbers, the Risks and the Response*, Sacramento (CA): California Sex Offender Management Board.

Minnesota Department of Corrections (2003) *Level Three Sex Offenders Residential Placement Issues*, St. Paul (MN).

Murphy, D. S., B. Fuleihan, S. C. Richards and R. S. Jones (2010) "The Electronic "Scarlet Letter": Criminal Backgrounding and a Perpetual Spoiled Identity", *Journal of Offender Rehabilitation*, 50: 101-118.

Mustaine, E. E. and R. Tewksbury (2011) "Residential Relegation of Registered Sex Offenders", *American Journal of Criminal Justice*, 36: 44-57.

Petersilia, J. (2003) *When Prisoners Come Home: Parole and Prisoner Reentry*, Oxford (UK): Oxford University Press.

Richards, S. C. (2009). "A Convict Perspective on Community Punishment: Further Lessons From the Darkness of Prison", in J. I. Ross (ed.), *Cutting the Edge: Current Perspectives in Radical/Critical Criminology and Criminal Justice* (second edition). Edison, NJ: Transaction, pp. 122-144.

Richards, S. C. and R. S. Jones (2004) "Beating the Perpetual Incarceration Machine", in S. Maruna and R. Immarigeon (Eds.), *After Crime and Punishment: Pathways to Offender Reintegration*, London: Willan Publishers, pp. 201-232.

Richards, S. C. and R. S. Jones (1997) "Perpetual Incarceration Machine: Impediments to Postprison Success", *Journal of Contemporary Criminal Justice*, 13: 4-19.

Richards, S. C. and J. I. Ross (2003) "Convict Perspective on the Classification of Prisoners", *Criminology & Public Policy*, 2: 243-252.

Richards, S. C. and J. I. Ross (2001) "Introducing the New School of Convict Criminology", *Social Justice*, 28: 177-190.

Richards, S. C., J. I. Ross, G. Newbold, M. Lenza, R. S. Jones, D. S. Murphy and R. S. Grigsby (2011) "Convict Criminology: Prisoner Re-entry Policy Recommendations", in I. O. Ekunwe and R. S. Jones (eds.), *Global Perspectives on Re-entry*, Tampere (FI): University of Tampere Press, pp. 198-222.

Ross, J. I., S. C. Richards, G. Newbold, R. S. Jones, M. Lenza, D. S. Murphy, R. G. Hogan and G. D. Curry (2010) "Knocking on the Ivory Towers' Door: The Experience of Ex-convicts Applying for Tenure-track University Positions", *Journal of Criminal Justice Education*, 21: 1-19.

Sandler, J. C., N. J. Freeman and K. M. Socia (2008) "Does a Watched Pot Boil? A Time-series Analysis of New York State's Sex Offender Registration and Notification Law", *Psychology, Public Policy, and Law*, 14: 284-302.

Sample, L. L. (2006) "An Examination of the Degree To Which Sex Offenders Kill", *Criminal Justice Review*, 31: 230-250.

Schram, D. D. and C. D. Milloy (1995) *Community Notification: A Study of Offender Characteristics and Recidivism*, Olympia (WA): Washington State Institute for Public Policy.

Spencer, D. (2009) "Sex Offender as Homo Sacer", *Punishment & Society*, 11: 219-240.

Tewksbury, R. (2005) "Collateral Consequences of Sex Offender Registration", *Journal of Contemporary Criminal Justice*, 21: 67-81.

Tewksbury, R. (2004) "Experiences and Attitudes of Registered Female Sex Offenders", *Federal Probation*, 68: 30-33.

Tewksbury, R. and J. Levenson (2009) "Stress Experiences of Family Members of Registered Sex Offenders", *Behavioral Sciences and the Law*, 27: 611-626.

Travis, J. (2005) *But They All Come Back: Facing the Challenges of Prisoner Reentry,* Washington (D.C.): The Urban Institute.
Zandbergen, P. A., J. L. Levenson and T. C. Hart (2010) "Residential Proximity to Schools and Daycares: An Empirical Analysis of Sex Offense Recidivism", *Criminal Justice and Behavior*, 37: 482-502.

ABOUT THE AUTHOR

Brian E. Oliver, PhD, is an ex-convict and member of the Convict Criminology Group. He received his PhD in Criminology and Criminal Justice from the University of Missouri – St. Louis in 2011. While in graduate school his course of study focused on several topics including intervention programming with at-risk individuals, collateral consequences faced by those with felony records, and the areas of recidivism and reentry. His work appears in *Child Abuse & Neglect, Trauma, Violence & Abuse, Justice Research & Policy* and *Dialectical Anthropology*. His current research explores whether variations in cumulative individual level characteristics associated with recidivism can be used to explain differences in recidivism rates across American states.

Interrelated Problems of Silencing Voices and Sexual Crime: Convict Criminology Insights for Reducing Victimization
D J Williams and James Burnett

INTRODUCTION

In western society few topics are as difficult to discuss and emotionally charged as human sexuality. Many people have significant personal issues with sexual identity, performance, and confusion about what is appropriate and legal. Given these widespread and diverse sexuality issues, it is not surprising that there are also substantial problems regarding common public understanding and interpretation of sexual violence and crime. This poses subsequent challenges concerning policy development. Indeed, over the past decade there has been a widespread focus on sexual crimes. Incidents of extreme sexual violence receive considerable media attention. Members of the public are disturbed and become fearful, and politicians feel the need to intervene. New restrictive laws and policies have been created with worthy intentions of protecting citizenry.

We believe that despite the best intentions, there are major interconnected problems that significantly impair progress in reducing actual sexual violence. The purpose of this paper is to identify and briefly discuss these problems. A common thread that tightly weaves these problems together is the silencing of voices, thus we advocate for theoretical and practical approaches that welcome and legitimately consider all perspectives. Therefore, in this paper we outline four specific issues related to sexual violence and suggest how Convict Criminology (CC) may help in addressing each of these challenges.

A central feature of CC is legitimizing and empowering voices, including the voices of prisoners. CC is a critical approach that promotes social justice and advocates for prisoners and their families (Richards and Ross, 2001; Ross and Richards, 2003; Jones *et al.*, 2009). A CC Perspective suggests that people should not be labeled by their mistakes or past events, as if nothing else matters. CC mentors and supports all ex-convict graduate students and professors that request assistance. Through collaboration, a new perspective on criminology, criminal justice and corrections may be developed (see Richards and Ross, 2001; Ross and Richards, 2003). Thus, we believe that CC may be valuable in addressing the major problems that impair progress in effectively addressing sexual violence. Before we proceed further let us be clear that we are fully against sexual violence and our concern is how communities can better *effectively* reduce this form of violence.

NORMALIZING SEXUALITY DISCOURSES AND SILENCING VOICES

Critical perspectives in the social sciences recognize that common knowledge about sexuality is constructed through social discourses that normalize. Historically, western religion has been instrumental and authoritative in determining which sexual practices are acceptable and which are not. During the 20th Century, scientific and medical discourses, built from positivist assumptions about knowledge, gained more influence and power governing sexuality and sexual practices (Foucault, 1978). Suffice it to say that sexual behaviors and practices are assigned meaning, and regulated by powerful social institutions and processes. Voices that are consistent with existing sexual scripts (see Simon and Gagnon, 2003), largely constructed historically from religion and science, are empowered, while opposing voices are silenced. At the same time, sexuality has been constructed with severe negative connotations.

According to many, sexuality and sexual practices should not be openly discussed. Compared to other topics, sex has been constructed as being substantially dangerous, adversarial and problematic. This is a major problem and it fuels the subsequent problems we identify here. If people in society cannot openly and safely discuss sexuality and sexual practices – similar to discussion of other topics – then how can various sexual issues and problems in that society be effectively resolved?

Despite scripts that allow a relatively narrow range of acceptable sexual behaviors, social scientists recognize that sexual interests and practices are extremely diverse across people and cultures (Popovic, 2006). CC can be helpful by being supportive of the recognition of sexual diversity, and by joining with other critical perspectives when such opportunities occur to legitimize and empower all voices specifically with respect to sexuality.

More effective solutions are always more likely to be realized when more, rather than fewer, voices and perspectives are recognized and considered. In contrast to popular accounts that normalize, critical accounts recognize that problematic sexuality, including violence, is less about labels that are assigned to specific sexual practices, and more about complex ethical issues related to mutual consent and safety.

ENTRENCHED MYTHS OF SEXUAL
OFFENDERS AND TREATMENT

When authoritative institutions and discourses restrict alternative voices and perspectives, it is easy for myths and stereotypes to be constructed and reified. Perhaps nowhere has this occurred more substantively than with issues involving sex offenders. Quinn *et al*. (2004) thoroughly documented the development and promotion of pervasive myths concerning sexual offenders and their treatment (e.g. sex offenders are the same, nearly all will re-offend, sex offender treatment is ineffective). Unfortunately, many law enforcement personnel and correctional therapists believe these myths, which are promoted through media and serve powerful political interests.

In contrast to popular myths that portray offenders as 'predators' that are unresponsive to treatment, the vast scholarly literature on this topic convincingly shows that sex offenders are a heterogeneous group with diverse motivations, needs and issues (ibid). It has been known for many years that most sex offenders are not strangers to their victims, but tend to be members of families and communities.

Large meta-analyses challenge myths about high sex offender recidivism rates. For example, Alexander (1999) found that across 79 studies (representing nearly 11,000 sex offenders), the re-arrest rate for sex offenders was 7.2 percent, compared to a 17.6 percent for untreated offenders. The federal Center for Sex Offender Management (CSOM, 2001) reported that sex offender recidivism rates are lower than those of other classifications of offenders. After reviewing scholarly literature on treatment efficacy, Marshall *et al*. (2006, p. 176) stated that "the evidence indicates that sex offenders can be effectively treated".

The existing scholarly literature is extremely valuable in countering pervasive myths about sexual offenders and the efficacy of psychotherapy. Scientific knowledge on this topic is important and, unfortunately, is often silenced due to political interests. Critical perspectives that help humanize all people in the justice system are further silenced and devalued. It can be easy, even among academics and professionals, to reduce sexual offenders, like other prisoners, from complex human beings to collections of risk factors, psychological test scores and various statistics. CC encourages collaboration among various community groups, along with the telling and listening of the stories of the criminalized. Stories provide emotional impact and remind us that offenders are human beings capable of changing behavior. Offender storytelling can be healing and is underutilized, both as a research and treatment method within rehabilitation (see Williams, 2006, 2009).

CURRENT POLICY IS MOVING FASTER IN THE WRONG DIRECTION

It is foolish to formulate social policies with the intention of protecting citizens, while failing to consider diverse needs and perspectives, including within academic institutions, in the process. However, this seems to be the case with respect to the quick development of more restrictive and punitive policies that regulate sex offenders. Griffin and Stitt (2010) discussed significant problems of recent legislation based on "memorial crime control", wherein strict, punitive policies are enacted based on a single or very few horrific cases (e.g. *Megan's Law, Jessica's Law*). These cases are truly tragic, yet it is inappropriate and unethical to over-generalize based on pervasive sex offender myths and extreme cases, and create legislation influencing thousands of offenders. This reflects gross injustice and will not protect citizens.

Recent research has shown that sex offender policies that restrict residency from close proximity to parks and schools have no effect in reducing recidivism (e.g. Duwe *et al.*, 2008; Maguire and Singer, 2010). Despite being ineffective in reducing sexual crimes, such restrictive policies are significant in terms of financial cost to communities. Sex offenders experience negative treatment because of their status, which then restrict successful reintegration into community (Robbers, 2009).

Furthermore, a recent study found that sex offender registration and notification laws may have a harmful effect on family members of sexual offenders (Levenson and Tewksbury, 2009). Levenson and Tewksbury discovered that family members of sex offenders were significantly more likely to experience threats and harassment from neighbors. The majority of children of sex offenders in the study reported being treated differently at school, and had experienced ridicule, teasing, depression, anxiety, fear or anger. In these cases, more injustice seems to be heaped upon injustice.

Academic voices that utilize traditional research methods, including those we have cited, are valuable and important. The voices of citizens are also valuable and important. So, too, of course, are the voices of victims and their families. Additionally, the voices of sex offenders and their families, which have been devalued and silenced in community dialogue concerning important policy issues, are also both legitimate and important. What important insights might sex offenders and their families have based on their real-world experiences that could be helpful in developing effective policies? Once again, drawing on the CC Perspective we emphasize that successfully reducing sexual violence is more likely to occur by finding solutions created from listening to and considering all voices and methods of knowing.

THE PRISON SYSTEM AND
VIOLENCE BETWEEN PRISONERS

While the prison system has an official classification of prisoners (Richards and Ross, 2003), there is also a convict subculture. Similar to life on the outside, sexuality and gender issues are interwoven into the convict subculture. Transgendered and homosexual individuals, particularly in male prisons, may be targeted for violence from other prisoners. Fear, prejudice and discrimination that are widespread outside of prisons concerning sexuality permeate prison walls. Violence and injustice are often the result.

The prison is a system of institutionalized abuse and violence where sex offenders are relatively powerless. The convict subculture, like mainstream society, places sexual offenders at the bottom of the totem pole. Institutional abuse and discrimination toward sex offenders is rampant in the prison system. These prisoners are commonly regarded as less than human, aberrations and irredeemable subjects. Prisoners convicted of sex offenses are commonly targets for severe violence from prisoners and prison staff.

Persons convicted of sex offenses may serve long sentences both in prison and the community. As prisoners on probation and parole they are subjected to electronic monitoring, along with restrictions on where they might reside, work, walk and interact with socially. Historically, they have been subjects for surgical or chemical castration, and various forms of sovereign violence at the hands of medical and social work professionals (Spencer, 2009). According to Spencer (2009, p. 225), sex offenders are believed to be "so depraved that normal cognitive-behavioral programs are unable to curb these individuals' insatiable desire to commit sex crimes". While the commission of sexual crime is completely unacceptable and must be reasonably addressed, it appears that myths and moral panic may be widening the scope of what constitutes sexual offenses (see Popovic, 2007). More people are becoming unfairly labeled, incarcerated and their lives ruined.

We have emphasized herein that all people deserve to be listened to, and to be treated humanely and fairly. Sex offenders are often not treated humanely and fairly in prisons and the community. They are also not given adequate support and opportunities to improve their lives. CC can continue to promote fairness, support and positive collaboration, both inside and outside of correctional institutions. The need for people in various roles and social spaces, including prisoners, public citizens, policymakers, professionals and academics, to welcome and apply critical thinking and reflection to sexuality, generally, and sexual crime issues, specifically, cannot be overestimated.

CONCLUSION

In this paper, we have identified and briefly discussed major interrelated problems that we believe prevent widespread progress in reducing sexual violence. Sadly, good intentions seem to contribute to the development of these problems as new cases of injustice and violence continue to be perpetrated in the process. We hope that CC and other important critical perspectives can gain support, and can be applied to help resolve these issues. If so, it is likely that sexual violence can be addressed more fairly and effectively, and thus be reduced.

REFERENCES

Alexander, M. A. (1999) "Sexual Offender Treatment Efficacy Revisited", *Sexual Abuse: A Journal of Research and Treatment*, 11: 101-117.

Center for Sex Offender Management (2001) *Recidivism of Sex Offenders*, Silver Spring (MD).

Duwe, G., W. Donnay and R. Tewksbury (2008) "Does Residential Proximity Matter? A Geographic Analysis of Sex Offender Recidivism", *Criminal Justice and Behavior*, 35: 484-504,

Foucault, M. (1978) *History of Sexuality* (volume 1), New York: Random House.

Griffin, T. and B. G. Stitt (2010) "Random Activities Theory: The Case for "Black Swan" Criminology", *Critical Criminology*, 18: 57-72.

Jones, R. S., J. I. Ross, S. C. Richards and D. S. Murphy (2009) "The First Dime: A Decade of Convict Criminology", *Prison Journal*, 89(2): 151-171.

Levenson, J. and R. Tewksbury (2009) "Collateral Damage: Family Members of Registered Sex Offenders", *American Journal of Criminal Justice*, 34(5): 4-68.

Maguire, M. and J. K. Singer (2010) "A False Sense of Security: Moral Panic Driven Sex Offender Legislation", *Critical Criminology*, 19(4): 301-312.

Marshall, W. L., L. E. Marshall and G. A. Serran (2006) "Strategies in the Treatment of Paraphilias: A Critical Review", *Annual Review of Sex Research*, 27: 162-182.

Popovic, M. (2007) "Establishing New Breeds of (Sex) Offenders: Science or Political Control?", *Sexual and Relationship Therapy*, 22: 255-271.

Popovic, M. (2006) "Psychosocial Diversity as the Best Representation of Human Normality Across Cultures", *Sexual and Relationship Therapy*, 21: 171-186.

Quinn, J. F., C. J. Forsyth and C. Mullen-Quinn (2004) "Societal Reaction to Sex Offenders: A Review of the Origins and Results of the Myths Surrounding Their Crimes and Treatment Amenability", *Deviant Behavior*, 25: 215-232.

Robbers, M. L. (2009) "Lifers on the Outside: Sex Offenders and Disintegrative Shaming", *International Journal of Offender Therapy and Comparative Criminology*, 53: 5-28.

Richards, S. C. and J. I. Ross (2003) "Convict Perspective on the Classification of Prisoners", *Criminology & Public Policy*, 2(2): 243-252.

Richards, S. C. and J. I. Ross (2001) "The New School of Convict Criminology", *Social Justice*, 28(1): 177-190.

Ross, J. I. and S. C. Richards (eds.) (2003) *Convict Criminology*. Belmont (CA): Wadsworth.

Simon, W. and J. H. Gagnon (2003) "Sexual Scripts: Origins, Influences and Changes", *Qualitative Sociology*, 26: 491-497.

Spencer, D. (2009) "Sex Offender as Homo Sacer", *Punishment & Society*, 11: 219-240.

Williams, D J (2009) "Turning Monsters Into People: A Reflexive Study of Sex Offenders and Leisure", *Journal of Unconventional Parks, Tourism and Recreation Research*, 2(1): 2-6.

Williams, D J (2006) "Autoethnography in Offender Rehabilitation Research and Practice: Addressing the "Us versus Them" Problem", *Contemporary Justice Review*, 9: 23-38.

ABOUT THE AUTHORS

D J Williams, PhD, is an Assistant Professor in the Department of Sociology, Social Work & Criminal Justice at Idaho State University. He is an interdisciplinary scholar and has several years' experience as a forensic psychotherapist.

James Burnett, PhD, is an ex-convict and Visiting Assistant Professor in the Department of Sociology, Social Work & Criminal Justice at Idaho State University. Dr. Burnett is a member of the Convict Criminology Group.

Detoured:
My Journey from Darkness to Light
Jesse De La Cruz

I am ignorant of how I was formed and how I was born. Through a quarter of my lifetime I was absolutely ignorant of the reasons for everything I saw, and heard, and felt, and was merely a parrot prompted by other parrots.

– Voltaire

FOLSOM STATE PRISON:
APRIL 2, 1996

I had been in prison for the past three years although it wouldn't be long before I was set free again. It was 7:55 a.m., but I'd been awake since 4:00 a.m., pacing in my cell, trying to make time move faster. Instead, it seemed to move in slow motion.

It was always like this whenever I was about to be released. The tension would mount each day as the date drew nearer. The nights would seem longer and it would get more difficult for me to sleep. My brain would suffer a persistent dull pain from all the questions that zipped through my mind, making my head hurt like the time Carlos Montes whacked me on my skull with a ball-pin hammer back in 1969.

Where would I live? How long would I stay out this time? Would I get a life sentence the next time I got busted? After all, the "Three Strikes You're Out Law" had taken effect in March of 1994 in California. I had read the language of the statute in the prison library when it had first been implemented, and it clearly stated that anyone with two prior felony convictions who was arrested and found guilty of any type of felony would be sentenced to life. The state was serious too. I had read a newspaper article about a guy from San Diego who had been sentenced to life for stealing nothing more than couple of slices of pizza. I had five prior felonies.

I really didn't think I could stay out either. The last time I had been cut loose I had been so nervous I had rushed to a liquor store and bought a half pint bottle of Smirnoff Vodka and a pint of orange juice as a chaser to calm my jitters. Even though I hated alcohol, I had guzzled the entire contents of the bottle trying to relieve my anxiety. When the Vodka hit my stomach, it had temporarily eased my fear, but it also tore down what little resistance I'd had about breaking the law. As soon as I reached my destination, I quickly located my Homeboy *Babo* and got a free shot of heroin from him. I started stealing after my $200 release money ran out a few days later.

I didn't want to drink alcohol, use heroin or steal anymore, but I didn't know how to live in the outside world. Sometimes I wanted to tell someone that I didn't know how I was going to survive on the streets without breaking the law. But there was no way I could tell any of my fellow prisoners I wanted to go straight or that I was terrified about being outside in the world without sounding weak. The very notion of being afraid of freedom seemed ridiculous – after all, getting out is what every prisoner dreams about.

Suddenly, I heard the echo of the Man's footsteps as he approached to cut me loose. "*Oralé Hueró*, it's time for me to get going", I said to my cellmate. "I hear you, Homie". "Come on, De La Cruz, we don't have all day", Officer Miller barked. Yeah, yeah, I thought, it was the same ole-game of hurry-up and wait.

Officer Miller stuck his big brass key into the lock and in one quick motion turned it to unlock the steel barred door. Everything was deathly quiet in the cellblock and I heard the door squeak as he swung it open. There was no one on the tier when I stepped out of my cell because the entire prison was on lock-down. An altercation between a northern California Mexican (*Norteño*) and a Southern California Mexican (*Sureño*) – violent prison rivals – a few days before had led prison administration to confine all prisoners to their cells 24 hours a day. Walking towards the stairway at the end of the tier, I briefly stopped in front of my road dog Prieto's cell. "Get laid and take a shot for me, Home-Squeeze", he said smiling brightly as he shook my hand through the bars. "*Simón, Ese*", I replied, as Miller and I continued on.

A guard sitting behind the desk situated inside the cage at the entrance of the cellblock hit a button hidden underneath the counter that unlocked the door leading to the main corridor. Officer Miller pulled the steel door open when he heard a loud buzzing sound, and we stepped onto the main hallway, wide and tall enough to drive three eighteen wheel trucks, side-by-side, through it. Normally, when walking down that corridor at any given time of the day, it was as packed as a crowded state fair at peak hour. You could barely hear the guy standing next to you speak because of the loud chatter created by many men talking and laughing at the same time. But now, Officer Miller and I were the lone two men and hearing the echo of our footsteps in that desolate, cavernous hallway made me feel like we were the last survivors in an abandoned underground nuclear bunker.

It wasn't until Miller unlocked the door to Receiving & Release (R&R) that I saw the other convicts who were being released as well. As soon as I walked into the room, I sensed the underlying nervous anticipation of everyone there. No one said anything, but it seemed as though we all knew we were about to embark on a difficult journey.

An R&R guard stood behind one of those doors that open the top half, turning the bottom closed door into a sort of counter. He handed me a large brown bag containing the street clothes Mama had sent me two weeks earlier. Mama hadn't forgotten the kind of clothes I liked either. She had sent me a stone gray long sleeve shirt, a pair of black dress slacks, a black belt, matching black socks, some boxer underwear, and a pair of gray-on-black Stacy Adams alligator skin shoes. Taking off my prison suit, I slipped on the clothes Mama had sent me and immediately felt that I was no longer a faceless member of the Orange Jumpsuit crowd.

Afterward, I sat down on the long wooden bench bolted to the wall. I tried to sit still as I waited for Officer Miller to call my name so I could sign my walking papers, but my nerves were on edge. I felt sweat run down my armpits underneath my shirt and my stomach hurt too. Unable to contain my apprehension, I strolled over to where the other prisoners were waiting to sign their release papers and when my turn finally came, I walked up to the counter where Officer Miller stood. I grabbed a pen and waited to sign my name on the forms he held in his hands. He was reading the paperwork slowly as if something was wrong. After a while Officer Miller looked up over the rim of his glasses, and slowly shook his head. "I don't think you're going anywhere this morning, De La Cruz", he scoffed.

For a brief moment, I stood there in disbelief. Then a wave of pain moved through my stomach, as if Officer Miller had stuck a knife in my gut and sliced from one side of my body to the other. I tried to keep my facial expression blank, attempting to hide that he had gotten to me, but in that instant, my world came crumbling down. What kind of game was this clown playing? First he tells me I'm going, and then he says I'm not. "What do you mean, I'm not going anywhere?" "Well, De La Cruz", Miller smirked, "These documents indicate you have an outstanding warrant".

I wanted to shout "No!" but my mouth felt dry. I glared at him, thinking that he had to be playing some kind of wicked mind game with me, but the cruel look in his eyes, and the contemptuous grin pasted on his face let me know he was dead serious and that he loved every second of goading me. Just as I was about to lose my cool and snatch him from behind the counter to beat the life out of him, he smiled at me and said, "Get laid and take a shot for me, Home-Squeeze".

Abruptly, I awoke, gasping for breath, in a cold sweat, disoriented and realized I'd been dreaming. I shook my head in an attempt to clear my thoughts and remembered that I was going to be released later that morning. And even though I should have been happy that I was finally getting out, I felt a knotted fist in the pit of my stomach.

Looking over at the lighted dial of the small clock sitting on the steel table in the corner of my cell, I saw it was only 4:00 a.m. I wouldn't be escorted to R&R until 8 a.m. Not wanting to wake my cellmate, I quietly slid off my bunk, took a leak, washed my face and brushed my teeth. I filled my tumbler with cold water and plugged the stinger (a device used to heat water) into the electrical socket in order to make myself a cup of instant Tasters Choice coffee.

Waiting for the water to boil, I recalled how at the beginning of my criminal career, and for many years after that, being cut loose from prison had always been like going on a vacation. As soon as I hit the streets, I would hook up with my old friends, start shooting heroin, which led to robbing drug dealers, boosting cigarettes from super markets, and breaking into homes to steal the TVs, stereos, jewelry or guns if there were any. And periodically, if I got angry or drunk enough, I would stab a man. Invariably, I would get caught and sent back to prison.

But things were different now. The last time I had been on the streets had been really tough. I hadn't been able to find a reliable crime partner because most of the guys who had been into crime with me were either dead, serving life sentences, or so sick from Hepatitis C that they couldn't rob or break into homes even if they wanted too. I had ended up homeless.

I remember feeling a sense of relief when I was arrested and ultimately returned to prison. It was as though I had come home. And why shouldn't I have felt relief? I had been shuttling in and out of prison for almost thirty years and confinement was now part of my nature. I had grown accustomed to the State of California telling me when and what to eat, when to move to the yard, when to shower, when to lock up, when to stand for count, when to get strip-searched and who to live with. In a perverse way, the prison walls had become part of my security.

On the other hand, whenever I was free, I could wake up in the middle of the night with a craving for donuts, walk down to the local 24-hour Safeway and get some. During the day I could pick and choose between a Chinese, Indian or Mexican restaurant to go for dinner. In the evening, I could go to a 16-Theater Cineplex and select any movie I wanted to watch. But along with all these choices came the responsibility of having and keeping a job, something I knew nothing about. As much as I hated to admit it, all those street freedoms had meant very little to me. After all, if staying out had been so important why did I always manage to return to the penitentiary? I clearly had become institutionalized.

But I had to stay out this time because it wasn't just about me anymore. Four years earlier I had fathered a baby girl and she needed me now. During this confinement, I had tried desperately not to reflect so much about my baby because thinking about her made me want to cry and there was no way I would cry in prison. But each day I had been haunted by the image of my little girl's face. She was the first thing I thought about when I woke up and the last thought that raced through my mind before I fell asleep.

As I sipped on my last cup of prison coffee, I thought about the morning she was born. I had been standing outside the door of the delivery room on the second floor of St. Joseph's Hospital in Stockton, California at 5:58 a.m. when I heard her cry out. A few minutes later I was invited in to see my daughter. I walked into a room and a nurse handed me my baby curled in a pink receiving blanket that was gently scented with baby powder. My baby's fragile pink fingers peeked out from the blanket and waved slowly in the air. Her full head of dark hair was covered with a white beanie, exposing only her rosy face as she slept. For a second, it appeared as though she instinctively smiled sweetly at me. I carefully brought her to my chest with tears streaming down my face. I remember asking myself how in the world I expected to be a father to my child if I was constantly in prison, but I felt powerless to change what seemed inevitable.

I had known lots of guys in the joint who had kids, and I had seen their children end up in prison, too. There was even a guy whose son had been his cellmate. I couldn't understand how he could live with himself knowing he had failed his son completely, but I never asked him how he dealt with it. What I did know was that I didn't want my child following in my footsteps. Holding her in my arms that day, I made a decision to straighten my life once and for all.

Unfortunately, my old patterns of behavior had been too difficult to change. Within months of her birth, I gave in to my habit of stealing and shooting heroin, and had wound up in prison again. So here I was, faced with having to go out to the streets and get straight, or risk being the father whose kid would only see him in prison visiting rooms, if I was lucky.

Lying back down on my bunk, in the dark quiet of my cell, I closed my eyes and tried not to think about all the changes I would have to make if I wanted to stay out. I tried not to think about the Three Strikes Law looming out there ready to snatch me up and take my freedom forever. I wished that I could snap my fingers and live a life similar to the ones I had seen in some of the afternoon soap operas. Damn, how had I gotten to a place where I was so terrified with something that so many people throughout the world strive for everyday – freedom?

LIFE TODAY:
OCTOBER 1, 2011

The journey to normalcy has been arduous, especially when I first started fifteen years ago. At that time, I didn't have a clue how I was going to navigate my way through the free world without breaking the law or using drugs. Furthermore, I didn't know how to socialize with so-called regular people. Everyone I had ever associated with was a criminal. Had it not been for education, and a few people who took an interest in me, I would of returned to prison and probably died inside.

Education opened my eyes to a completely different world and gave me an opportunity to enter professional life, something I would have never would have been able to do without a Master's Degree. There is no way I would have ever been considered to partake in half the things I participate in today without my educational degrees. I would have simply been an ex-con who talks and writes well. Today, I teach Criminal Justice and am working on obtaining my Ed.D, which I will complete in 2013.

In the Fall of 2010, I had the privilege of making contact with Dr. Stephen Richards – a Professor of Criminal Justice at the University of Wisconsin, Oshkosh. I was interested in meeting him after I learned he was a member of a unique group of men and women who call themselves "Convict Criminologists" (Richards and Ross, 2001; Ross and Richards, 2002, 2003, 2009). This group, I later learned are ex-cons with Ph.Ds who teach at universities. Dr. Richards and I have spoken on the phone numerous times and I always leave our phone conversations feeling rejuvenated. There is nothing more motivating than one ex-con talking to another about how to get from point A to point B. I had the pleasure of meeting Dr. Richards and a few other members of "Convict Criminology" in November of 2010 at an American Society of Criminology conference, and have since become a member. I am honored to be part of such an exceptional group of academics whose mission is to school the general public about the importance of rehabilitation, and the power of educating prisoners at our nation's colleges and universities. I have also had the opportunity to raise my child and instill in her the value of education: not by telling her, but by showing her as I journeyed through the educational system while obtaining an AA, BA, Masters, and now my Ed. D.

REFERENCES

Richards, S. C., and J. I. Ross (2001) "The New School of Convict Criminology", *Social Justice*, 28(1): 177-190.
Ross, J. I. and S. C. Richards (2009) *Beyond Bars: Rejoining Society After Prison*, New York: Alpha/Penguin Group.
Ross, J. I. and S. C. Richards (eds.) (2003) *Convict Criminology*, Belmont (CA): Wadsworth.
Ross, J. I. and S. C. Richards (2002) *Behind Bars: Surviving Prison*, New York: Alpha/Penguin Group.

ABOUT THE AUTHOR

Jesse De La Cruz is an ex-convict raised in the barrios of California. At the age of twelve he began a journey that would eventually lead him to heroin addiction, crime, gangs and prison. He served approximately thirty years going in and out of the California prison system. After his final release from Folsom State Prison in 1996, he enrolled in college, graduated with his Baccalaureate in Sociology in 2001, a Master's of Social Work Degree in 2003 and is now completing a Doctorate in Education. He is the founder of the Jonah Foundation, a sober living house for men transitioning from the inside to the outside world. He lives in Stockton, CA with his daughter and grandson.

PART III:

CONVICT CRIMINOLOGY
BEYOND BORDERS

Developing a Convict Criminology Group in the UK
Andreas Aresti *

INTRODUCTION

This article explores the idea of developing Convict Criminology (CC) in the UK as a means to educate policy makers and the general public about prisons and prisoners. Since its inception in the United States in 1997, CC has grown with increasing momentum (Richards and Ross, 2001; Ross and Richards, 2003; Jones *et al.*, 2009). Led by former prisoners, this theoretical perspective and social movement takes a critical approach to criminal justice issues, challenging the traditional understandings and representations of crime, the criminal justice process, prisoners and ex-convicts.

CC approaches existing policy, research and political commentary with a critical lens (Jones *et al.*, 2009, p.152). Additionally, and equally important, CC also has a generative element, whereby Convict Criminologists also act as mentors, guiding and supporting former prisoners who have recently entered into academia. Whilst CC is a refreshing alternative to the typically 'managerial' research generated in the United States (for a critique see Austin, 2003) two significant questions that beg consideration are first, whether there is a need to develop CC in the UK. More specifically, is there a need for a UK based CC movement with its own physical presence and identity? And second, even if there is a demand for such a movement in the UK, how viable is it to develop CC here? Specifically, are the resources present and what structural constraints are likely to impede its development? This paper seeks to address these questions.

AN INSIDER PERSPECTIVE:
THE AUTHOR'S BACKGROUND

It seems a little strange to me that I am advocating CC as you know little about my background. Arguably, the two are inseparable so here is some context. In 1998, I walked out of the prison gates, straight into a university unaware of what lay ahead and what course my life was to take. One thing is for sure – I was out of my comfort zone and as I walked through the university gates I thought "*what the f--k am I doing here*". At this point, my old life appeared quite attractive despite my general discontent for it, and my strong urge to change and lead a more fulfilling life.

Whilst I would not say crime was my profession as such, as a tradesman working as a roofer since leaving school at age fifteen, I was always involved in some form of 'illegal activity' with my mates. Typically, these activities were usually motivated by the desire for financial gain, but of course, were also inextricably linked with other complex factors, such as status, identity and masculinity – a relationship that has been well documented by a variety of criminologists (Irwin, 1970; Messerschmidt, 1993; Katz, 1988; Collinson, 1996). Therefore, violence and aggression were also part of my life, manifesting themselves in a variety of ways. Having had such experiences, and subsequently having made that transition into 'conventional life', I believe that like many others before me, I can utilise this personal experience to, as many a Convict Criminologist has commented, *"tell it like it is"*.

The benefits of personal experience when studying prisons, prisoners and criminal justice issues have been articulated in detail by a number of CC authors (see Ross and Richards, 2003), and whilst I may retrace these steps a little, my primary aim is to strengthen my argument as to why it is necessary to have a CC group in the UK. To do this I will use the current state of affairs in the criminal justice system / penal system as the background context. And I will mainly utilise my experiences and observations of working in the 'field'.

My opportunity to work in the field of prisoner / former prisoner resettlement came in the latter stages of my PhD and was a result of a combination of two things: my status as a former prisoner and my doctoral research topic. The PhD focused on former prisoners' experiences of self-change and identity negotiation. Moreover, it explored what it is like to live with the status of ex-prisoner (ex-convict), exploring how these 'forced' identities are negotiated in everyday life. And whilst the combination of these two things (ex-convict status / PhD in desistance) arguably gives me some credibility in the field, it was not an area of interest originally. In fact it had not even crossed my mind as my academic background is not criminology. Rather I have an undergraduate degree in psychology and master's degree in cognitive neuropsychology.

So why the switch many have asked? This is a question I find difficult to answer when replying to people who do not know about my past. Indeed, as Jones (2003) and Goffman (1963) before him have articulated, the stigmatised often live in two worlds, one where everyone knows of the stigmatising condition and another where no one knows. After completing my master's degree it became apparent that my past criminal convictions were preventing me from pursuing careers in my chosen field. In other words, my convictions for drug trafficking and violent behaviour meant I was prohibited from working with vulnerable populations such as children, the mentally ill and patients with damaged brains or brain abnormalities. As a consequence I could not be licensed to be a clinical psychologist or clinical neuropsychologist. Of course, my criminal convictions have no direct relevance to these cohorts or any other vulnerable population, but regardless I am prohibited from working with them professionally, as current legislation, including the *Rehabilitation of Offenders Act* (1974) and *Enhanced Disclosures Act* (1996) dictates.

Despite the dramatic pro-social changes I have made in my life there are still legal impositions, dictating what I can and cannot do in terms of career and social activities. It was this social exclusion and prejudice that led me to follow the line of inquiry that I did, exploring self-change and desistance, undoubtedly a means of making sense of my situation as well as a career move. Of course, in many respects I am glad that my path took this turn, because the combination of my academic training and personal experience have given me insight into the appalling state of affairs of the criminal justice and penal system. This insight is used in my consultancy work, where I conduct research in prisons, primarily focusing on prisoner resettlement and ex-convict reintegration / resettlement and desistance. Additionally, I am also involved with and have strong associations with UNLOCK (National Association for Reformed Offenders), a charity that works to improve the lives of those in prison and 'reformed offenders', via their advocacy work, projects, and services. I argue that my insider perspective allows for a better understanding of the criminal justice process, as seen through my experientially based critical lens.

Therefore, for me this provides further evidence that we need a CC group here in the UK, with the courage to expose issues and concerns through their research and advocacy, disseminating this knowledge, and bringing it into the public domain and into mainstream society's consciousness. We need to weave the CC Perspective into the fabric of the criminal justice system, following a more authentic approach as articulated by Richards and Ross (2001, p. 1) when talking about the American corrections crisis: "We need to be more honest and creative with respect to the research we conduct and the policies we advocate, implement and evaluate". Whilst applicable to all areas of the criminal justice process, it is as these authors comment, particularly important in the resettlement and 'rehabilitation' field, the need for greater transparency and scrutiny of the evidence base utilised to inform policy, resettlement initiatives and strategies are long overdue. This change, in my view, can only come about by developing a CC movement in the UK. The time for a refreshing, new radical approach to criminal justice issues is now and I will support this argument through the use of my personal experiences, as well as some research based evidence. The following observations reinforce this.

THE STATE OF PLAY

The UK prison population (England and Wales) is currently peaking at over 86,000 (Ministry of Justice, 2011) and is showing no signs of a decline, with reconviction rates of adults aggregating at 49 percent within one year of being released from prison. For those serving sentences of less than twelve months, reconvictions increase to a staggering 66 percent. Those who have served more than ten previous custodial sentences have a rate of reoffending of 79 percent (Ministry of Justice, 2010a, 2010b). The National Audit Office (2010) has estimated that reoffending by former prisoners costs the economy £9.5 to £13 billion a year.

The overall average cost per prison place, including prison related costs, but excluding health and education expenditure, is £45,000 per annum (Hansard, 2010). Despite this substantive drain of public monetary resources and clear evidence prisons are ineffective and counter-productive, as evidenced in the reconviction rates, but also by many authors (see Burnett and Maruna, 2004; Cavadino and Dignan, 2006; Liebling and Maruna, 2005), the UK boasts one of the highest rates of imprisonment in comparison to our European counterparts (Walmsley, 2008). Arguably, this reflects the on-going trend for successive British governments to take a more punitive approach to penal issues, apparent in their right wing ideologies and conservative policies.

Yet similar to the United States, a consequence of the rising prison population here in the UK, is the growing number of prisoners or former prisoners turning to academia. Although the numbers are unquantifiable, as presently there does not appear to have been a systematic attempt to explore just how many people have shifted in this direction, some evidence of the growing numbers are apparent in the numerous voluntary sector initiatives that have 'sprung up' with the aim of assisting and/or supporting prisoners and ex-convicts with gaining entry to higher level education, primarily university (e.g. The Prisoners Education Trust and The Longford Trust). Moreover, a few universities facilitate prisoner or ex-offender entry / learning by providing long distance courses and/or widening participation schemes (e.g. Open University and the Open Book Project at Goldsmiths College, University of London). And whilst the amount of ex-convicts entering graduate studies is likely to be smaller than in the United States, the numbers appear to be growing.

Further evidence of this comes from my personal experiences, first, through my engagement with the 'ex-offender' circuit (conferences, advocacy work, research and so on) where I have met a number of university-educated ex-convicts, and second, through individuals contacting me. In the last five years a number of ex-convicts undertaking undergraduate or post graduate degrees have contacted me primarily because of my research on desistance, but also as a means of making a connection with another ex-con in academia.

Importantly, whilst a number of ex-convicts have undertaken undergraduate degrees or master's degrees, some have used them as a springboard for careers in the voluntary sector, delivering services to prisoners or ex-convicts, campaigning on their behalf for advocacy groups and/or working with penal reform groups. These individuals have much to offer organizations that clearly recognise the importance of direct experience, and see such individuals, or "professional-ex's" as Maruna (2001) describes them, as an invaluable resource.

Although in my experience the numbers are limited, a small yet growing number of former prisoners have PhDs or are working towards completing a PhD. Therefore, whilst these may lead the way for an evolving CC movement in the UK, it is paramount that over here, just like in the United States, the core of our British CC Group be the ex-convict graduate students and academics, supported by a larger group of non-con academics and knowledgeable practitioners, with or without a 'past'. The crucial thing is that we all share the same critical perspective and the intellectual orientations of the CC movement.

FINDING MY INTELLECTUAL HOME
IN CONVICT CRIMINOLOGY

I first came across CC a few years ago when I was still doing my PhD, courtesy of a colleague at UNLOCK. Coming into criminology from psychology things were pretty new to me, and in many respects quite different, but what surprised me the most was the number of former prisoners I met. Some were in the early stages of their academic careers, whilst others had used academia as a springboard for their careers in other domains such as the voluntary sector. Typically, these individuals worked in some generative capacity with prisoners, ex-convicts and/or (former) substance abusers. Consequently, I thought that as a group these 'enlightened' individuals could be a useful resource, using their direct experience and academic skills / knowledge to inform our existing, and often misguided understandings of crime, criminal justice issues, the penal system and resettlement / desistance. Of course unbeknown to me, such a group had already been formalised and was fully functioning a decade or so earlier, much to my joy and delight, but also to my great relief. Instantly, I felt some kinship with my peers in the United States and when reading the accounts of ex-convict academics many of their experiences resonated with mine.

Similarly, like many of the Convict Criminologists in America, one of the biggest issues for me and other former prisoners I have spoken to was the disparity between our lived experience of crime, prisons and life thereafter, and the mainstream criminological literature. This disparity has been voiced by many a Convict Criminologist and neatly articulated by Mobley (2003) who points out that much of the criminological research conflicts with the former prisoners' lived experience. He goes on to point out how existing taxonomies are used to categorize social phenomena and that these have been refined with scientific 'precision' over the years, to the detriment of 'real' substantive knowledge and insights (i.e. the flesh and bones of human lives). To me this rings true, especially in my given area criminal desistance. Yet despite this strong conceptual argument, I have often wondered why CC has not been pushed forward over here in the UK. I like many others am frustrated, angry and dissatisfied with the way things are with the state of affairs. Why is CC not having more of an impact here?

I think this is down to a number of reasons, but primarily because whilst exceptional work is being produced from members of the group over in the United States, little of this work appears to be filtering over to here in the UK. Moreover, criminology students are not being exposed to CC in the UK. Why? Possibly because the work generated by Convict Criminologists in the United States is arguably more relevant to the American criminal justice process and not always translatable to issues in the UK. Furthermore, the lived experiences of prison life, whilst universally resonant on many levels (see Gaucher, 2007), can be and is more divergent locally. Therefore, not only do we need research accounts by ex-convict academics to enrich our understandings of prisons and criminal justice issues (Ross and Richards, 2003), we also need ex-convict academics that have experienced them in different jurisdictions. In doing so, a strong evidence based challenge and critique, by 'informed experts', can be directed at the existing dominant forms of dealing with criminal justice/penal issues both in government and academia.

Whilst there are some highly regarded and prestigious criminologists producing critical work that directly challenges the dominant models, policies and practices utilised by the government and its associative agencies, in my experience the impact this is having is negligible. This is not a reflection of the individuals generating this exceptional work or the work itself. Rather, it is a reflection of the outdated and misinformed ideologies maintained by successive governments and the 'mechanical mindset' of many of those working in the departments dealing with criminal justice issues (e.g. Ministry of Justice (MOJ), National Offender Management Service (NOMS), Probation, resettlement departments).

For example, despite the strong evidence that a strengths based approach (Burnett and Maruna, 2006; Maruna and LeBel, 2003) to resettlement and desistance can and does significantly reduce reoffending (see Maruna, 2001; Maruna and LeBel, 2003; Veysey *et al.*, 2009) current 'evidenced based models' utilized to facilitate prisoner reintegration and reduce reoffending (i.e. deficit models) are typically used with knowledge of their ineffectiveness. Unlike strengths based approaches, which view the ex-convict as a stigmatised person, requiring a range of opportunities to facilitate and develop a meaningful, pro-social self-concept (Maruna, 2001), deficit models utilise risk-needs based strategies in an attempt to contain or control the 'problem' person. In other words, they view the prisoner or ex-convict as a set of risk factors, rather than a human being, who has strengths and skills, and the potential for self-change.

Undoubtedly, there is a small group of enlightened academics and civil servants that work to improve prison conditions and help prisoners. Unfortunately, they are outnumbered by a much larger group of academics and public servants that do their work without caring what happens to prisoners or ex-convicts. The failure of rehabilitation and resettlement strategies provides them with job security and career promotion in a penal system that grows on failure (Richards and Jones, 1997, 2004).

In my view we need to develop our own CC movement in the UK. This will be an academic movement with the passion and drive to 'take the bull by the horns' and directly challenge as Ross and Richards (2003) put it, managerial criminology, criminal justice and corrections. We clearly need a group of academics, working collectively who like the group in the United States, will take a critical stance and challenge existing (mis)representations of crime, prisons, the criminal justice system, prisoners and ex-convicts. Moreover, we need a CC group that will push forward alternative strategies and initiatives that are more cost effective and humane.

DEVELOPING CONVICT CRIMINOLOGY IN THE UNITED KINGDOM

So with the earlier arguments in mind, I, along with some colleagues have set on the path to developing CC in the UK. My initial attempts to do this involved 'testing the water' and asking colleagues what they thought about the idea of starting a CC group in the UK. This was received well, and there is some talk of trying to find CC a 'physical' home at a London based academic institution. Naturally, the criminologists in this department are of a critical orientation, with some familiar with CC and its intellectual underpinnings. My conversations have also extended to others and unsurprisingly, there is much interest and excitement at the prospect of developing CC here in the UK, by both ex-convicts in the early stages of their academic careers and non-con academics.

Moreover, as the word begins to spread and as a direct result of a presentation a colleague and I gave on CC at the British Society of Criminology (BSC) conference in July 2011, more and more people are being exposed to it. I am finding that CC is of particular interest to ex-convicts who are now undertaking master's degrees or completing their PhDs. Importantly, this has two significant implications. First, the more people involved in the group the more robust its physical presence or identity, and second and relative to this, the stronger the group identity the stronger the collective action. Specifically, the group on one level provides a 'sense of belonging' to a cohort of individuals who in many respects share similar experiences of (and are resisting) social exclusion (Leary, 2007) and a morally deficient label. On another level, it reinforces an individual's identity, attitudes, morals and values, motivating them to act accordingly (Ellemers *et al.*, 2002) in a proactive manner for just causes and for social benefit.

Yet despite the overwhelming psychological benefits of being part of this group, the 2011 BSC conference presentation, although well received, highlighted some issues. Before I outline these, I should briefly mention that the presentation included my colleague Rod Earle describing his transition from prison to university. He also talked about his research on prisons and reflexivity. I presented on the intellectual and historical underpinnings of CC, and then provided an argument as to why it was important for CC to have a physical presence and identity in the UK. The presentation generated much interest and a number of academics passed on their contact details, asking us to keep them up to speed with the group's development.

However, a few academics, including an ex-convict academic, whilst positive about developing CC in the UK, also raised concerns. They approached the idea with caution, primarily because they are concerned with how it may impact on their ability to gain research funding or employment. This experience resonates with the experiences of some of the ex-convict academics in the United States, in particular when the CC book was being put together, as articulated by Ross and Richards (2003, p. 8): "professionally, a number of convict professors expressed concerns that by appearing in this book they might be denied access to government research grants".

So an issue here is whilst a CC cohort in the UK appears to be a very good idea, some people may be a little cautious when considering whether to associate themselves with such a group. Considering that the number of former convicts with PhD's are likely to be considerably less than in the United States, this could be a problem. In my experience, those former prisoners that have recently entered academia or are on their way to obtaining PhD status, are more forthcoming than the more established academics with a 'past'. Therefore, my one concern relates to how many people will join and be actively involved with the group.

THE IVORY TOWER IN THE
UNITED KINGDOM

Whilst, the services on the ground require radical reform, and in many instances need to be more transparent and open to scrutiny, it is the systems in place at a senior level that require dramatic reformation. For changes to occur on the ground, significant changes need to be made at the top level of the criminal justice system. Drawing parallels with the United States and considering the notion of managerial research (Austin, 2003; Richards and Ross, 2001), arguably much of the prison research in the UK is dominated by government funding and/or carried out by researchers who subscribe to conservative ideologies. Until recently, researchers employed by the MOJ or Home Office conducted much of this research internally. It is only now that the MOJ are working towards 'farming' this research back out to the academics, rather than the researchers they employ or ones that are on their 'payroll'. This shift came to light at the 2011 BSC conference I attended, where representatives of the MOJ talked about reforming the CJS, their new strategies for rehabilitation and research funding.

My first reservation was well, who would get the funding for this research? Of course many of the people the MOJ had funded over the years are established academics that have a 'good' working relationship with the MOJ and churn out research that is in keeping with the pre-existing government's key ideologies. Any research that does not fit with these is likely to be 'under publicized'. Moreover, I very much doubt that they would entertain a bid from a group of researchers that come from a critical tradition, particularly ones that are pushing forward a radical new approach like CC.

My second reservation concerns the internal workings of the system. The MOJ and many of the other government departments are quite insular and dare I say incestuous. In my experience, employees are usually graduates from top tier universities, are typically white and middle class, and arguably have little grasp on the reality of the social worlds of those at the lower end of the social hierarchy. In contrast, the vast majority of prisoners in jail or prison in the UK are from the working class, the unemployed, ethnic minorities, the socially deprived and the socially excluded (Jacobson *et al.*, 2010; Cavadino and Dignan, 2006). Considering this, and as articulated by many a Convict Criminologist, most of the politicians and many of the researchers, are far removed from the realities of prisons, prisoners and life after prison (Austin, 2003; Mobley, 2003). Therefore, it is difficult to see how, without the involvement of 'us', the knowledgeable experts (ex-convict academics), policy makers can devise and implement effective policies and strategies to improve prisons and resettlement.

Senior level staffs at the MOJ, the politicians and many of the researchers who are typically of similar a background, but more importantly of a particular 'mind set', determine the 'rules' and dictate what is 'best' for the 'uneducated majority'. This is particularly distressing to me when I walk into prison and observe their ineffective policies and strategies based on 'managerial research'. To me the solution is simple. All the MOJ and politicians need to do is employ some ex-convict academics, who could use their 'expertise' to help devise effective and humane means of dealing with the pre-existing penal and rehabilitative issues (see Richards and Ross, 2003a, 200b).

Rather than do this, government administrators are more concerned with job security. The system in my view maintains the power status quo by moving its 'specialised workers' (i.e. civil servant) from one department to the other and typically only recruiting individuals of a particular 'social constitution', thus in many respects maintaining the 'old boys club'. Therefore, what we have here are people in senior positions that are arguably not suited to the job, and new employees with little experience with prisons and prisoners.

The former point was apparent at the recent BSC conference when of the head of research for the MOJ stated that a few years earlier she was head of research at the treasury. And whilst research skills are transferable, intimate knowledge of one domain does not make you an expert in another that has little or no relation. Despite the many issues with this, importantly, this has grave implications for the type of research that gets funding and who gets that funding. Moreover, when commissioning research, it is my view that much of the funding will out of habit go to the same people, because they have a 'proven track record'. This is regardless of the fact that the scientific inquiry, and subsequent policies and the strategies generated by these individuals have been ineffective. But if a senior level official lacks expertise in the area, in this instance criminal justice issues, it makes sense to stick with convention, rather than take a refreshing alternative approach.

Again applying what Richards and Ross (2001, p. 177) state about American corrections to the UK, if we are serious about addressing the crisis facing criminal justice and the penal system, "Then we need to be more honest and creative with respect to the research we conduct and the policies we advocate, implement and evaluate'. To do this we need a CC group here in the UK that will push forward such radical reform.

So my point is that if the MOJ or other government departments dealing with criminal justice issues, penal issues and resettlement/desistance are not willing to hire ex-convicts with university degrees or fund ex-convict academics to do honest and creative research, then I can foresee our failing approach to criminal justice and our penal system reaching the point of 'no return'. The implications of this for society in terms of economic and public welfare are catastrophic.

A LIGHT AT THE
END OF THE TUNNEL?

Yet contrary to what I have been arguing, the MOJ and Home Office do appear to recognise the value of personal experience. Recently, I was part of a delegation that went to the MOJ to talk about my experiences of the disclosure process (Criminal Records Bureau). I was also part of a delegation that went to the Home Office to talk about the *Rehabilitation of Offenders Act* (ROA, 1974) and its impact on our lives as 'ex-offenders'. Additionally, some high profile former prisoners in 'the field' have acted as consultants, advising government, politicians and judges on numerous issues (e.g. policy, prison conditions, resettlement issues) and have been key advisors on public inquiries commissioned by the government. A perfect example is Bobby Cummines OBE, an ex-gangster and currently the chief executive of UNLOCK, who boasts an impressive list of key advisory roles (see UNLOCK, 2011). But importantly, as far as I am aware, these positions are always temporary and short-lived. Surely, in addition to the ex-convict researcher, the ex-convict advisor would be an invaluable resource to the MOJ, and of course by employing him or her as a full time civil servant, the MOJ would be setting a good example to others. Specifically, to actually employ an ex-convict in a full time position would set a precedent and would demonstrate good practice to other employers.

PEER RESEARCH

The use of personal experience in the research process and its benefits has been articulated by many authors, particularly in the realms of qualitative research (Kvale, 1996) and of course is a defining principle of CC. Whilst in the UK, I am only aware of a handful of former prisoners who have actually obtained PhD's and a few others that are about to start a PhD. I am also aware of the growing number of ex-cons that are being employed on research projects as peer researchers. The level of peer researcher involvement varies depending on their research skills although regardless, their contributions are invaluable.

The use of peer research is becoming increasingly popular, in a variety of domains, for example, in studies of homelessness (e.g. de Winter and Noom, 2003), sexual behaviour (e.g. Price and Hawkins, 2002) and more recently studies focusing on prisons and prisoner resettlement (Sheffield Hallam, 2005; Jacobson *et al.*, 2010). In all these instances, the 'ex' is typically viewed as the expert and is involved in the design, data collection and other intellectual activities, using their expertise to inform the projects. In the context of prisons, prisoners and resettlement, and conducive with the CC Perspective, former prisoners are viewed as 'experts'. Whilst the intellectual contribution peer researchers provide is priceless, of equal measure, is her or his ability to engage with the participant and to establish rapport. In my experience as a peer researcher in the past, I believe I brought to the table a level of authenticity and trust. Disclosure of my ex-convict status meant that I was seen as trustworthy and genuinely there for the right reasons, for the benefit of prisoners and ex-convicts.

The peer research interviewer and the prisoner or ex-convict interviewee have a shared understanding of crime and prisons, and can usually identify with each other on a number of levels. Hence, these interviews generate high quality in-depth data. This includes significant insights that non-con interviewers may have not been able to evoke, due to issues of trust or lack of familiarity or connection to the interviewee's life world. Indeed, research participants have stated that they would not have been so forthcoming in their responses if I had not disclosed my ex-convict status prior to the interview.

Yet despite this ability for peer researchers to bring us closer to the 'lived experience' of the phenomena, thus providing a more in-depth understanding of our 'object of inquiry', the sustainability of this invaluable resource is uncertain in prison research. Well at least for me and a few of the other ex-convicts that are involved in prison research. Whilst I have been able to visit a number of prisons over the past year or so, as part of a research team, this may be coming to an end. In the past, all the prisons we have visited have been given full details of our criminal records and we were given access to each individual prison at the governor's discretion. Recently, I made an application to the MOJ for a generic security clearance. This is a standard procedure, where a prison researcher may apply to the MOJ for security clearance to most prisons, thus overcoming the complications of going through the same access and security process with each individual prison when doing research there. I, along with another ex-convict, was refused, yet the principal investigator, a non-convict academic got clearance.

So here we have the contradiction. On the one hand, the use of ex-convicts experiences is viewed as invaluable not only by liberal minded academics, but also by those in authority (i.e. politicians, the MOJ, the Home Office, policy makers and the like). On the other hand, its these very people that devise and implement the policies and other initiatives (e.g. security clearances) that constrain ex-convicts by excluding them from a myriad of social events, institutions, and social systems. Clearly, Johnson (2002) hits the nail on the head when he states that former prisoners suffer from a presumption of moral contamination.

Yet interestingly, the immorality of those in the corridors of power go unnoticed or if noticed is met with little consequence. You do not have to look to far to see these 'blatant double standards'. For example, look at the 'out of control' traders and speculators who brought the economy to its knees, the super rich tax cheats (Barber, 2011), the recent problem regarding fraudulent expenses claims made by some Members of Parliament, not to mention the scandalous allegations against Rupert Murdoch's News Corporation group.

So clearly in light of this and the other issues considered in this article we need to push forward CC here in the UK. As with the main group in the United States, the principle concerns that need to be addressed here are captured in the passage by Jones *et al.* (2009, p. 152) below:

> How the problem of crime is defined; the solutions that are proposed; the devastating impact of these decisions on the men and women labeled criminals who are locked in correctional facilities, separated from loved ones, and prevented from fully reintegrating into the community; record high rates of incarceration, overcrowding of penal institutions, and a lack of meaningful programming inside and outside the prison; and the structural impediments to successful re-entry that results in a revolving door criminal justice system.

CONCLUSION

This article supports the idea that there is a need to develop CC in the UK, with its own physical presence and identity. And whilst undoubtedly there is much overlap and similarity between criminal justice and penal systems in the United States and the UK, there are clearly some significant differences that are untranslatable. These differences manifest themselves in a variety of ways, for example in terms of policies, legislation, prison conditions and regimes, resettlement services and strategies, and dominant models of rehabilitation. Therefore, it is clear that whilst we can learn much from the main CC Group in the American context, we also need to follow our own unique modes of scientific inquiry, utilising these to develop our 'local' understandings of crime and criminal justice issues, and using this research to improve our prisons, policies and resettlement / rehabilitative strategies. It is clear that this is the only way forward if we are going to make radical changes to our failing penal system.

However, whilst I advocate a UK based CC group, it must be noted that that this group would need to be part of the 'mother' group in the United States, naturally following the same underlying principles and intellectual orientations. Therefore, CC UK would be part of the wider CC social movement and only differ in the fact that it deals with issues unique to the UK. Like the wider movement, British CC should consist of ex-convict academics, non-convict academics and practitioners in the 'field', who share the CC philosophy. This collection of individuals with diverse backgrounds will provide a solid foundation for the group and be an invaluable resource when it comes to taking a critical lens to, as well as challenging, pre-existing ways of understanding and dealing with criminal justice and penal issues. Indeed, I have worked with many a non-convict academic, some from more 'privileged' backgrounds, who have given me much insight and knowledge. So diversity in the group is critical.

So now the time has come to push CC forward here in the UK and whilst I am excited, I am also apprehensive because I am uncertain of how things will work out. I know that there is a growing interest in CC, not only from ex-convicts going through academia, but also established academics. Therefore, I believe the time has now come for a radical and refreshing alternative approach to come into to play.

ENDNOTE

* The views expressed in this article are the authors alone and not particularly representative of the other academics working to develop the British Convict Criminology group in the UK.

REFERENCES

Aresti, A., V. Eatough and B. Brooks-Gordon (2010) "Doing Time After Time: An Interpretative Phenomenological Analysis of Reformed Ex-prisoners' Experiences of Self-change, Identity and Career Opportunities", *Psychology, Crime & Law,* 16(3): 169-190.

Aresti, A. (2011) "Is There a Place for Convict Criminology in the UK?", paper presented 4 July 2011, *British Society of Criminology*, Northumbria University, Newcastle Upon Tyne.

Austin, J. (2003) "The Use of Science to Justify the Imprisonment Binge", in J. I. Ross and S. C. Richards (eds.), *Convict Criminology*, Belmont (CA): Wadsworth, pp. 17-36.

Barber, B. (2011) *The Government is Wrong on the Riots* (Trade Unions Congress conference). Retrieved from <http://touchstoneblog.org.uk>.

Burnett, R. and S. Maruna (2006) "The Kindness of Prisoners: Strengths-based Resettlement in Theory and in Action", *Criminology and Criminal Justice,* 6(1): 83-106.

Burnett, R. and S. Maruna (2004) "So 'Prison Works', Does It? The Criminal Careers of 130 Men Released from Prison under Home Secretary, Michael Howard", *Howard Journal of Criminal Justice,* 43(4): 390-404,

Cavadino, M. and J. Dignan (2006) *The Penal System* (third edition), London: Sage.

Collison, M. (1996) "In Search of the High Life: Drugs, Crime, Masculinities and Consumption", *British Journal of Criminology,* 36(3): 428-444.

De Winter, M. and M. Noom (2003) "Someone Who Treats You as an Ordinary Human Being... Homeless Youth Examine the Quality of Professional Care", *British Journal of Social Work,* 33(3): 325-338.

Ellemers, N., R. Spears and B. Doosje (2002) "Self and Social Identity", *Annual Review of Psychology,* 53: 161-86.

Gaucher, B. (2007) "Carceral Universals", *Journal of Prisoners on Prisons,* 16(2): 1-7.

Goffman, E. (1963) *Stigma: Notes on the Management of Spoiled Identity,* Englewood Falls (NJ): Prentice Hall Inc.

Hansard, HC, 3 March 2010, c1251W.

Hansard, HC, 23 March 2010, c115.

Irwin, J. (1970) *The Felon,* Englewood Cliffs (NJ): Prentice Hall.

Jacobson, J., C. Phillips and K. Edgar (2010) *'Double Trouble': Black, Asian and Minority Ethnic Offenders' Experiences of Resettlement,* London: Clinks.

Johnson, R. (2002) *Hard Time* (third edition), Belmont (CA): Wadsworth.

Jones, R. S. (2003) "Ex-con: Managing a Spoiled Identity", in J. I. Ross and S. C. Richards (eds.), *Convict Criminology*, Belmont (CA): Wadsworth, pp. 191-208.

Jones, R. S., J. I. Ross, S. C. Richards and D. S. Murphy (2009) "The First Dime. A Decade of Convict Criminology", *Prison Journal,* 89(2): 151-171.

Katz, J. (1988) *Seductions of Crime: Moral and Sensual Attractions in Doing Evil*, US: Basic Books.

Kvale, S. (1996) *Interviews: An Introduction to Qualitative Research Interviewing*, London: Sage.

Leary, M. R. (2007) "Motivational and Emotional Aspects of the Self", *Annual Review of Psychology,* 58: 317-344.

Liebling, A. and S. Maruna (eds.) (2005) *The Effects of Imprisonment*, Cullompton, Devon: Willan Publishing.

Maruna, S. (2001) *Making Good: How Ex-convicts Reform and Rebuild Their Lives,* Washington (D.C.): American Psychological Association.

Maruna, S. and T. P. LeBel (2003) "Welcome Home? Examining the 'Reentry Court' Concept from a Strengths-Based Perspective", *Western Criminology Review*, 4(2): 91-107.

Messerschimdt, J. W. (1993) *Masculinities and Crime: Critique and Re-conceptualization of Theory*, Lanham (MD): Rowman & Littlefield.

Ministry of Justice (2011) *Ministry of Justice Statistics Bulletin: Population in Custody monthly tables September 2011*. Retrieved from <www.justice.gov.uk/publications/population>.

Ministry of Justice (2010a) *Reoffending of Adults: Results from the 2008 Cohort*, London: Ministry of Justice.

Ministry of Justice (2010b) *Compendium of Reoffending Statistics and Analysis*, London: Ministry of Justice.

Mobley, A. (2003) "Convict Criminology: The Two-legged Data Dilemma", in J. I. Ross and S. C. Richards (eds.), *Convict Criminology*, Belmont (CA): Wadsworth, pp. 209-225.

National Audit Office (2010) *Managing Offenders on Short Custodial Sentences*, London: NAO.

O'Keeffe, C. (2005) *Women into Work Pilot Project*, Sheffield: Sheffield Hallam University.

Price, N. and C. Hawkins (2002) "Researching Sexual and Reproductive Behaviour: A Peer Ethnographic Approach", *Social Science and Medicine,* 55(8): 1325-1336.

Richards, S. C. and R. S. Jones (2004) "Beating the Perpetual Incarceration Machine", in S. Maruna and R. Immarigeon (eds.), *After Crime and Punishment: Pathways to Offender Reintegration*, London: Willan Publishers, pp. 201-232.

Richards, S. C. and R. S. Jones (1997) "Perpetual Incarceration Machine: Structural Impediments to Post-prison Success", *Journal of Contemporary Criminal Justice*, 13(1): 4-22.

Richards, S. C. and J. I. Ross (2003a) "Ex-convict Professors Doing Prison Research", in *The State of Corrections: 2002 Proceedings ACA Annual Conferences*, Lanham (MD): American Correctional Association, pp. 163-168.

Richards, S. C. and J. I. Ross (2003b) "Convict Perspective on the Classification of Prisoners", *Criminology & Public Policy*, 2(2): 243-252.

Richards, S. C. and J. I. Ross (2001) "Introducing the New School of Convict Criminology", *Social Justice*, 28(1): 177-190.

Ross, J. I. and S. C. Richards (eds.) (2003) *Convict Criminology*, Belmont (CA): Wadsworth.

Veysey, B. M., D. J. Martinez and J. Christian (2009) "Identity Transformation and Offender Change", in B. M. Veysey, J. Christian and D. J. Martinez (eds.), *How Offenders Transform their Lives*, Cullompton, Devon: Willan Publishing, pp. 1-11.

Walmsley, R. (2008) *World Prison Population* (eight edition), London: International Centre for Prison Studies.

ABOUT THE AUTHOR

Andy (Andreas) Aresti, PhD, is an ex-convict. He completed his doctorate in December 2010, and currently works as both a research consultant and lecturer. Andy has published in *Psychology, Crime & Law*, and has also worked on and authored a number of published research reports. He is currently the Chair of Trustees for UNLOCK and lives in London.

An Ugly Fairy Tale with an Ending of Hope:
The Founding of KRIS in Finland
Matti "Kid" Hytönen

INTRODUCTION

Once upon a time there was an immature, self-indulgent man who had been in prison for a long, long time for many criminal activities. He had been unable to find any suitable place in society in which he could fit. He had come to believe that normal life was just for other people – for real people, not for him. So he went on drinking and using drugs. Alcoholism and drug addiction did provide him focus and drive in his life, a purpose sometimes so intense he would do whatever was necessary to feed his addictions. They were not kind masters. If he failed to satisfy them, they turned his own body against him with such torturous agonies of withdrawal, he would do what his body demanded. Do whatever he must to get more. Rational plans of action were a luxury. If plan A failed, physical need quickly drove him to plan B or C, which were not so much plans as acts of desperation. These acts eventually always ended with the same result: back to prison with another new sentence.

During those nineteen years behind bars, he had understood one underlying motivational force: drugs and booze. For him, this became all consuming and left room for little else. In prison, he had moments of clarity in which he saw a connection between his addictions and his behavior. He came to carry some weak ideas of sobriety – that if he would stop with all that stuff, maybe he could be one of the normal human beings, one of the real people. But he did not have enough guts to take the step or see a way out the abyss.

He went in and came out from different Scandinavian correctional institutions during the 1960s, during the 1970s and even during the 1980s. The world changed dramatically outside the prisons over these decades, so much it seemed impossible to for him to grasp and understand the world now surrounding him. In the late 1990s, this unhappy creature made the big step. He put all his power and will into leaving narcotics and alcohol behind him. Against the odds, he succeeded. He became one-hundred per cent sober.

SUDDEN IMPACT

The man described above was I. Sober, I discovered a new way of living. But it was not easy to combine one's needs with the responsibilities in the free world outside of prison. I carried a deep emptiness inside of me that was matched with the loneliness of my new situation. I was a sober being within a world I did not yet really have a purpose in. No longer living a life consumed by drugs, I had all the time in the world to think. I wanted to do something good. I realized it was not so easy to get other people to see inside me, to understand I was no longer that thief, that liar – that jerk. I started to study. I tried desperately to find rules of life to guide me. I read a lot, but I still found I had nothing to fill the emptiness of my soul.

One day I happened to read an article in some Finnish newspaper, about an organization in the neighboring country of Sweden. All the members in that organization were ex-cons. They had survived imprisonment and made successful re-entries into society. They were now using the experiences of their criminal past in their present work, helping others who still were swimming in the swamp they had escaped.

I felt a sudden impact. It was like a bolt of lightning through my brain. This was just what I had been thinking during these difficult, lonely years. How could I use my experiences and knowledge of drug addiction and crime to assist others to find their way to a life of freedom? It simply seemed so right. I felt an immediate kinship with this group. I was so eager to be able to use my experiences from those decades in prison, and my years of addiction and crime to find my place in society, and most of all to help others!

A TELEPHONE CALL

That newspaper article was published sometime in the shift to the millennium. I had started my new life after moving back from Sweden to Finland. I considered moving back to Sweden to be able to work with former Swedish ex-cons I read about, but wondered whether similar work could take place in Finland for the same purpose and for Finnish convicts. As I reflect on this I felt I had truly found my purpose and was filled with a sense of destiny that this would come be true.

In summer 2001 I got a telephone call from Katariina Pousi who had gotten much help from this Swedish organization called CRIS (Criminals Return Into Society) during and after her last sentence. She wanted to start a new life after all those years of addiction in Stockholm and in several Swedish prisons – but this time in Finland. She wanted to start CRIS, with the same guiding principles in her home country. She had been speaking with Christer Karlsson, the President of CRIS in Sweden, who promised to give all possible spiritual support to get CRIS started in Finland.

Katariina called me and some others she knew that had changed their lifestyles. A meeting was held on September 22, 2001. About a dozen CRIS people arrived from Stockholm and 7 to 8 from Finland. My role was to translate the rules and the principals of CRIS into Finnish. *Translation changed the acronym CRIS to KRIS.* Katariina had handmade 150 sandwiches. There was coffee and tea. The discussion floated in optimistic waves. During that evening, KRIS was born in Finland!

DON'T LOOK BACK

There's an old saying: "Don't look back". But I have to look back to those first years to give insight on the difficulties we met as we tried to build KRIS in Finland. First of all, we did not have any funds. Money, the lack of it, would be one of the main obstacles on our journey creating KRIS. So we started begging. We went to every possible place to tell about our mission and to ask for support. In our meeting with the Ministry of Justice, they were listening, smiling and seemed to be interested. The passion burned bright and powerful as a half-dozen or so of us ex-convicts with burning hearts stood in the room and told them, "We together have been sentenced for over a hundred years – now we want to help our brothers and sisters for more than a hundred years!"

Afterwards we felt a bit disappointed. They had not given any direct answer. However, a few weeks later we started getting positive signals from the Ministry. They had been talking to important people. Our job now was to write requests to get money, which we did. In December 2003 we got a message from the main financing institution. We would get 15,000 Euros to start. We did not look back to the past anymore and looked towards a brand new horizon. Our thoughts on what we could accomplish knew no limits.

Everyone who was an active volunteer during those first shimmering months can remember one certain night where we happened to take three long trips to different prisons. You have to be at the prison gate at seven in the morning to be able to pick up and help one who is being released because at seven o'clock the gate opens. Prisoners are released whether their support person is there or not. An addict or criminal being released from prison without a knowledgeable support person to be there with them is more likely to wander back into what they knew. Those that know can find narcotics or other action surprisingly fast once they are released. That night during those long drives, we were calling each other with our mobile phones. "Where are you?", one asked. "Oh, still 400 kilometers!", another responded. But the long cold distance did not matter at all. We were burning with the passion of knowing that we were doing something new and good in Finland. We were quite sure we were going in the right direction with our three cars driving into the winter night. During next two to three years, there were several new KRIS organizations created in Finland. The phenomenon was easy to describe with the word "avalanche". We would often get 40 telephone calls per day asking us about KRIS and what we could do to help someone coming out of prison.

WHAT IS THE MAGIC OF KRIS?

Today, we are about one thousand members. Approximately, one-hundred have a daily working space and job in KRIS. We work successfully in the reentry process together with the authorities. How was it possible? What is the magic in this model? When an addict or criminal stops the lifetime-long 24/7 Tivoli with different kinds of drugs and action, he or she has to redevelop all the moments of daily life, including his or her relationship with time itself. Without one's days and nights pressing relentlessly in a search for drugs, fixing, using, recovering, swindling, stealing or cheating to get more, one is suddenly swimming in 24 hours of new time every day. It can be daunting, even devastating, as one has to fill those many empty hours anew each day.

Now here is the magic! What could be more suitable for an ex-con who had been deeply addicted to drugs or crime, but is now free of them? He or she can start helping their brothers or sisters with their own experiences, those unique sequences in his or her own life that opened new ways to see and experience life. This knowledge on how to reshape time, fill the moments of one's life without drugs or crime not only can provide another with knowing guidance on what they are facing, but it also can fill one's own emptiness with new purpose. This, the experience of ex-addicts and ex-criminals on ways to deal with the struggles newly released prisoners face, is a commodity nobody can buy. This is the magic and the most valuable thing in the KRIS philosophy, the power of our solidarity recycling, empowering itself through nonjudgmental acceptance of our brethren as we share our experience, knowledge and understanding of rebuilding time with the promise of a new life.

The core ideas behind KRIS are honesty, solidarity and comradeship, and abstinence from drugs. They are the foundation from which we built a reentry program that was not about surveillance, continual stigmatization, and erecting barriers between communities and released prisoners. Instead, we created a reentry program that was about welcoming ex-prisoners into a community that valued their knowledge and experience for the promise it holds for helping others. Honesty is protected by confidentiality, so our clients can discuss their issues and problems, and find solutions to them before they cause harm. Solidarity and comradeship helps us view ourselves within and act as a community.

We begin helping prisoners before they are released with housing, understanding of the support programs available and getting them the assistance they may need. We meet them at the prison gates as they are released, welcoming them back. We provide them with mentors with a common background and cell phones for both so they may talk anytime, as well as a broader peer support network. We assist them with job programs and training, drug treatment, and a special program to help them learn to live a crime free life. We have an outreach community service program that people or organizations in the wider community can call for KRIS members for help in the community. We established activity centers for individuals, families and children. We have sport programs, movies, group activities, holiday celebrations and meals. We also encourage participants to just drop-in to enjoy talking and networking with others in our community.

KRIS TODAY

Today's KRIS in Finland is a result of hundreds of mistakes, hundreds of misunderstandings, and also hundreds of gains and hundreds of successful decisions. Of course, it is also the result of work with thousands of clients. Our brothers and sisters are called clients when we write requests to get money. But they are friends when we are together. During the ten-year history of KRIS in Finland, we have been giving different kinds of support to thousands of prisoners reentering society.

My narrative represents a transition from a life of drugs and crime to the founding of KRIS in Finland and the passion behind establishing this reentry program, which was developed and run by ex-convicts in its early years. The only policy was work, work and more work. Actually, we did not know how we should solve the problems on the way, but we acquired this knowledge through experience. We started keeping statistics without knowing what to keep or how to utilize them. So we wrote down everything. Week-by-week, month-by-month we learned from our clients and ourselves. We started to understand the structure, but we still had to ask many questions of ourselves and of this organization we were building. Nonetheless, in the beginning we had to make decisions without much organizational experience. Mostly, we were guided by our interactions with our clients who were like ourselves, searching for paths towards a new life. Nowadays we have better educated ex-convicts who have risen to top positions in the organization and who are good captains for the future. Moving forward, I want to point out the burning passion that led to the founding of KRIS continues on to this day. Without that nothing would have happened.

I retired this year after having served as the Executive Manager of KRIS in Finland for its first decade. Seventy years old is a suitable age for that. But I will carry the history and the policies of KRIS in my heart forever. This kind of organization is necessary if the problems of reentry and aftercare are to be solved. I can recommend with a warm heart our short philosophy to everyone who is interested about this work. Our three principals – 1) honesty, 2) comradeship and solidarity, and 3) abstinence from drugs – have proven their value as the foundation for a true community oriented reentry program. The experience and knowledge of the older members on how one can fall into and rationalize the spiraling vortex of a criminal way of life, and above all, how to break free from it, is the basis of how KRIS tries to help other people facing similar circumstances. Not surprisingly, we are a remarkably successful reentry program that now enjoys strong support and trust from the Ministry of Justice in Finland.

NOTE FROM THE SPECIAL ISSUE EDITORS

During June 2010, the International Scientific Conference on Global Perspectives on Reentry was held at the University of Tampere, Finland (Ekunwe and Jones, 2011). Through the efforts of Ikponwosa Ekunwe and Richard Jones and the support of the University of Tampere, a number of Convict Criminologists from the United States were able to attend. In Tampere we met Matti "Kid" Hytönen and many members of KRIS Finland as we presented papers at the conference, spending many hours just talking together. We discussed KRIS with Finland's Ministry of Justice, hearing firsthand their appreciation and support for the excellent work they were doing. Perhaps more importantly, we recognized in our discussions how similar our two organizations were. Members of both KRIS and Convict Criminology have worked to find ways to fuse their criminal experience with knowledge and vision. The ex-convicts of Convict Criminology at the conference were honored to be inducted as members of KRIS Finland in recognition of our similar journeys through life and our shared struggle to build a better future for us all.

REFERENCES

Ekunwe, I. O. and R. S. Jones (eds.) (2011) *Global Perspectives on Re-entry*, Tampere (FI): University of Tampere Press.

ABOUT THE AUTHOR

Matti "Kid" Hytönen is an ex-convict. He has just retired at age 70 after serving as the Executive Manager of KRIS Finland. Though retired he continues to serve as Chairman of the Board of KRIS Central Organization in Finland, as well as Chairman of the Board for KRIS Southern in Finland. KRIS maintains an English version of their website at <http://www.kris.fi/?id=163>. KRIS is the translated acronym for the original Swedish program CRIS and one may see either acronym when researching the program in Finland.

Finnish Criminal Policy: From Hard Time to Gentle Justice

Ikponwosa O. Ekunwe and Richard S. Jones

INTRODUCTION

It can be argued that Finland possesses one of the most advanced and efficient systems of criminal justice policy ever implemented. As far as methods of punishment go, the Finns believe in fines, short sentences, open prisons and heavy emphasis on gentle social rehabilitation, yet the rate of recidivism is one of the lowest in the world. The question at hand is how did such a system emerge? Prior to 1960, criminal justice policy had its roots in the Russian authoritarian model of the nineteenth century. Around 1960, a social revolution took place in Finland, which led to sweeping changes in social welfare and criminal justice policies. The result was that the old Finnish system was replaced by a forward looking, socially aware new way of thinking. One of the reasons behind this radical change was the desire to minimize the costs of the criminal justice system and to move closer to the Nordic philosophy of criminal justice. Finnish policy makers were heavily influenced by a growing body of research that raised serious questions about the efficacy of harsh penal policies. Instead, these policy makers were struck by the growing body of literature from Nordic countries that supported the idea that recidivism could be greatly reduced by policies that focus on maintaining the connection between prisoners and the outside world, as well as providing them with tools to survive in it.

Academic debates on the methods of treating convicts have been an on-going process in Finland, leading to significant changes in the way that the country responds to the problem of crime. The result of this shift in criminal justice policy is that Finland has one of the lowest per capita crime rates in the world, as well as significantly lower rates of recidivism as well. The focus of this paper is on the shift in social policy in Finland and the factors related to this country becoming one of the leading jurisdictions in criminal justice and penal reform.

FINNISH CRIMINAL JUSTICE POLICY PRIOR TO 1960

After the Second World War, a committee was formed to study the state of Finnish prisons and it was ascertained that serious problems were evident, including the shortage of space, food, healthcare and clothing, which was a reflection of the unstable situation found in Finnish post-war society. Although these deficiencies led to a willingness to improve the conditions in prison, the decision makers did not want to act without due consideration to the increase in the rate of criminality. In 1945, a reformation committee comprised of prison administrators proposed modest reforms regarding prisoners' clothing, smoking and food provisions. These reforms were implemented without exception and a gradual shift in perception of the role of prison administration followed shortly. Rather than simply controlling prisoners, the role of prison administration shifted to the goal of transforming and rehabilitating prisoners to become better citizens able to adhere to societal norms and abide by its rules (Matinpuro, 1981).

In the turbulent aftermath of the Second World War, Finland experienced a large increase in crime, with crimes of theft heavily represented (Hannula, 1981). In response to this situation, the criminal policy of the time concentrated on punishment and crime prevention through longer sentences. This was reflected in the 1940s and 1950s when Finnish criminal policy experienced a temporary halt in reforms, which resulted in a general toughening of the system. One example of this can be found in the actions of the Honkasalo Committee appointed to investigate prison conditions with special regard to guard safety. The committee found that the atmosphere of Finnish prisons had deteriorated over time due to influence from socially subversive elements and unfounded outside criticism of the system. Measures were taken to counter this development, including returning to the use of harsher sentences for first time offenders. Individual treatment of prisoners was heavily criticized by the Committee, for it was thought to cushion the system excessively, thus weakening its crime preventive element. The consequences of radical change were also deemed too unsure to form any basis for policies (Matinpuro, 1981). It has been suggested that the proposals of the Committee effectively amounted to a return to the 1930s in Finnish penal practices (Hannula, 1981).

However, even during the immediate post war times there were significant voices in Finland demanding the reform of penal policy. The Prison Administration Statute of 1950 was for the first time based on the recognition of human dignity for all prisoners and placed a heavy emphasis on education in prisons, albeit this education was to be more ethical and moral in nature according to the traditional progressive idea of a prisoner making himself eligible for society again through work and worship. The length of the workday in prisons was shortened from ten to eight hours following the shortening of the workday of guards, for even though working was held in very high regard it was seen as beneficial from a productivity angle to gradually allow prisoners more spare time (Matinpuro, 1981). Already during the late 1940s Finland adopted its own version of convict labor colonies as a form of punishment, which had no guards and in which the prisoners were paid for their work. According to Anttila (1981), these colonies were not directly based on any foreign examples. Valentin Soine, the reform minded head of Finnish prison administration was very proud to demonstrate them in a Geneva conference in 1958. The Honkasalo Committee itself was highly criticized by advocates of a gentler school of thought, mainly comprised of psychologists and senior officials of the prison administration such as Soine, and the implementation of the committee's proposals was withdrawn in the late 1950s (ibid). International cooperation in penal policy had naturally been delayed during war-time but already in the 1950s Finland was actively taking part in international policy conferences, which allowed new ideas to emerge. Especially important for later Finnish development was the Nordic connection, for the Scandinavian countries were already in the process of reforming their prison systems along gentler lines and Finland had a longstanding tradition of cooperation with them. The mention of human dignity in the 1950 Statute came directly from a Swedish example, with the first Finnish statement concerning the lack of social rehabilitation capabilities of its prisons being made by a Finnish psychiatrist during a conference in Sweden.

At the end of the 1950s, new attitudes to crime control were developed by inter-Nordic research on juvenile crime. At times, however, the Finnish intellectual climate became so hostile to the gentler school for what was perceived to be excessive leniency that foreign connections became vital for its survival (Anttila, 1981). Moreover, it was made clear that Finnish penal policy could not extend to the same level as Swedes due to post-war living conditions in Finland. It was believed that more attention needed to be paid to raising the standard of living of society as a whole than to the state of the country's prisons (Matinpuro, 1981).

THE CHANGES OF THE 1960s

Policies in the criminal justice system in Finland, embedded with the principles of legality, equality and humaneness by making rehabilitation the central value, have created an encouraging situation for offenders in desisting from crime. The initial high numbers of confined criminals in Finland by the beginning of the 1960s subsided to the Nordic level of 50 to 60 prisoners per 100,000 inhabitants by 1998 as seen in the figure below.

Table 1:
Prisoner Rates (per 100 000 inhabitants)
in Four Scandinavian Countries (1950–2000)

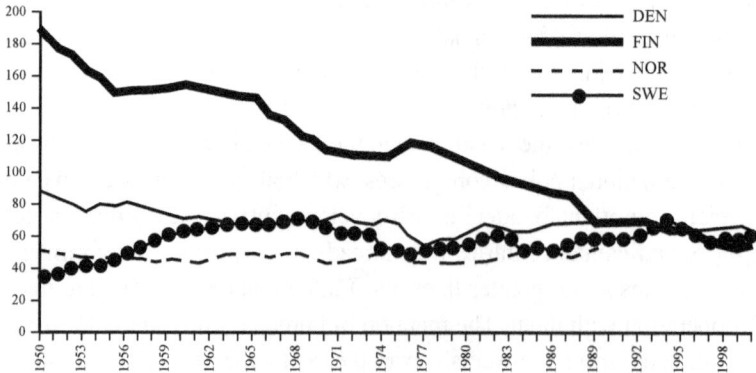

* Compiled from Falck, von Hofer and Storgaard , 2003.

The fact that Finland has been a relatively peaceful and safe society with a low level of crime facilitated the adoption of liberal policies in crime control. It can also be argued that this factor has a rather restricted explanatory force. For example, during the 1960s, Finland experienced severe social and structural changes in its development from a rural / agricultural economy into an industrial urban welfare state. This rapid development had its positive impact on its low crime rate. Finnish penal policy may also be described as *exceptionally expert-oriented*: reforms have been prepared and conducted by a relatively small group of experts whose thinking on penal policy has followed similar lines. The impact of these professionals was reinforced by close personal and professional contacts with senior politicians and with academic research.[1]

The new social outlook connected penal policy with overall social policies in Finland, stressing that it should never be viewed as something separate from the fabric of the society. To demonstrate the changes of the intellectual climate an example is in order. In 1964, a committee was set to evaluate the Finnish use of confinement, but by the time its report was published in 1969 its findings, recommending adoption of more individual treatment for prisoners and increased use of open prison sentences, were already considered old fashioned and outdated, while the so-called neoclassical school, ready to take the reforms even further, advocating common crime deterrence and social re-acclimatization, was gaining popularity. In 1968, Paavo Uusitalo demonstrated in his influential research that less restrictive conditions would not lead to increased recidivism, but could in fact have the opposite effect. Overall, the socio-politically influenced Finnish penal policy adopted a new kind of orientation. In the future, the policy would aim at minimizing the suffering and social costs incurred by criminal activity and the measures used to combat it, and for sharing these costs fairly among the parties involved (Matinpuro, 1981). This era gave birth to the neoclassical interpretation of the functionality of prisons, with explicit stress laid on the general instead of individual inhibitory effect of criminal policy, identical treatment of cases, guaranteed legal protection and new criminology (Hannula, 1981). A sign of changing thinking taking practical shape was to be found in the appointment of permanent prison psychologists, the first of which began working in Turku and Helsinki in 1968 (Anttila, 1981), while the prison conditions saw tangible improvements and led to a decrease in the overall amount of prisoners. This was achieved in 1969 through decriminalization of drunkenness and a reform in fine legislation, which drastically changed the conversion of imprisonment for non-payment and practically removed fine offenders from prisons (Aho and Karsikas, 1980).

The emerging social awareness can be demonstrated very well through the example of formation of societies based on critique of the prison system. Most notable of these were the so-called November Movement of 1967 and the National Convict Alliance Krim (Valtakunnallinen Vankiliitto Krim) of 1968. These organizations for the first time brought a lot of media attention to the ills of the Finnish prison system, even managing to attract the political parties of the day to their cause. A book published by the November Movement, which contained prisoners' narratives of their own experiences within the Finnish prison system, received a lot of attention in the media (Matinpuro, 1981). These writings brought the experience of prisoners closer to ordinary people, and helped the public to better understand some of the problems inherent in the prison system.

Among the achievements of the November Movement was starting a debate on what prisons produce (Myllylä, 1998). One important idea that emerged was that prison cures nobody. As a result policies were enacted that prison sentences should rarely be used in smaller crimes and other penalty systems should be developed instead (Pajuoja, 1998).

The influence of these movements was soon felt, when prison rules were reformed at the end of the 1960s where many unnecessary formalities were abandoned and censorship of outgoing convicts' letters was relaxed. Vocational prison education began replacing the purely moral and ethical teaching prisoners had been receiving, while compulsory church visits were abolished in 1971 (Matinpuro, 1981). The old work and worship ideology was being replaced by the new re-socialization principles.

Again the international dimension played a significant part in influencing these Finnish national reforms. The existing international discussion was centered more and more on the scientific aspects of crime in the form of academic criminology, with the Council of Europe starting to sponsor criminology expert meetings in 1963. In just such a meeting in 1964, British criminologist Roger Hood demonstrated that people charged with fines rather than short term prison sentences were much less likely to continue committing crimes, a lesson to which Finns heeded. Even more important was the Nordic criminology seminar in 1965, which concluded that the more closed prisons are kept the worse convict atmosphere they produce, thus greatly hindering the overall performance of the prison system. A general reworking of attitude was called for, since it was determined that even in Nordic countries prisons that were supposed to provide social treatment for the prisoners were still dispensing punishment masquerading as treatment. Attitude transformation was to be a long and gradual process.

In the 1970s international cooperation received even more attention with the practice of study trips to prisons in other countries, particularly Nordic ones. With the generational shift in universities, the former criticism of the Swedish system eventually declined, while the Finnish system was increasingly seen as backward in contemporary publications such as the *Vankeinhoito* magazine.

This series of reforms was brought to a formalized close with the advent of the Finnish Prison Administration Reform of 1975. Statements issued by the Finnish government postulated that the moralizing attitude of prison education was to be abandoned in favor of social acclimatization. To facilitate this, prison education was to be transformed to support the vocational skills of convicts. It was made clear that prison sentences should constitute purely a loss of freedom, which meant that prisoners were sent to prison as punishment, not for punishment. The continued use of freedom limiting sentences was stated to be based on two principles. On one hand, it limits the danger to society from prisoners assessed as dangerous. On the other hand, it keeps an air of common crime deterrence in effect through the very existence of such sentences. To demonstrate the long road the Finnish prison administration had walked to reach these goals and to signify the fact that these ideas were the product of gradual development, one could observe the comments of the Chief Director of the Finnish Prison Administration, who implied that the Reform of 1975 was practically a formalization of and final recognition for policy that had in principle already been followed for many years (Matinpuro, 1981).

In the beginning of 1960s the department of prison administration established a committee to examine how deprivation of liberty could be developed. As a result, the committee suggested proceeding to analogous deprivation of liberty, giving up on the progressive system and extension of an open prison system. They also suggested that handling prisoners should become more individualistic whereby prisoners entering into prison should be examined carefully. The main goal was to formulate a process that would offer the best possible conditions for the persons who had committed a crime to readjust to living in society. The deprivation of liberty committee published a list of reformist proposals in 1969.

One could say that the Finnish criminal policy changes of the 1960s and 1970s came into being through a combination of significant outside influence especially in the form of Nordic ideas concerning prisoner treatment, with a local school of thought advocating a gentler approach. In the 1950s the development of penal policy experienced a temporary halt with a hard line faction wishing to thwart the gentle approach. However, after the important change of generations even the prison system was accepted as a part of the emerging Finnish welfare state and developed as such. Combined with the changing societal landscape of the 1960s and 1970s, these influences were bound to carry through to creating the modern Finnish criminal justice system, the basis of which remains unchanged to the present day. These policy changes have been quite successful. From a post war crime boom and relatively high incarceration rates, Finnish prisons have emerged to be counted among the most humane correctional facilities in the world and yet, recidivism is very low compared to international standards.

It is important to note that Finnish policy makers are not satisfied with the results produced by the criminal justice system and continue to work to improve their system. Finland has relied heavily on science in guiding its social policies. The principles guiding Finnish penal policy are aimed at preserving the rights of offenders while also ensuring that people are punished for their criminal acts.

FINNISH RECIDIVISM STUDY

Recidivism as a term is broadly used to refer to re-offending within a specified period of time after discharge from imprisonment and in this research, following the international praxis, persons sentenced to at least two unconditional prison sentences are usually considered as recidivists. One of the most significant discoveries in the study of recidivism by Anssi Keinänen and Tuukka Saarimaa in their research "Empirical Analysis of Recidivism of Finnish Prisoners" is that a relatively large number of crimes in Finland are committed by a small number of individuals,[2] which leads to a controversial belief that if it would be possible to identify those likely to commit crimes, the crimes could be prevented by selective incapacitation. The Penal Code of Finland grants the courts a choice between applying conditional or unconditional sentences, leaving it to the discretion of the judge, except for cases where seriousness of the offence, the guilt of the offender as manifest in the offence or the criminal history of the offender necessitates the application of an unconditional prison sentence.[3]

Recidivism is influenced, besides legislation and court praxis, by the length of the follow-up. The longer the released prisoners are followed by the authorities the higher the proportion of those caught committing a new crime. A part of those released are left outside the follow-up because of immigration. These fractions that are not the nationals of the country, upon their release can be deported to their native country, while some may be in institutional care making the likelihood of recidivism smaller.

Notwithstanding, the research carried out by Kimmo Hypén, a senior officer in the Criminal Sanctions Agency in Finland, on Finnish Recidivism shows that the rate is falling:

> Of the offenders for the first time in prison back to prison return 35% but only a few of them end up in the actual prison cycle. Based on the results, the idea of the great probability of ending up in prison cycle is false.[4]

Hypén's research was based on offenders who had been convicted to an unconditional prison sentence and who had been released between 1993 and 2001. His data was collected from the central prisoner register, which includes data on 30,000 separate individuals and their 100,000 prison terms. In his research on *Fewer Offenders Than Thought Caught in Prison Cycle*[5] he points out that in "the years 1993-1997, 40 per cent of the released first-timers started a new, unconditional prison sentence during five years after release".[6]

According to records from the Finnish prison data bank, the Criminal Sanctions Agency stipulated that "[t]he probability of re-entering prison many times is extremely small: under ten in a hundred of the first-timers return to prison over six times".[7] This low rate in comparison to the Western world is due to the humane treatment of prisoners in compliance with the country's penal code system. With a recidivism rate of 35 percent, Finland has one of the lowest rates of repeat offenders, which can be attributed to various sources. Patrik Törnudd[8] notes that the low recidivism rate is a result of the fact that "those experts who were in charge of planning the reforms and research shared an almost unanimous conviction that Finland's internationally high prisoner rate at the beginning was a disgrace and that it would be possible to significantly reduce the amount and length of prison sentences without serious repercussions on the crime situation". This attitude is currently shared by civil servants, the judiciary, prison authorities and even the politicians.[9]

Crime control has never been a central political issue in Finnish election campaigns, unlike in many other western countries. Finnish politicians rarely relied on populist rhetoric, such as 'three strikes' and 'truth in sentencing'. The industrial urban welfare state of Finland, coupled with the good judgment of the Finnish politicians to interact and coexist with the penological experts could be attributed to less interference of politicians (partisan politics) in the Finnish criminal policy making. This is reflected in the *Sentences Enforcement Act* sets the following requirements on the Prison Service, which emphasizes human dignity:

1. Punishment is a mere loss of liberty: The enforcement of sentence must be organized so that the sentence is only loss of liberty. Other restrictions can be used to the extent that the security of custody and the prison order require.
2. Prevention of harm, promoting of placement into society: Punishment shall be enforced so that it does not unnecessarily impede but, if possible, promotes a prisoner's placement in society. Harms caused by imprisonment must be prevented, if possible.
3. Normality: The circumstances in a penal institution must be organized so that they correspond to those prevailing in the rest of society.
4. Justness, respect for human dignity, prohibition of discrimination: Prisoners must be treated justly and respecting their human dignity. Prisoners may not be placed without grounds in an unequal position because of their race, nationality or ethnic origin, skin color, language, gender, age, family status, sexual orientation or state of health or religion, social opinion, political or labor activities or other such similar things.
5. Special needs of juvenile prisoners: When implementing a sanction sentenced to a juvenile offender, special attention must be paid to the special needs caused by the prisoner's age and stage of development.
6. Hearing prisoners: A prisoner must be heard when a decision is being made concerning his/her placing in dwelling, work or other activity and some other important matter connected to his/her treatment.
7. Prisoners have a right to vote and they exercise this right in prisons.

LIFE IN FINNISH PRISON

Finland is a country that imprisons fewer of its citizens than any other country in the European Union. An ex-inmate from a Finnish prison rightly illustrates the gentleness of the country's penal institutions by saying: "*If I have to be a prisoner again, I will be happy to be one in Finland because I trust the Finnish system*". Looking at Finland's penal institutions, whether those systems are categorized as "open" or "closed" prisons, it is hard to tell when you have entered the world of custody. A warden in the Hameenlinna penitentiary, a Finnish prison, normally says when welcoming visitors to the institution: *"this is a closed prison, but you may have noticed you just drove in, and there was no gate blocking you"*.

Walls and fences have been removed in favor of unobtrusive camera surveillance and electronic alert networks. Instead of clanging iron gates, metal passageways and grim cells, there are linoleum-floored hallways lined with living spaces for prisoners that resemble dormitory rooms more than lockups in a typical prison. Guards in Finnish prisons are unarmed and wear either civilian clothes or uniforms free of emblems like chevrons and epaulettes. As the warden proudly explained *"there are 10 guns in this prison, and they are all in his safe, and that the only time he takes them out is for transfer of prisoners"*.

At "open" prisons where gentle justice is highly transposed, prisoners and guards address each other by first name, contrary to the prison cultures in most countries, where prisoners are addressed by numbers (Ekunwe, 2007). Prison superintendents in Finland go by non-military titles like manager or governor, and prisoners are sometimes referred to as *clients* or, if they are youths, *pupils*. Kirsti Nieminen, governor of the Kerava prison that specializes in rehabilitating young offenders normally explains to the guest visiting the institution that they play the role of parents to these prisoners.

Prison officials can give up to twenty days solitary confinement to convicts as punishment for infractions like fighting or possessing drugs, though the usual term ranges from three to five days. The guards even try to avoid that by first talking out the problem with the offending prisoner, as was highly emphasized by a supervisor at Hameenlinna Prison (ibid). In one of her discussions the supervisor stated that in Finland we *"believe that the loss of freedom is the major punishment, so we try to make it as nice inside as possible"*. She went on to explain that thirty years ago Finland had a rigid model inherited from neighboring Russia and one of the highest rates of imprisonment in Europe. But then academics provoked a thoroughgoing rethinking of penal policy, relying principally on the argument that it ought to reflect the region's liberal theories of social organization.

As noted by Tapio Lappi-Seppala, director of the National Research Institute of Legal Policy, Finnish penal policy is exceptionally expert-oriented. He explained in his article "The fall of the Finnish prison population", that Finland believes in the moral-creating and value-shaping effect of punishment instead of punishment as retribution. He asserted that over the last two decades, more than 40,000 Finns had been spared prison, $20 million in costs had been saved, and the crime rate had gone down to relatively low Scandinavian levels. Finland is a relatively classless culture with a Scandinavian belief in the benevolence of the state and a trust in its civic institutions, representing something of a laboratory for gentle justice. The kinds of economic and social disparities that can produce violence largely do not exist in Finland's welfare state society where street crime is low and law enforcement officials can count on support from a supportive public.

Markku Salminen, the former director general of the Finnish prison service once said, "*I know this system sounds like a curiosity, but if you visit our prisons and walk our streets, you will see that this very mild version of law enforcement works*". He also accredited the politicians with keeping the law-and-order debate civil and not strident. He pointed out that in Finland the newspapers are not full of sex and crime as in other countries, and due to this, there is no pressure on him to get tough on criminals from populist-issue politicians like there would be in other countries.

Finnish courts dispense four general punishments: a fine, a conditional sentence, which amounts to probation, community service and an unconditional sentence. The last category, which is widely used, is made less harsh by a practice of letting prisoners out after only half their term is served. Like the rest of the countries of the European Union, Finland has no death penalty. According to the Ministry of Justice in Helsinki, in 2006, there were a little more than 2,700 prisoners in Finland, a country of 5.2 million people, or 52 for every 100,000 inhabitants. This rate of incarceration is considerably lower than many European Union countries and is much lower than rates in Russia and United States.

DEVELOPMENT OF SUPERVISORY PROBATIONARY FREEDOM IN FINLAND

The gentleness of Finnish justice extended further to include Supervised Probationary Freedom. This system was first implemented in Finland in October 2006, where prisoners are released from prison up to six months prior to the actual parole date if certain prerequisites are met. The framework for probationary freedom enables individual methods of implementation according to the needs of the specific prisoner.

The preconditions for probationary freedom are defined in the Penal Code (39/1889). Firstly, probationary freedom must promote the implementation of the individual sentence plan, which describes the terms for serving the sentence, for the release from prison and for parole. Secondly, prison personnel evaluate whether the prisoner in question will probably follow the terms defined for his/her probationary freedom. This evaluation is based on the information concerning the conduct of the prisoner during his/her sentence, on his/her personality and on his/her criminal background. In addition, the prisoner has to agree to follow the terms defined for him/her, to be supervised and to let the officials be in contact with each other, as well as private communities and persons in matters having to do with the probationary freedom of the prisoner.

When granted probationary freedom, the prisoner is required to live at home, at a half-way house or at a rehabilitation institution, and is expected to take part in constructive activities such as work, studying and rehabilitation. They are supervised by correctional officers via mobile phone tracking, visits to home and workplace, as well as phone conversations. Case-specific restrictions are defined for each person granted probationary freedom. Usually, the person is allowed to move in a restricted area (e.g. within city limits) and he/she must remain at home during night-time. In addition, the use of alcohol and other intoxicants is prohibited.

The background for introducing probationary freedom into the Finnish penal system lies in certain redefinitions of penal policy, as well as the development of related international laws such as human rights conventions. The aim of the Finnish penal policy has been to transform serving a prison sentence into a more predictable and systematic process in which a prisoner is given the chance of gradually gaining license to greater freedom of movement. The implementation of probationary freedom may also be seen as a manifestation of the shift of focus in correctional services towards so-called "community punishments" (e.g. community service). One of the main objectives is to decrease the use of incarceration by emphasizing sanctions that both cost less and are more effective in preventing recidivism.

DISCUSSION

Comparative research poses numerous challenges, but one does wonder if the remarkable results produced in Finland over the past half century could be replicated elsewhere such as the United States. What is interesting is that in the early 1960s, both Finland and the United States embarked on liberal social and criminal justice models, with an emphasis on expanding the rights of offenders, the rehabilitation of offenders, limiting the use of incarceration to serious offenders, and assisting in the reentry of ex-offenders back into society.

However, the 1970s produced divergent paths for the two countries (Ekunwe and Jones, 2011). For the United States, there was a conservative backlash, both for social and criminal justice policy, which shifted the blame for social problems on the individual and produced the 'war on drugs', mass incarceration with long prison sentences, and a subsequent reduction in prison programming due to the cost of building new prisons. The size of the American prison population increased dramatically, representing more than one-third of the entire population of Finland. For Finland, they have continued on the path begun in 1960. Avoiding the harsh rhetoric of political conservatives, Finnish criminal justice policy is directed by sound research and is aimed at preserving the rights of defendants and prisoners, while also ensuring that people are punished for their criminal acts.

So, how does one explain these divergent paths? First, the United States has a history of reliance on individual responsibility, a distrust of government, and as a result, there is no inherent belief that people have a right to health care or that one should expect government to provide basic social support for its citizens. In addition, capitalism embraces a competitive ideology, which produces winners and losers, and it is the goal of winning that sustains one's belief in the system. Finland, on the other hand, embraces democratic socialism and demonstrates tremendous faith in government institutions to preserve the human rights of all of its citizens, which includes health care, education, and meeting one's basic needs for survival.

This paper has demonstrated the effects of liberal policies in Finland that have produced gentle justice and low recidivism rates. Not completely satisfied with their current low rates of recidivism, Finland continues to seek ways to continue to improve their system, as is evidenced by the creation of supervised probationary freedom and the intention of reducing the number of closed prisons and replacing them with open prisons. But, what about the implications of the United States returning to harsh punishment? Richards *et al.* (2004) have referred to a "perpetual incarceration machine", a system that recycles offenders in and out of prison in an endless cycle. One reason for this is referred to as the collateral consequences of incarceration, which includes the stigma of a prison record, numerous job restrictions and the loss of voting rights, which make it difficult for ex-offenders to successfully re-enter society (see Mauer and Chesney-Lind, 2002). Most men and women in the United States leave prison with few job prospects, without adequate housing, and with few prospects for change. It is no surprise, then, that prison staff often tell ex-cons as they leave the prison that "we will see you back soon".

While it is unlikely that the United States will ever adopt policies similar to those of Finland, it could learn much from what has worked in Finland. First, reduce the profit from political rhetoric, as well as from the prison industrial complex. American criminal justice policy could benefit from relying on empirical research, rather than political rhetoric or ideology. Secondly, Finland has demonstrated that gentle justice can produce positive results and that harsh punishment produces the opposite outcome. It is no wonder that long and harsh sentences would make it much more difficult on a person attempting to re-enter society and the recidivism rate in the United States supports that notion. Finally, reducing the negative impact of a felony conviction and the stigma that is associated with it would go a long way in helping ex-offenders begin life anew with a clean slate. When President Eisenhower warned the American public to beware of the military-industrial complex, he could have easily been speaking about the prison industrial complex. While wasting billions upon billions of dollars on weapons that will never be used, the United States also spends billions upon billions of dollars on a criminal justice system that does not reduce crime, but instead maintains it (Reiman and Leighton, 2009).

ENDNOTES

[1] Several of Finnish Ministers of Justice during the 1970s and 1980s were in direct contact with research work. Indeed, one of them, Inkeri Anttila, was a professor of criminal law and the director of the National Research Institute of Legal Policy at the time of her appointment as Minister.

[2] See Anssi Keinänen and Tuukka Saarimaa article on "Empirical Analysis of Recidivism of Finnish Prisoners" online at <http://www.joensuu.fi/taloustieteet/ott/scandale/copenhagen/keinanen_anssi_and_saarimaa_tuukka%20NEW.pdf>.

[3] The Penal Code of Finland, chapter 6, section 9.

[4]   See <www.rikosseuraamus.fi/25232.htm>.

[5]   Ibid.

[6]   Kimmo Hypén further stipulates that the number of convicts receiving a new prison sentence hardly grew after five follow-up years even when this period was extended up to ten years (see ibid).

[7]   See "The released from prison in Finland 1993-2001 and the re-entered" online at <http://www.rikosseuraamus.fi/25234.htm>.

[8]   Patrik Törnudd, a Finnish criminologist, stressed the importance of the political will and consensus in bringing down the prisoner rate in his book Fifteen Years of Decreasing Prisoner Rates in Finland (1993) available online at <www.unicri.it/ wwk/documentation/lmsdb.php?id_=911&vw_=f>.

[9]   Finnish politicians do not oppose the reform proposals prepared by the Ministry of Justice, but instead work with the experts on penological matters without making it a political campaign issue.

REFERENCES

Aho, T. and V. Karsikas (1980) "Vankien taustaan ja vankilukuun liittyviä tilastoja 1881–1978", *Vankeinhoidon historiaprojektin julkaisu* (3),   Helsinki (FI): Oikeusministeriön vankeinhoito-osasto.

Anttila, I. (1981) "Kansainväliset vaikutteet Suomen vankeinhoidon kehityksessä", in E. Suominen (ed.), *Suomen vankeinhoidon historiaa, Osa 1*, Helsinki (FI): Valtion painatuskeskus,

Ekunwe, I. O. (2007) *Gentle Justice: Analysis of Open Prison Systems in Finland: A Way to the Future?*, Tampere (FI): University of Tampere Press.

Ekunwe, I. O. and R. S. Jones (2011) "Doing Re-entry: Accounts of Post-prison Release in Finland and the United States", in I. O. Ekunwe and R. S. Jones (eds.), *Global Perspectives on Re-entry*, Tampere (FI): University of Tampere Press, pp. 443-469.

Falck, S., H. von Hofer and A. Storgaard (2003) *Nordic Criminal Statistics 1950-2000, Report 3*, Stockholm: Department of Criminology – Stockholm University.

Hannula, I. (1981) "Vankeinhoitoon liittyvän lainsäädännön historiaa 1881–1975", in E. Suominen (ed.), *Suomen vankeinhoidon historiaa, Osa 1*, Helsinki (FI): Valtion painatuskeskus.

Keinänen, A. and S. Tuukka (2006) *Empirical Analysis of Recidivism of Finnish Prisoners*, available online <http://www.joensuu.fi/taloustieteet/ott/scandale/ copenhagen/keinanen_anssi_and_saarimaa_tuukka%20NEW.pdf>.

Lappi-Seppälä, T. (2000) "The Fall of the Finnish Prison Population", *Journal of Scandinavian Studies in Criminology and Crime Prevention*, 1(1): 27-40.

Lappi-Seppälä, T. (1982) "Teilipyörästä terapiaan –piirteitä rangaistusjärjestelmän historista", *Vankeinhoidon historianprojektin julkaisu*, 9, Helsinki (FI): Oikeusministeriön vankeinhoito-osasto.

Matinpuro, R. (1981) "Vankien oikeudet ja vankilajärjestys 1918–1975", *Vankeinhoidon historiaprojektin julkaisu*, 4, Helsinki (FI): Oikeusministeriön vankeinhoito-osasto.

Mauer, M. and M. Chesney-Lind (eds.) (2002) *Invisible Punishment: The Collateral Consequences of Mass Imprisonment*, New York: The New Press.

Myllylä, A. (1998) "Vankeiopiston lyhyt historia", *Suomalaisen kontrollipolitiikan arviointia marraskuun liikkeen täyttäessä 30 vuotta*, Vantaa (FI): Tietosanoma oy.

Pajuoja, J. (1998) "Marraskuun liike seuraavan sukupolven silmin", *Suomalaisen kontrollipolitiikan arviointia marraskuun liikkeen täyttäessä 30 vuotta*, Vantaa (FI): Tietosanoma oy.

Pyykkönen, L. (1998) "30 vuotta Marraskuun liikkeen jälkeen", *Suomalaisen kontrollipolitiikan arviointia marraskuun liikkeen täyttäessä 30 vuotta*, Vantaa, FI: Tietosanoma oy.

The Penal Code of Finland (39/1889; amendments up to 650/2003 as well as 1372/2003, 650/2004 and 1006/2004 included): Unofficial translation Ministry of Justice, Finland. Available online at <http://www.finlex.fi/en/laki/kaannokset/1889/en18890039.pdf>.

Reiman, J. (2009) *The Rich Get Richer and the Poor Get Prison: Ideology, Class, and Criminal Justice*, Upper Saddle River (NY): Prentice Hall.

Richards, S. C., J. Austin and R. S. Jones (2004) "Kentucky's Perpetual Prisoner Machine: It's About Money", *Policy Studies Journal*, 21(1): 93-106.

Törnudd, Patrik (1993). "Fifteen Years of Decreasing Prisoner Rates in Finland", *Research Communication*, 8, Helsinki (FI): National Research Institute of Legal Policy. Available online at <www.unicri.it/wwk/documentation/lmsdb. php?id_=911&vw_=f>.

ABOUT THE AUTHORS

Ikponwosa O. Ekunwe, PhD, is an ex-convict now Academy of Finland Postdoctoral Research Fellow at the School of Management/Politics, University of Tampere, Finland. His current research project "Making It in the Free World: Strategies for Successful Re-entry", which is being funded by the Academy of Finland, is a study of the reentry experience of ex-convicts in Finland who have made a successful transition into the free world.

Richard S. Jones, PhD, is an ex-convict now Professor of Sociology at Marquette University. He is the author of the books *Doing Time: Prison Experience and Identity* (with Tom Schmid) and *Global Perspectives on Re-entry* (with Ikponwosa O. Ekunwe). He has also published in the areas of prison experience, social identity and the problems of reentry faced by previously incarcerated individuals.

RESPONSE

John Irwin and the Convict Criminology Code
Katherine Irwin

This issue of the *Journal of Prisoners on Prisons* (JPP) is dedicated, in part, to my father John Irwin, who was many things to many people. To some, he was the original felonious criminologist, a member of the Prisoners' Union, and the founder of Project Rebound, a program to turn former prisoners into college students. To others, my father was a prison scholar, with several seminal books to his name. And to Convict Criminologists and convicts, he was a talkative and interested guy who felt more comfortable circulating with outlaws than with straight folk. As Dad's daughter, it is an honor to respond to this issue of *JPP* in the spirit of my father's life and work.

As indicated by all of the manuscripts in this edition, Convict Criminology (CC) research offers several insightful contributions to the literature on punishment with the potential to correct the many misconceptions about convicts and imprisonment. Despite my academic support for the CC work and my excitement about the future of CC scholarship, my reaction to the achievements in this volume is personal. In fact, I see several moral threads that tie my father's most closely held beliefs to the CC tradition. After serving a five-year sentence for armed robbery, Dad organized his life around overcoming the degradation of prison on an individual and collective level. Moreover, Dad's agenda as a scholar, activist, and father was dedicated to clearly articulating a path away from the indignities of incarceration and towards a consequential life. It is not surprising then that I should read these fine manuscripts by other CC scholars and recognize the lessons that many of us learned from John Irwin. In the following, I outline a few of Dad's many instructions – or as his children refer to them, Dad's "lectures" – about how to live a useful and meaningful life.

BE A HUMANITARIAN

In his writing and talks, my father communicated a humanitarian message succinctly and clearly. What most criminologists did not, and still often do not realize, is that convicts are not psychologically damaged, emotionally sick and dangerous predators. They are human beings. While simple, this insight is profoundly instructive. When Dad started writing about prison in the late 1960s and 1970s, he dedicated his work to the "more than 200,000 convicts presently 'doing time' in the United States". Not surprisingly, scholars who were worried about the treatment of prisoners during this period also comprised a minority group. Today there are more than two million convicts "doing time" and, consequently, prison has become a fashionable topic among criminologists. Being a humanitarian means caring about prison as a central moral concern regardless of whether two, two hundred thousand or two million people are incarcerated.

My father argued that prison is a problematic institution deserving critical attention because imprisonment is a dehumanizing experience not only for prisoners, but also for their families, friends and communities. Here, the humanitarianism of CC scholars comes to the fore in the idea that our lives are inextricably intertwined with others. Therefore, it is more than just the individual prisoner who serves time. His or her children, partner, parents, neighbors and many others are all variously doing their own time as well.

Dad believed that solutions to the problems of prison were also based in humanist principles, including interconnection and mutual respect. In Project Rebound, my father supported the "each one teach one" model of mentorship in which each ex-convict college student can be a resource for others who are re-entering. Dad's collectivist approach, however, went deeper than mentorship or organizing a social movement and, instead, cut to the core of his effervescent personality and lifestyle. My father and my stepmother Marsha loved parties, conversation, and celebrations. As a result, the family home was a central location for gatherings of all kinds, including meetings, dinner parties, dance parties, football parties, and regular Friday night get-togethers that included family, students, friends, colleagues, ex-convicts, local activists, and Project Rebound members. A good measure of laugher, discussion, and storytelling helped to grease the wheels of camaraderie and mutual trust among this diverse collection of collaborators.

Dad's social ease did not diminish with age. Up until the last few weeks of his life, he regularly visited local prisons to hang out with new and old friends. On occasion, one of my father's friends would be released, and Dad was often there to help in the transition by locating jobs and places to live, as well as introducing these ex-cons to his circle of friends and colleagues. This goes beyond mentorship, entering the realm of companionship and connection that Dad believed was necessary to overcome prisonization.

It is not surprising to me, therefore, that the CC movement is more than a research tradition. It is also a support group. There is great power in a collective, and my father would be the first to advocate that each of us sustain an intellectual community by reaching out to like-minded people on the other side of prison walls and the academy. Although the criminal justice system often prohibits prisoner organizations, and connections between and among ex-cons, convicts are certainly not the only individuals dedicated to combating the negative effects of incarceration. In the 1970s, Dad and other prisoners' rights activists acknowledged the contributions of lawyers, students, researchers, and religious leaders. Dad would be the first person to advocate for those who are re-entering to make connections with justice advocates, concerned individuals and other sympathetic people within their communities. Moreover, as the CC community illustrates, our everyday lives, thoughts and work are richer, more rewarding, and certainly more plentiful when we nurture a collection of people who are dedicated to the same goals.

BE A ROGUE

Believing that the only occupation appropriate for ex-cons involved manual labor, members of the California Board of Parole consistently encouraged my father to learn a trade while in prison and give up his dream of going to college. Being a bit of a rogue, my father usually did not follow the advice of those in the "establishment" and he certainly did not concern himself with what others thought about him. He was driven by his own moral proscriptions and, thus, he ignored the Parole Board's advice. Upon release he enrolled in college and later in a PhD program. Even in the late 1950s and 1960s, when the U.S. prison population was relatively small, he knew that he would encounter considerable derision, and he was prepared to forge new and unpopular pathways. For criminologists and those exiting prison, Dad's tradition of being a bit of a rogue exemplifies how individuals can buck the current system and speak out or write against the status quo.

Despite Dad's habit of saying and doing unpopular things, he acknowledged that it was much harder to be a rogue today than it was in the 1960s and 1970s – a time when there was a certain amount of tolerance for social movements and rule breakers. Today, convicts are one of the most feared and hated groups in society, leading my father to argue that convicts are treated as "whipping dogs for others' sadistic and psychopathic hatred". The common condemnation of convicts means that being a rogue might not be an option for those who fear for their survival, inside and outside of prison.

Given the contemporary climate, the CC movement has more than just the potential to dramatically change prison scholarship – it is also instrumental for millions who have re-entered society. For example, last year, I had five students separately tell me that they had criminal justice records and none wanted the rest of the class to know. In addition, another ten students discussed having family members who had been in prison. America's incarceration binge has brought prison closer to our homes and classrooms, and I am so thankful to have a large collection of CC scholarship to prove that each of these apprehensive students is not alone. This would not be possible if previous CC scholars had listened to the voice of the establishment by avoiding college and had remained quiet about their experiences. For their courage, I am most thankful.

BE RESPONSIBLE

My father consistently espoused the belief that we all have to accept responsibility for our mistakes. He understood that humans make many mistakes, some of which could have been avoided with careful consideration and good decision-making skills – but not all. As an example, in the early years of Dad's criminal justice work, he and his colleagues were convinced that the discretionary powers of judges was to blame for punitive sentencing decisions in the 1970s, and they vociferously campaigned against non-equitable, arbitrary and indeterminate sentencing. Twenty years later, Dad and many others learned that with determinate sentencing after the 1980s came more and harsher punishments. He and his colleagues quickly spoke out about the downsides of their early policy stance and revised their recommendations.

Being responsible also means that my father encouraged others to consult with as many individuals as possible before advocating for any particular policy. Although he had experienced prison first hand, Dad never felt comfortable relying exclusively on his personal biography to make sense of criminal justice theory, policy or practice. In fact, CC scholars and prisoners' rights advocates have embraced the idea that including a diverse cross-section of voices in policymaking can only lead to better policies and practices. In the 1970s, for example, one of the founding principles of the Prisoners' Union was that individuals who are serving time should have a say in the practices that affect them, including visitation, research on prisoners, grievance systems, pay for prison labor, access to adequate health care and access to meaningful programming, to name just a few. This just seemed like sane policymaking.

Being responsible by considering as many viewpoints as possible also points to future directions for the CC movement. The CC papers in this volume include some voices but not others. I am especially eager to hear more from women and juveniles, whose experiences have been a cornerstone of prisoners' rights advocacy in the past. Also, I am eager for Latinos, Asians, and indigenous people of America, the Pacific Islands, and the Caribbean to offer their narratives to the expanding CC story. I have no doubt that as this tradition continues Convict Criminology will be able to draw more diverse voices and perspectives into the fold.

ABOUT THE AUTHOR

Katherine Irwin, PhD, is an Associate Professor of Sociology at the University of Hawaii, Manoa. She has conducted research in the areas of youth culture, women and drug use, youth violence, girls in the juvenile justice system, and youth violence prevention programs. Her work has been published in a number of journals such as *Contemporary Drug Problems*, *Critical Criminology*, *Qualitative Sociology*, *Sociology Compass*, *Sociological Spectrum*, *Symbolic Interaction*, *Youth and Society*, and *Youth Violence and Juvenile Justice*, among others.

Reflections on Convict Criminology
Robert Johnson

In response to this thorough and thoughtful issue of the *Journal of Prisoners on Prisons* (JPP), I would like to reflect on how I came to appreciate this valuable, indeed essential, perspective on prisons and imprisonment. I came to study Convict Criminology (CC) because of several key people, and through those people, hundreds of prisoners who were willing to talk and write about their experiences behind bars.

The first person to expose me to the theoretical perspective that eventually became known as CC was Hans Toch, who showed me how to do prisoner interviews and listen carefully to what the prisoners had to say about their world, a world very different from my own. Toch helped me to listen to prisoners as they grappled with the "pains of imprisonment" on their own terms – terms we tried to present in our work together, notably *The Pains of Imprisonment* (1982) and *Crime and Punishment: Inside Views* (2000). The second person was John Irwin, honored in this journal issue. As a graduate student, I admired John's first book, *The Felon* (1970), but thought he was too hard on the prison staff. At the time, I was doing a study of officers who formed what I came to call "informal helping networks" to assist prisoners in crisis. John rather patiently listened to me, and suggested I sample a broader range of officers before I came to conclusions on the nature of prison staff and their effectiveness. By the same token, John was willing to look at the work I was doing and factor it into his thinking. For me, that was an early lesson in open-mindedness, which reinforced nicely what Hans Toch was trying to teach me and his other students.

Among those other students of Toch's was Tom Bernard, also honored in this issue of the *JPP*, who studied at State University of New York Albany with me in the 1970s. Tom was the third person in my education about Convict Criminology. Some years back, Tom discovered a thoughtful prisoner named Victor Hassine, who asked Tom to read a manuscript he was writing. Tom agreed and the end result was the first edition of *Life Without Parole: Living in Prison Today* (1996). A few editions later, Tom asked me to come on board and help edit Victor's work. Eventually, I took over the main editorship, working with graduate students at American University – first Ania Dobrzanska (on the fourth edition, 2008), now with the Department of Justice, and then Sonia Tabriz (on the fifth and current edition, 2011), now a law student at the George Washington School of Law. None of these subsequent editions would have been possible without the original work of

Tom Bernard. I knew Victor, in particular, was deeply grateful to Tom and proud to have a book published by Oxford University Press.

The fourth person who was integral to my thinking about Convict Criminology was Victor Hassine. Over the years we became friends, talking over the phone every week. We wrote fiction individually and together, much of that creative writing found in the book, *Lethal Rejection: Stories on Crime and Punishment* (2009). Victor also contributed to a small press I run, *BleakHouse Publishing*, one goal of which is to give a voice to the voiceless including, of course, convicts. Two notable examples are Charles Huckelbury, who published a book of poetry with the press entitled *Tales From The Purple Penguin* (2008), and Erin George, whose book of poetry, *Origami Heart* (2009) was also published by my press. Sadly, Victor took his life in 2008, during the twenty-seventh year of his confinement. The current edition of Victor's book features an examination of his prison journey as a whole, from its difficult beginnings to its tragic conclusion. The new title, *Life Without Parole: Living and Dying in Prison* (2010), captures the sad trajectory of Victor's life, and indeed the likely fate of all prisoners sentenced to life without parole, who are serving what I and other authors have called "America's other death penalty". Victor's death was a blow to many convicts and to all of us who knew and admired him. It is hard to imagine a person who worked harder to earn a shot at freedom and who, moreover, had clearly established that he had much to contribute to society. To honor his life, we at *BleakHouse Publishing* created an award in his name, The Victor Hassine Memorial Fellowship, generously funded by the Hassine family.

There are now several key figures in the CC Group, notably Stephen C. Richards and Jeffrey Ian Ross, who coined the term "Convict Criminology" and have pushed hard to get recognition for this original and important work, and those who contribute to their voices. Richards and Ross (2001, 2004) co-authored the article "The New School of Convict Criminology" and then co-edited the seminal book *Convict Criminology* (2003), which features eight autobiographical chapters by ex-con professors. This wonderful edition of the aptly named journal, the *Journal of Prisoners on Prisons*, would not have been possible without them and the many writers they have supported and encouraged over the years.

Over the past 15 years, the CC Group has worked to promote and expand the collaboration of academic criminologists and convicts. This Group is composed of ex-con professors and "noncon" professors, like myself.

The CC Perspective includes a remarkable collection of published work, which has profoundly improved what we know, not just about the prison world, but also about how a small number of prisoners survive the ordeal of imprisonment and then go on to work their way through graduate degrees to join the academic ranks. The ex-con professors took on the hard work mentoring and advising prisoners exiting prison to enter universities, and eventually complete their doctorates. This effort has produced a growing number of hybrid authors, convicts that became criminology professors, like many of the authors in this collection of articles.

I am honored to have the opportunity to write about my experiences studying CC, and to be associated with so many original and important voices that have shaped my continuing education on crime and punishment. In addition to those persons mentioned above, I would like to offer a special thanks to Susan Nagelsen, an original creative writer and frequent writing partner of Charles Huckelbury, noted briefly above, himself an award-winning creative writer, and Erin George, also noted briefly above, who, in addition to her evocative poetry, has written *A Woman Doing Life* (2010), a remarkable ethnography of her life in a prison published by Oxford University Press. Happily for me, Nagelsen, Huckelbury and George serve as staff members for *BleakHouse Publishing*, together working to give the press a distinctive and inclusive voice on matters relating to crime, punishment, and social justice.

Today, prisoners have many venues for their voice to be heard. The *JPP*, CC Group publications and website, as well as *BleakHouse Publishing*, all provide space for the creative and intellectual expression and aspirations of these men and women, who have much to teach us about prison life and the dream of freedom that sustains them.

REFERENCES

George, E. (2010) *A Woman Doing Life: Notes From a Prison for Women*, Oxford (UK): Oxford University Press.

George, E. (2009) *Origami Heart: Poems by a Woman Doing Life*, Washington (D.C.): BleakHouse Publishing.

Hassine, V. (2011) *Life Without Parole: Living and Dying in Prison Today*, Oxford (UK): Oxford University Press.

Huckelbury, C. (2008) *Tales From the Purple Penguin*, Washington (D.C.): BleakHouse Publishing.

Irwin, J. (1970) *The Felon*, Berkeley: University of California Press.
Johnson, R. and S. Tabriz (eds.) (2009) *Lethal Rejection: Stories on Crime and Punishment*, Durham (NC): Carolina Academic Press.
Johnson, R. and H. Toch (1982) *The Pains of Imprisonment*, Los Angeles: Sage Publications.
Johnson, R. and H. Toch (2000) *Crime and Punishment: Inside Views*, Oxford (UK): Oxford University Press.
Richards, S. C. and J. I. Ross (2004) "The New School of Convict Criminology", *Journal of Prisoners on Prisons*, 13: 11-26
Richards, S. C. and J. I. Ross (2001) "The New School of Convict Criminology", *Social Justice*, 28(1): 177-190.
Ross, J. I. and S. C. Richards (eds.) (2003) *Convict Criminology*, Belmont (CA): Wadsworth.

ABOUT THE AUTHOR

Robert Johnson is a Professor of Justice, Law and Society at American University and Editor of BleakHouse Publishing. Johnson is a widely published author of fiction and non-fiction. His short story, "The Practice of Killing", won a national fiction contest sponsored by *Wild Violet* magazine. Johnson's best known work of social science, *Death Work: A Study of the Modern Execution Process*, won the Outstanding Book Award of the Academy of Criminal Justice Sciences.

A Challenge From and
A Challenge to Convict Criminology
Mike Larsen and Justin Piché

In criminology, attempts to destabilize the field are frequent (Hil and Robertson, 2003, p. 91), as old debates are rehashed in an attempt to reconstitute the raison d'être and the modus operandi of the discipline (Martel *et al.*, 2006, p. 636). Often, these discussions focus on methodological practice (e.g. Austin, 2003) or the application of social theory (e.g. Matthews, 2009). Agenda setting conversations outlining specific questions that require criminological attention (e.g. Zedner, 2007), as well as whether and how scholars should engage in normative politics (e.g. Chancer and McLaughlin, 2007), also feature prominently in the literature. Rare, however, are interventions that put into question the whole enterprise in a manner that challenges the core assumptions of the discipline itself and provokes a reorientation of the way scholars conduct research (e.g. Taylor *et al.*, 1973; Cohen, 1988).

Convict Criminology (Ross and Richards, 2003; Richards, 2009) is among the most recent attempts to provoke such a discussion. As gleaned in this issue, those who identify as Convict Criminologists generally critique their mainstream colleagues for uncritically making use of state constructed descriptors (e.g. 'crime', 'community corrections') and categories (e.g. 'criminal') in their analyses, for marginalizing and/or completely silencing the voices of the criminalized, and for deploying theories and methodologies that produce knowledge that does not map onto the realities of victimization, criminalization, and punishment that they themselves have encountered. To differentiate themselves from their mainstream counterparts Convict Criminologists integrate their firsthand experience as criminalized individuals into their criminological analyses. In so doing, the argument is advanced that a richer understanding of penality is produced and a new school or perspective of criminology emerges.

As Co-managing Editors of the *Journal of Prisoners of Prisons*, a forum that aims "to bring the knowledge and experience of the incarcerated to bear upon [...] academic arguments and concerns, and to inform public discourse about the current state of our carceral institutions" (Gaucher, 1988, p. 54), we certainly agree with the need for, and importance of, having the voices of the criminalized at the centre of debates on punishment. The emergence of Convict Criminology has challenged many to revisit the questions of *who can know* or *who can be the knower* in criminology and Convict Criminologists are to be commended for this important contribution.

With this being said, we question claims that Convict Criminology currently represents a new school of thought or operates as a distinct perspective within the discipline. Our position is based on three particular observations. First, there appears to be a lack of a common vocabulary amongst the various contributions attributed to the Convict Criminology perspective. This suggests that there is an absence of a broader set of theoretical commitments that unifies them in a manner consistent with other approaches in criminology (e.g. Functionalist, Interactionist, Marxist, Feminist, Foucauldian).

Second, the diversity in research methods deployed, including autoethnography and surveys, has implications for the broader epistemological claim made by Convict Criminologists that experience – in this case the experience of victimization, criminalization and punishment – constitutes knowledge. In studies that veer away from methods that explicitly place experiential knowledge at the centre of research endeavors, it is unclear how it is incorporated into scholarship. This undermines the ability to maintain methodological coherence that is the cornerstone of scholarly perspectives. On a related note, if an emphasis on experiential knowledge is understood to be central to the Convict Criminology perspective, it is important to reflect on *whose* experiences and voices are consistently represented and whose are under-represented. As Katherine Irwin (this issue) notes, this collection and the collaborative intellectual project that gave rise to it would benefit from the inclusion of voices of women and other marginalized groups. In saying this, we acknowledge that the Convict Criminology Group is expanding, and we appreciate that maintaining an inclusive movement or initiative is an ongoing – and often challenging – undertaking.

Third, while it is clear that Convict Criminologists are involved in concrete actions on the ground as a matter of practice, the degree to which some authors reproduce the language of the state and its penal institutions in their own discourses, and as part of their participation in benevolently-couched programs of social control, needs to be addressed if Convict Criminology is to fulfill its promise of offering alternative understandings of victimization, criminalization and punishment. We note that many contributions are informed by critical or radical criminologies, incorporating critiques of organized oppression and class conflict, and working to demystify the languages and logics of the carceral. Others, including some contributions to this special issue, make use of elements of official vocabularies and 'controltalk' (Cohen, 1985) without problematizing them.

The Group's website, drawing on Ross and Richards (2003), proposes that "Convict Criminology represents the work of convicts or ex-convicts, in possession of a Ph.D. or on their way to completing one, or enlightened academics and practitioners, who contribute to a new conversation about crime and corrections" (see http://www.convictcriminology.org/about.htm). We suggest that this definition accurately reflects the body of work that is associated with Convict Criminology. It emphasizes the importance of shared experience and the pursuit of a novel conversation, without making explicit the theoretical and epistemological commitments of the Group. Accordingly, as it currently stands, Convict Criminology appears to be more of an example of standpoint theory than a fully-fledged scholarly perspective. This observation, like recent critiques concerning Cultural Criminology as a 'new' approach to criminological research (see Spencer, 2011), should not be read as an indictment. Nor should it be interpreted as an argument in favor of stultifying rigidity or uniformity in scholarly work. Rather, the issues we have raised here offer as an opening for proponents to clarify what is understood by Convict Criminology – theoretically, methodologically and normatively – as they continue to work towards developing a distinct perspective or new school of criminology. Such reflections would likely not only sharpen the critical edge of Convict Criminology, but also the discipline as a whole, which would benefit from more perspectives that are not intimately connected to the ideological and material reproduction of state repression.

REFERENCES

Austin, J. (2003) "Why Criminology Is Irrelevant", *Criminology and Public Policy*, 2(3): 557-564.
Chancer, L. and E. McLaughlin (2007) "Public Criminologies: Diverse Perspectives on Academia and Policy", *Theoretical Criminology*, 11(2): 155-173.
Cohen, S. (1988) *Against Criminology*, New Brunswick (NJ): Transaction Publishers.
Cohen, S. (1985) *Visions of Social Control*, Cambridge: Polity Press.
Gaucher, B. (1988) "The Prisoner as Ethnographer: The Journal of Prisoners on Prisons", *Journal of Prisoners on Prisons*, 1(1): 49-62.
Hil, R. and R. L. Robertson (2003) "What Sort of Future for Critical Criminology?", *Crime, Law and Social Change*, 39(1): 91-115.
Martel, J., B. Hogeveen and A. Woolford (2006) "The State of Critical Scholarship in Criminology and Socio-legal Studies in Canada", *Canadian Journal of Criminology and Criminal Justice*, 48(3): 634-662.
Matthews, R. (2009) "Beyond 'So What?' Criminology: Rediscovering Realism", *Theoretical Criminology*, 13(3): 341-362.

Richards, S.C. (2009) "A Convict Criminology Perspective on Community Punishment: Further Lessons from the Darkness of Prison", in J. I. Ross (ed.) *Cutting the Edge: Second Edition*, New Brunswick (NJ): Transaction Publishers: 105-120.

Ross, J. I. and S. C. Richards (eds.) (2003) Convict Criminology, Belmont (CA): Wadsworth.

Spencer, D. (2011) "Cultural Criminology: An Invitation... to What?", *Critical Criminology*, 19: 197-212.

Taylor, I., P. Walton and J. Young (1973) *The New Criminology: For a Social Theory of Deviance*, London: Routledge and Kegan Paul.

Zedner, L. (2003) "Pre-crime and Post-criminology", *Theoretical Criminology*, 11(2): 261-281.

ABOUT THE AUTHORS

Mike Larsen is an Instructor in the Criminology Department at Kwantlen Polytechnic University and Co-managing Editor of the *Journal of Prisoners on Prisons*.

Justin Piché is an Assistant Professor in the Department of Criminology at the University of Ottawa and Co-managing Editor of the *Journal of Prisoners on Prisons*.

COVER ART

Michael Lenza, PhD, is an ex-convict who is now an Associate Professor of Criminal Justice at the University of Wisconsin-Oshkosh. He has published on the death penalty, research ethics, medical marijuana, a historical political view of the development of mass incarceration in the USA, as well as theory and research methods. He is currently working on the institutional foundations of violence in the American context, and utilizing postmodern autoethnograpic theory and methods to provide voice to prisoners.

Front Cover: "When harmony fails, I go to where the rocks sleep"
Back Cover: "And become"

The poem and paintings were done when I was serving time and was still in max. As prisoners we had little choice but to deal with the contradictions within – who am I? Events out in the free world or a mere policy change could redefine us and our sentences like earthquakes roving through time. It could knock down flat that head trip of who we believed ourselves to be. Problem is you cannot exist as a man or women in any world without that 'me' or 'I'. In that crush of the quakes knocking down our worlds we would regularly arise to create self once more – thereby become. Problem was, even in our hard fought for delusions of our lives, we knew more quakes were roving our world. Sometimes it was good for one hell of a laugh, other times not.

CALL FOR CONTRIBUTIONS

25TH ANNIVERSARY OF THE *JOURNAL OF PRISONERS ON PRISONS*

The Journal of Prisoners on Prisons (JPP) published its first issue in 1988. 21 Volumes later, we are looking forward to our 25th anniversary in 2013. We are seeking submissions for an issue commemorating a quarter-century of the *JPP*. We are particularly interested in submissions that address one or more of the following themes:

Writing as Resistance
Contributions on this theme could include reflections on the past, present, and future of prison writing. This has been a central theme in the *JPP* since its inception. We welcome contributions that discuss the importance of prison writing, the use of prison writing as a vehicle to counter-inscribe the prison industrial complex, and the status of prison writing as a distinct genre. We also welcome contributions that discuss the role of prison writing, prisoner ethnography, and the *JPP* in the classroom.

The Carceral
Contributions on this theme could address continuities and changes in the prison industrial complex. The pages of the *JPP* have served as a venue for the critical analysis of the socio-politics of incarceration, and as a space to describe the impact of changes in carceral policy and practice on the everyday lives of prisoners. We are particularly interested in contributions that speak to broad trends and major currents in carceral policy and practices.

Theorizing Prisons
Contributions on this theme could address theoretical perspectives on prisons and the organized deprivation of liberty. The *JPP*'s intellectual tradition has been informed by conflict criminology, early and recent contributions to critical criminology, abolitionist theory, standpoint theories, critical race theory, and political economy, among other schools of thought. We welcome contributions that offer new theoretical resources for making sense of the carceral, as well as contributions that review concepts and theories of enduring value.

Submission deadline: December 1, 2012

Please consult our submission guidelines and send submissions to:

Journal of Prisoners on Prisons
c/o Justin Piché, Assistant Professor
Department of Criminology, University of Ottawa
Ottawa, Ontario, Canada K1N 6N5

We also accept submissions by email, to Mike Larsen and Justin Piché, at jpp@uottawa.ca.

www.ingramcontent.com/pod-product-compliance
Lightning Source LLC
Chambersburg PA
CBHW020611270326
41927CB00005B/276

* 9 7 8 0 7 7 6 6 0 9 4 0 9 *